Insolvency Law
Made Clear

A Guide For Debtors

Daniel Kessler

BATH PUBLISHING

Published June 2021

ISBN 978-1-9163023-4-1

Bath Publishing Limited
27 Charmouth Road
Bath
BA1 3LJ
Tel: 01225 577810
email: info@bathpublishing.co.uk
www.bathpublishing.co.uk

Bath Publishing is a company registered in England: 5209173

Registered Office: As above

Dedication

For Tash

I grant thou wert not married to my Muse,

And therefore mayst without attaint o'erlook

The dedicated words which writers use

Of their fair subject, blessing every book.

Acknowledgments

I owe special thanks to all those who helped me write or proofread this book. I thank my colleagues in chambers for their support, particularly Guy Olliff-Cooper and Hossein Sharafi, with whom I have discussed the text. Guy was kind enough to let me use his checklist of rules applying to bankruptcy and winding up petitions and statutory demands, which is set out in Annex 2. The clerks and staff at 4 Stone Buildings led by David Goddard have also helped in the production of the book and offered an external perspective. My parents, James and Jane Kessler both reviewed the text and made helpful comments; as did Natasha Pein, Adrian Hogan and Dominic Olins.

In pre-pandemic times I would ask my mini-pupils to research chapters of the book. Thanks go to Hamish Levick (challenges to Trustees); Tom Hemming and Elena Margetts (insolvent estates); Aabynn Cha (corporate insolvency); Kit Holliday (directors' guarantees); Maha Ahmad and Miriam Sadler (bankruptcy offences); Sahar Khan (when to go bankrupt); and Rabin Kok (directors' disqualifications). Matthew Gold proofread the entire text. I wish them all success in their legal careers.

Finally, the text went from manuscript to book thanks to Helen Lacey at Bath Publishing.

Important notice

This book tries to help 'litigants in person': people who do not have lawyers. It explains legal words, rules and procedure as clearly as possible. Because the book is written for litigants in person, it sacrifices accuracy for clarity. For example, it provides the basic rules without giving all the exceptions, and it provides the underlying principles without a full explanation of the legal test. Almost every page is 'wrong' through omission. It follows that this book is not a replacement for legal advice.

The author does not accept any legal liability or responsibility in respect of any errors or omissions from this book.

DANIEL KESSLER

Contents

Acknowledgments   v

Important notice   v

Preface: the effects of the pandemic   xix

Legal terms defined   xxi

Introduction and aim of this book   xxix

PART 1   BANKRUPTCY

Chapter 1   Alternatives to bankruptcy   3

1.1   Individual Voluntary Arrangements   3

Box 1:   Who is bound by an IVA?   3

1.1.1   The IVA process   4

Box 2:   Interim Order FAQs   6

1.1.2   Failure of the IVA   7

1.1.3   Conclusion   7

1.2   Debt relief orders   7

Box 3:   What if the debtor nearly qualifies for a DRO?   9

1.3   County Court Administration Orders   10

Chapter 2   Effect of bankruptcy   13

Box 4:   Pre-bankruptcy   13

2.1   Stages of bankruptcy   13

2.2	The estate of the bankrupt		14
	2.2.1	Exceptions	14
	2.2.2	Legal claims	15
	2.2.3	Trusts	16
	2.2.4	Pensions	16
	2.2.5	Jointly held property	16
	Box 5:	*How much of the house does the bankrupt own?*	
			17
2.3	Sale of the estate		17
	2.3.1	Sale of shares	18
	2.3.2	Sale of house	18
2.4	Disclaimer of property		18
	Box 6:	*Relationship with the Trustee*	19
2.5	Review of the conduct of the bankrupt		20
2.6	Increasing the asset pool		20
	Box 7:	*Validation orders*	24
2.7	Calculating the debts of the bankrupt		25
	Box 8:	*Proof of debt*	26
2.8	Effect on the bankrupt's career and business		26
	Box 9:	*Bankruptcy and employment*	27
2.9	Inability to obtain credit		28
2.10	Running the bankrupt's business		29
2.11	Effect on immigration status		29
2.12	After-acquired property		30
2.13	Income payments orders		30
2.14	Distribution to creditors		33
2.15	Publicity of bankruptcy		34
2.16	Investigations by the Trustee in Bankruptcy		35
	2.16.1	Investigation powers	35
	Box 10:	*Bankruptcy offences*	37
2.17	Length of bankruptcy and effect of discharge		37

Contents

Chapter 3 Should a debtor go bankrupt? 39

3.1 Is the debtor solvent on the 'balance sheet' basis? 39

3.2 Other factors 41

Box 11:   Immigration reasons 43

3.3 Voluntary bankruptcy 43

Chapter 4 Statutory demands and unsuccessful execution of judgments 45

4.1 Types of debt 45

4.2 What is a statutory demand? 47

4.3 Service of a statutory demand 48

4.4 Consequences of a statutory demand 49

Box 12:   Time limits if the debtor is outside England and Wales 49

4.5 Expedited demand 49

4.6 Application to set aside the statutory demand 50

4.6.1   How to make the application 50

4.6.2   Contents of application 50

Box 13:   Challenging HMRC tax assessments 53

Box 14:   Applications out of time 56

4.7 Statutory demands in respect of debts not immediately payable 57

4.8 Initial review by the court 57

Box 15:   Court delays 58

4.9 The first hearing 58

4.10 The substantive hearing 59

4.11 Orders at the hearing 59

4.12 Challenging the statutory demand 60

Box 16:   Execution of judgment 62

Chapter 5 Bankruptcy petitions and bankruptcy hearings 69

5.1 What is a bankruptcy petition? 69

5.2	Jurisdiction	69
	Box 17: *Forum shopping*	74
5.3	Debts	75
5.4	Statutory demand	75
5.5	Court choice	76
5.6	Additional steps	78
5.7	Withdrawal of petition	79
5.8	Service of the petition	79
5.9	Timing of the hearing	82
5.10	The hearing of the petition	82
	Box 18: *When to file a notice of opposition*	83
5.11	Outcomes of the hearing	83
5.12	Adjournment of the petition	83
	5.12.1 Technicalities	83
	5.12.2 Enable evidence to be fully heard	84
	5.12.3 Enable debtor to satisfy the court of their power to pay debts	85
	Box 19: *Staying the petition*	88
	5.12.4 Running multiple arguments	88
5.13	Grounds to oppose a bankruptcy petition	89
	5.13.1 Serious procedural irregularities	90
	5.13.2 The debtor has no assets	91
	5.13.3 Bankruptcy would be disproportionate	92
	5.13.4 The debt is not for a liquidated sum	92
	5.13.5 The debt is disputed	93
	5.13.6 The debtor has made an offer to settle	93
	5.13.7 The petition is an abuse of process	96
	5.13.8 The creditors are guilty of improper behaviour towards the debtor	99
	5.13.9 Bankruptcy would have a serious psychological impact on the debtor; or the debtor is very elderly or unwell	99

5.13.10   The petitioner does not attend the hearing of
           the petition   100

5.13.11   An Individual Voluntary Arrangement has been
           approved   100

5.13.12   The court has no jurisdiction to make the
           bankruptcy order   100

5.13.13   Debtor lacks capacity   100

Box 20:   Other grounds for dismissing petitions   101

5.14   Substitution   102

5.15   Change of carriage   103

5.16   Bankruptcy order   103

5.17   Appeals   103

5.18   Other forms of bankruptcy   103

Chapter 6   Possession hearings   105

6.1   Overview   105

Box 21:   What if the bankrupt was renting?   106

Box 22:   Coronavirus and evictions   107

Box 23:   Caution   108

6.2   Role of Trustee   108

Box 24:   Summary of the bankrupt's rights   108

6.3   Orders for possession   110

6.3.1   Rights of occupation when the bankrupt lives
          with children   110

6.3.2   Rights of occupation when the bankrupt lives
          with a spouse or civil partner   111

Box 25:   'Common law wives'   112

6.3.3   Rights of occupation when the bankrupt co-
          owns the property with a third party   113

6.4   Low value homes   113

6.5   Mortgage payments   113

6.6   Objecting to sale   114

6.7   Dismissal of Trustee's application for possession   115

Chapter 7	**Bankruptcy offences**	117
7.1	Bankruptcy offences in the Act	117
7.2	Defence of innocent intention	119
7.3	Punishment	120
7.4	Effect of annulment and discharge	120
7.5	Prosecution	120
7.6	Application for an arrest warrant	120
7.7	Contempt of court	121
7.8	Bankruptcy offences outside of the Act	122

Chapter 8	**Challenges to the Trustee in Bankruptcy**	123
8.1	General control of the Trustee by the court	124
8.2	Compensation for breach of duty	127
8.3	Complaints to the regulator	129

Chapter 9	**The conclusion of bankruptcy: discharge and annulment**	133
9.1	Discharge	133
	9.1.1 Effect of discharge	134
	9.1.2 Bankruptcy restriction orders	135
	Box 26: *Contesting a bankruptcy restriction order*	137
	9.1.3 Insolvency register	138
	9.1.4 Income payments order or income payments agreement	138
	9.1.5 Long term impact	138
9.2	Annulment	139
	9.2.1 The order should not have been made	139
	9.2.2 The debts and expenses have been paid	139
	Box 27: *Other challenges to the Trustee's fees*	142
	Box 28: *Annulment and divorce proceedings*	143
	9.2.3 An IVA has been signed	144
9.3	Effect of annulment	144

Contents

Box 29:   Removing entries at the Land Registry   145

Chapter 10   Death and Bankruptcy   147

Box 30:   Key terminology   147

10.1   Death before the presentation of a bankruptcy petition 148

Box 31:   What happens if the PR refuses to pay an admitted debt?   148

Box 32:   Sources for the law   149

10.1.1   Out of court   149

10.1.2   CPR Part 64 application   150

10.1.3   Insolvency Administration Orders   150

Box 33:   'Survivorship' and jointly owned property   151

10.2   How to choose between the three options – from the perspective of the PR   152

Box 34:   What if the petitioning creditor does not know the debtor has died?   152

10.3   Death after presentation of the bankruptcy petition   153

10.4   Death after bankruptcy order is made   153

Chapter 11   Guarantees   155

11.1   What is a guarantee?   156

11.2   Why guarantees might be unenforceable   156

11.2.1   Does the guarantee apply to the debt?   156

11.2.2   Has there been a proper demand under that guarantee   157

11.2.3   Is the guarantee valid?   158

Box 35:   Independent legal advice   158

Box 36:   Other reasons to challenge a guarantee   160

11.3   Evidence to present to the bankruptcy court   160

PART 2   CORPORATE INSOLVENCY

Chapter 12   Companies going insolvent   165

Box 37:   Terminology   165

12.1	Corporate insolvency in general	166
12.2	Limited liability and exceptions to limited liability	167
Box 38:	Coronavirus changes to wrongful trading	168
12.3	Before a company goes into liquidation	170
12.4	Administration	170
Box 39:	What is a floating charge?	171
12.5	Moratorium outside of administration	172
12.6	CVA or CVL?	173
12.7	Process of an insolvent company going into liquidation	173
12.8	Review of transactions and duties of directors	174
Box 40:	Coronavirus and transaction avoidance	175

Chapter 13 Compulsory liquidation 177

13.1	Winding up petitions	177
Box 41:	Coronavirus and winding up petitions	178
Box 42:	The Company Insolvency Pro Bono Scheme	181
13.2	What happens next?	182

Chapter 14 Directors' disqualification hearings 185

14.1	What is director's disqualification?	185
Box 43:	Director's disqualification and bankruptcy	188
14.2	How to avoid disqualification proceedings	188
14.3	What to do if the Secretary of State brings proceedings	189
14.3.1	Disqualification undertakings	189
14.3.2	Disqualification hearings	191
14.4	Application for permission to be a director	192

PART 3 APPEALS

Chapter 15 Appeals 197

15.1	Reviews	197
15.2	Appeals	199
Box 44:	Stay of judgment	202

15.3   Annulment of a bankruptcy order   202

Box 45:   *Failure to attend court*   204

PART 4   COSTS

Chapter 16 Costs   207

16.1   Costs at different stages   208

Box 46:   *A word of warning*   208

16.1.1   Solicitors' fees   208

16.1.2   Barristers' fees   211

Box 47:   *What about winding up petitions?*   213

16.1.3   Court fees   213

Box 48:   *Help with court fees*   214

16.1.4   Process server's fees   214

Box 49:   *Litigants in person can claim for their costs*   215

16.2   Principles of costs awards   215

Box 50:   *Third party costs orders*   216

Box 51:   *Costs of the bankruptcy or winding up petition* 217

Box 52:   *Costs schedules*   219

16.3   Fees of the Trustee in Bankruptcy or liquidator   220

PART 5   LITIGATION

Chapter 17 Litigation tips for those with legal representation   225

Box 53:   *Legal aid*   225

17.1   How to choose a lawyer   226

17.1.1   What kind of lawyer?   226

17.1.2   How to find an appropriate solicitor   227

17.1.3   How to find an appropriate direct access barrister   228

Box 54:   *Word of mouth*   229

17.2   How to best use a lawyer   229

Box 55:   Hearings where the parties have agreed what the
            outcome should be   231

Chapter 18 Representing yourself   233

18.1   Writing to the petitioning creditor   233

    18.1.1   Settlement   234

    18.1.2   Disputed debt   236

    18.1.3   Sending documents   236

    Box 56:   Who to contact   236

    18.1.4   'Pre-action' correspondence   237

    Box 57:   Using the creditor's resources wisely 238

18.2   Written documents for the court   238

    Box 58:   Making applications   240

18.3   Skeleton arguments   240

    Box 59:   Court bundle   241

    Box 60:   Sending documents to court   241

18.4   Appearing in court   242

    18.4.1   Cross-examination   243

    Box 61:   Remote hearings   243

    18.4.2   Addressing the court   244

    Box 62:   What should I wear?   245

    18.4.3   Order of proceedings   245

PART 6   ANNEXES

Annex 1   Model Documents   249

    Box 63:   How to use these documents   249

Letter of settlement   250

Application to set aside a statutory demand on the grounds
that the debt is disputed   253

Notice of opposition   259

Application for a validation order   260

Statement of costs   265

Contents

Skeleton argument opposing the making of a bankruptcy order   267

Grounds of appeal   273

Annex 2   **Checklists**   275

Statutory demand for bankruptcy   276

    The Demand   276

    Service   279

    Certificate of Service   282

Bankruptcy Petition   284

    The Petition   284

Corporate Insolvency   288

    Winding Up Petition   288

    Witness Statement   289

    Filing Checklist   290

    Service Checklist   290

    Certificate of Service   291

    Gazette   292

    Opposing the Petition   293

    Certificate of Compliance   293

    List of Appearances   294

Sources of help   295

Table of cases   297

Table of legislation   299

Index   303

Preface: the effects of the pandemic

This book was written and is being published during the Covid-19 pandemic. The pandemic affects this book in three ways.

Firstly, and most importantly, through an increase in the number of people and companies going insolvent. The Office of National Statistics estimated that there was a 10% fall in GDP in 2020, and the central forecast of the Office of Budget Responsibility in March 2021 predicted that the rate of unemployment will peak at almost double its pre-pandemic level. The impact will not be felt evenly throughout the economy: companies and people working in certain sectors, such as accommodation and food services, are forecast to be most affected. To some degree, the country has been protected from the impact of the recession through Government spending on schemes like the Coronavirus Job Retention Scheme and Local Restrictions Support Grants. This has allowed the private sector to repay its creditors using public funding. However, as the United Kingdom returns to 'the new normal' and the emergency funding stops, some debtors will be unable to repay their debts. Creditors will consider bankruptcy and winding up petitions as a means of seeking a return on their debts when other means fail.

Secondly, the Government has made changes to English insolvency law in response to the pandemic, sometimes with retroactive effect. The law might have changed following publication of this book. The most likely candidates for change are the rules for possession proceedings, the presentation of winding up petitions, and the application of wrongful trading provisions. These rules have already changed more than once since March 2020. If the law does change, it is likely to be more generous to debtors as the Government seeks to provide short term protection while the economy recovers from the pandemic.

Finally, this book presents insolvency statistics to offer context to the rules it describes. Statistics from 2020, where they are available, are likely to mislead: neither the court nor creditors acted in the same way from March 2020 as they did in 2019. In particular, there are presently restrictions on putting a company into compulsory liquidation (see Chapter 13) and, although there are not similar restrictions on bankruptcy proceedings, many creditors are avoiding insolvency proceedings. HMRC, for example, has permitted the deferment of VAT and income tax payments, and it did not petition for bankruptcy or winding up orders unless it suspected criminal activity. As a consequence, there were relatively few bankruptcy and winding up orders made in 2020. For example, in November 2020 the number of personal and corporate insolvencies was down by about a third from November 2019. This book presents figures from before the pandemic in order to be more representative of how the system operates.

This book seeks to state the law as of March 2021.

Legal terms defined

'The Act': to save time, this book refers to the Insolvency Act 1986 as 'the Act', or 'IA 1986'. It can be found here: https://www.legislation.gov.uk/ukpga/1986/45/contents. A section of the Act is referred to as s123; multiple sections are referred to as ss12 and 13 or ss12 to 25.

'Adjourning' means 'postponing for another occasion'.

'Administration' is a legal process which only companies can go through. An Insolvency Practitioner working as an 'administrator' runs the company in place of the directors.

'After-acquired property' refers to property which is received by an undischarged bankrupt: for example, if they received an inheritance. A Trustee can acquire this property for the creditors.

The 'annulment' of a bankruptcy order is when it is cancelled. Annulment can happen if the debts of the bankrupt are paid, if the bankruptcy order should not have been made or if the bankrupt signs an individual voluntary arrangement.

An 'asset' is something of value. For example, cash, cars and houses are all assets.

'Bankruptcy' has a precise legal meaning which is the process by which an individual's estate is run for the benefit of their creditors. A 'bankrupt' is someone who has been the subject of a bankruptcy order.

A 'bankruptcy restrictions order' (BRO) continues certain bankruptcy restrictions even after the bankruptcy is discharged. Bankruptcy restrictions undertakings (BRU) may be accepted instead of needing to obtain an order.

A 'claim', if made to the court, is a formal request to ask the judge to make an order to protect a legal right.

A 'class' of creditors is a group of them. Bankruptcy is often described as a 'class' remedy: this is because its focus is the creditors as a group.

A 'company voluntary arrangement' (CVA) is the formal process which, if 75% of creditors agree, can lead to the debt of a company being reduced or the company being given more time to pay.

'Corporate' is an adjective, and it means 'of a company'.

'Costs' refer to the lawyers' fees, court fees and other fees to bring or defend a claim.

The 'court' is a polite way of referring to the judge who is in charge of making decisions in a case.

'Credit rating agencies' are companies which assess how likely it is that someone can afford to repay a debt. They work behind the scenes. Professional lenders will almost certainly check an individual's credit rating with an agency before agreeing to a loan.

A 'creditor' is someone who is owed a debt. For example, if a bank makes a loan to an individual the bank will be a creditor.

A 'creditors' voluntary arrangement' (CVA) is a process where creditors agree to restructure the debts of an insolvent company. See Chapter 12.

A 'debt relief order' (DRO) is a type of streamlined bankruptcy which only applies for debtors who have few assets and small debts.

A 'debtor' is someone who owes a debt.

To 'default' on a loan is not to repay it on time.

A 'directions hearing' is a court hearing which aims to make orders about the conduct of the case rather than to determine its outcome. For example, it might set a timetable for the exchange of evidence.

'Directors' are those individuals who are responsible for running a company in the eyes of the law. They do not need to have the job title 'director', and they are (or should be) listed in Companies House. Some but not everyone who has the title 'director' is a director for the purposes of this book: only those with a particular legal role with the company are directors. The rest are senior employees of the company.

The 'discharge' of bankruptcy is when the bankruptcy order ends.

A company is 'dissolved' after the process of liquidation is finished: it is struck off the list of companies in Companies House. Whatever assets remain become the property of the Queen ('*bona vacantia*').

A 'disposition' of an asset is when that asset is sold or given away. It would include where security is given over that asset.

A 'distribution' is a payment. For example, the Trustee in Bankruptcy may make a 'distribution' to creditors, if the bankrupt held sufficient funds.

The 'equity' in a house is the value remaining after the mortgage. This will be the only meaning of the word 'equity' in this book.

'Estate' has two distinct meanings. For most of this book, 'estate' is used to refer to the belongings of a bankrupt which they do not keep after the making of a bankruptcy order. This would include cash in the bank, but exclude their tools of trade. However, 'estate' has a wider meaning in Chapter 10 if someone dies, and refers to all their possessions.

'Execution' of a judgment is enforcing it: typically this is a bailiff attending to remove property to sell and pay off the judgment creditor.

A 'guarantee' is an agreement to pay someone else's debts.

A 'hearing' is when the parties speak in front of a judge in a court.

An 'income payments agreement' (IPA) is an agreement where someone who is bankrupt agrees to pay future earnings to their Trustee in Bankruptcy. If the bankrupt does not agree, the Trustee can apply for an 'income payments order' (IPO).

An 'individual voluntary arrangement' (IVA) is a formal process which, if 75% of creditors agree, can lead to the debt of a person being reduced or the debtor being given more time to pay.

'Insolvent' means either 'unable to pay debts as they fall due'; or alternatively 'debts are greater than assets'. The first definition is usually easier to prove: if someone is meant to pay a debt but cannot, they are technically insolvent.

An 'Insolvency Practitioner' (IP) is a qualified professional, similar to a chartered accountant who specialises in insolvency matters.

An 'interim order' protects an individual from their creditors while they try to pass an individual voluntary arrangement.

'Interest' can be either a) additional money which needs to be repaid when taking out a loan, or b) the right to some part of property. For example, someone's interest in a house might be the first £50,000; or an interest under the Family Law Act 1996 which entitles them to live there. 'Interest' can also be used as an abstract noun, meaning 'what is good for somebody', as in "this is not in my interests".

A 'judgment' is the decision of a judge.

A 'judgment debt' is a debt which arises out of a court judgment. If person A is ordered to pay person B, A is the judgment debtor and B is a judgment creditor. The difference between a judgment debt and a regular debt is only in the difficulty of disputing a judgment debt, since the court would already have heard the arguments and made its decision.

The 'jurisdiction' of the court is whether the court has the ability to do something.

A 'liability' is a legal obligation which someone owes to someone else. It could be an outstanding debt, but it could also be an obligation to make future payments or a non-monetary obligation such as to maintain insurance on a flat.

A 'liquidated' debt is one that can be quantified. A promise to pay £10,000 is a liquidated debt, but a claim for damages resulting from an accident is not liquidated until the court determines its value.

'Liquidation' is an entirely different concept, and is the word used to describe the 'bankruptcy' of a company.

A 'liquidator' is an Insolvency Practitioner who is appointed to run a company's liquidation.

'Listing' is when the court finds time in its diary for a hearing.

A 'litigant in person' is someone who does not have professional legal representation.

'Litigation' is when someone brings a claim in court.

A 'moratorium' is a period when nobody can bring a claim or enforce a debt.

A statement given under 'oath' is one where the witness swears to tell the truth, either while holding a Bible or another sacred text. A non-religious witness can instead 'affirm' their evidence. The difference between an oath and an affirmation is of no legal importance.

An 'offence', as used in this book, is a crime.

The 'Official Receiver' (OR) is a qualified Insolvency Practitioner who works for the Government. The Official Receiver is the first person who takes control after a bankruptcy order is made, but a private Insolvency Practitioner can replace them if the creditors wish.

An 'order' is when the court requires something to happen or not happen.

A 'party' to a claim is someone who participates in that claim. For example, the debtor and petitioning creditor are parties to a bankruptcy petition.

The 'PDIP' is the 'Practice Direction - Insolvency Proceedings'. This forms part of the procedural rules which the court will follow. It can be found at https://www.justice.gov.uk/courts/procedure-rules/civil/rules/insolvency_pdf.

A 'personal representative' is in charge of the estate of someone who has died.

'Personal service' means that a document must be physically handed to its addressee, as opposed to posted or sent by email. If personal service is not possible, the court may permit 'alternative' or 'substituted' service – typically service by post.

A 'petition' is a request for the court. In this book, it refers to a request to bankrupt someone, except in Chapter 12 where a winding up petition is to put a company into liquidation. When the request is submitted to the court, the petition is said to be 'presented'.

The 'petitioning creditor' is the creditor who brings a petition, as opposed to any other creditor who might support or oppose the petition, or not be involved at all.

A 'privileged' document is one which does not need to be disclosed to the other side of a dispute. Legal advice is usually privileged, and so is a document which is sent 'without prejudice'.

'Pro bono' legal advice is legal advice given for free.

'Proceedings' is shorthand for 'the court process when a claim is made'.

A 'process server' is someone whose job is to serve documents, i.e. to deliver court documents to individuals. They are frequently used when a document requires personal service.

'Property' means something similar to 'an asset'. It refers to someone's possessions. Property does not need to be land (this is known as 'real property'). For example, a car is a type of property.

'Proving' a debt means demonstrating to the Trustee in Bankruptcy or liquidator that the individual or company owed the creditor the debt. It can be as simple as sending them an invoice. Only certain debts are 'provable': the list is set out on in Box 8 on page 26.

To 'realise' property is to sell it.

The 'respondent' is the defendant to an application. If a debtor applies to set aside a statutory demand, the debtor is the applicant and the creditor is the respondent.

The 'Rules' refer to the Insolvency (England and Wales) Rules 2016. If a reference is in the form (r[number]), it will be to the Rules. They can be found at https://www.legislation.gov.uk/uksi/2016/1024/contents/made.

The 'Secretary of State' is shorthand for the Secretary of State for Business, Energy and Industrial Strategy. In practice, the Minister's decisions will be made through the Insolvency Service.

'Security' for a loan is when, if the debtor defaults, the lender has some claim over an item. The lender can then sell that item and repay their own debt. The most common example is a mortgage, where the lender has a right to the house on which the mortgage is secured if the debtor does not pay. To 'secure' a debt is to provide security for it.

'Secured' creditors hold security. 'Unsecured' creditors do not.

'Service' of a court document means how it is to be given to its recipient. Two examples are service by post and 'personal service' where the recipient is given a document in person. It is usually enough to send a document by email. Certain documents, in particular statutory demands and bankruptcy petitions, have special requirements and must be served personally.

A 'statement of truth' is a formal declaration by someone that the contents of the document is true to the best of their knowledge and belief.

A 'statutory demand' is a formal request for payment. It must state that it is a statutory demand.

A 'stay' of a claim, application or an order is when the court decides that it should be paused.

'Solvency' is the opposite of 'insolvency'. If someone is solvent, they can pay their debts, and their total assets are greater than their debts.

A 'third party' is a stranger to either a) a transaction or b) a legal claim. For an example of each: a) if a lender makes a loan with a debtor, the debtor's spouse is a 'third party' to the loan; and b) if a creditor applies to make the debtor bankrupt, the debtor's family are 'third parties' to the bankruptcy petition.

The 'Trustee in Bankruptcy' or 'Trustee' is the Insolvency Practitioner who takes control over the bankrupt's financial affairs. This will be the only way in which the word 'Trustee' is used in this book.

A transaction at an 'undervalue' is one where the asset is transferred for less than it is worth: for example, if something of value is given away for free.

An 'undischarged bankrupt' is someone whose bankruptcy is continuing; but a 'discharged bankrupt' has completed the process.

A 'validation' order is where the court gives permission for a transaction to take place. This is necessary if the transaction took place after the presentation of a bankruptcy or winding up petition.

'Vests' refers to the transfer of ownership of property, e.g. if I sell a car, the car vests in the purchaser.

The 'winding up' of a company is the same as its liquidation.

A 'without prejudice' document is a confidential communication which tries to settle a dispute. Without prejudice communication is privileged: it cannot be shown to the judge.

A 'witness statement' is a formal written account of events. Witness statements typically contain an exhibit with documents as supporting evidence. It is the primary way in which someone gives the court information.

Symbols and acronyms

Numbers in square brackets are usually paragraph references to a judgment.

Legal cases have standard ways of being referred to ('cited'). The most common, and the version this book uses where possible, is the 'neutral citation'. An example is [2021] EWHC 222: this means that judgment was given in 2021, in the England and Wales High Court, and it was the 222nd judgment that year. Sometimes the letters (Ch) appear afterwards: this refers to the 'Chancery' division of the High Court. Another example could be [2021] EWCA Civ 123 where EWCA refers to the England and Wales Court of Appeal and Civ means that it is a civil, as opposed to a criminal, case.

The name of a legal case is usually underlined, bold or in italics to distinguish it from the names of the people involved. For example, *Donoghue v Stevenson* refers to the case between a Mrs Donoghue and a Mr Stevenson. After the first instance, it is common to refer to a case using just one of the names, for example simply *Donoghue*.

The 'CPR' are the Civil Procedure Rules 1998: http://www.justice.gov.uk/courts/procedure-rules/civil/rules.

Alongside the CPR, there are civil procedure Practice Directions ('PD') which are, in effect, further rules of civil procedure.

The 'IR' are the Insolvency (England and Wales) Rules 2016: https://www.legislation.gov.uk/uksi/2016/1024/contents/made.

The 'CDDA' is the Company Directors Disqualification Act 1986: https://www.legislation.gov.uk/ukpga/1986/46/contents.

The 'OR' is the Official Receiver (see above).

The 'PR' is the Personal Representative (see above).

Introduction and aim of this book

This book is for individuals who are facing bankruptcy and those whose companies are facing insolvency.

The book is divided into six parts. Part 1 deals with individual bankruptcy and what happens to the bankrupt and their families during the bankruptcy; Part 2 covers the equivalent process when companies go insolvent; Part 3 focuses on how to appeal a decision of the court; Part 4 explains how costs may be awarded against parties in different situations; Part 5 provides information on how best to use a lawyer if resources are limited, and litigation tips if the debtor has to represent themselves; and finally, Part 6 consists of two annexes which contain model documents and checklists. These documents and checklists are also available as text documents so the reader can amend the templates as they wish (the files are provided within the digital download pack).

Part of the difficulty people face when having problems with debt are technical terms used without an explanation. 'Insolvency' is the word used when a person or a company has more debt than assets; or who/which cannot pay a debt which has fallen due. If that someone is a person, this can lead to them going bankrupt.

Bankruptcy is a court process where a stranger, the 'Trustee in Bankruptcy', takes control of the financial affairs of the bankrupt, selling most of the available assets to pay off the creditors. 'Bankruptcy' can be used loosely to mean 'insolvency', or precisely to refer to the court process where a bankruptcy order is made. This book tries to find a balance between using the correct legal terms – which are essential to understand since they will be the words used in court and in legal documents – and being comprehensible.

Bankruptcy is not the only insolvency process an individual can enter: see Chapter 1. The processes for a company are different and are set out in Chapter 13.

For some, bankruptcy is a way to escape debts and start again. How to do this voluntarily is explained in Paragraph 3.3. Others look for an alternative. Chapter 3 also discusses when to contest and when not to contest the making of a bankruptcy order.

Many people cannot afford legal advice or need to be careful with how they use the resources they have for legal advice. Chapter 17 offers guidance to those who can only afford limited legal advice, or who cannot afford any. The book should also be useful for volunteers in legal advice centres, or for professional lawyers who do not often encounter insolvency problems. It exclusively covers the law of England and Wales.

The book cannot cover every situation. It tries to cover the most common problems which individuals face. There is plenty of material available to help debtors. This book is different because it focuses on court processes. It describes what happens at a late stage of a debtor's financial problems, if these problems are not resolved sooner. Most other available books advise on financial management before the problem proceeds to court. Resolving debt issues before they come to court will lead to a better outcome for the individual, but often this advice comes too late. It may not be enough for someone who has received a statutory demand to think about financial management: they also have to understand and participate in the bankruptcy process or they could be made bankrupt within two or three months.

Fortunately, creditors typically prefer to avoid going to court (also known as 'litigation'). Litigation is expensive. It commonly happens that the people litigating ('the parties') spend more on lawyers than their original dispute was worth. However, some creditors are reluctant to compromise. Chapter 18 discusses strategies for negotiating with those creditors who are prepared to settle a case without making a debtor bankrupt. One of the key messages of this book is that debtors should use the fact that the English legal system is expensive and slow to their advantage to achieve a realistic settlement. It may also be useful for debtors to know what is likely to happen if they cannot resolve their debt problems any other way.

Insolvency is common for both individuals and companies. Statistics from the Insolvency Service show that approximately 122,000 people went insolvent in 2019, which is 1 out of every 400 adults in England and Wales. Of these, about 78,000 signed an 'individual voluntary arrangement' (see Chapter 1), 27,000 had a 'debt relief order' (again, see Chapter 1) and 17,000 went bankrupt. These three processes all have similarities. More is known about individuals who voluntarily go bankrupt than those who are forced to do so. The most common causes of bankruptcy for people who voluntarily go bankrupt are the debtor living beyond their means; relationship breakdown; reduction of the bankrupt's income or loss of their employment. The typical debtor has approximately £35,000 of debt.

This book focuses on bankruptcy even if it is the less common outcome. It is necessary to understand what bankruptcy is (and is not) to understand how to approach the other processes.

A further 17,000 companies went insolvent in 2019. Of these, 12,000 were voluntary liquidations (see Chapter 12); 3,000 were compulsory (see Chapter 13); and 2,000 were administrations (Chapter 12)[1]. The most common sector for the companies is construction, followed by wholesale and retail trade. This book tries to help directors of companies going insolvent; and advise individuals who are facing 'directors' disqualification orders' as a result (see Chapter 14).

Principles of insolvency law

Describing some basic principles behind insolvency law will put the rules and arguments which follow in this book into their proper context.

The purpose of bankruptcy is to transfer management of the bankrupt's assets to an independent professional, known as a 'Trustee in Bankruptcy'. The Trustee can then organise the sale of these assets, gather information about who the creditors are, and distribute the proceeds according to the scheme set out in the Insolvency Act 1986. The Trustee can also recover assets by reviewing transactions made by the bankrupt before bankruptcy. A Trustee can undo the transactions which unfairly harm the creditors, or favour one creditor over the others. Finally, the Trustee can investigate the circumstances of the bankruptcy and the conduct of the bankrupt. If necessary, the Trustee can refer any possible criminal offences to the Insolvency Service for prosecution or for an order that certain restrictions continue to protect any future creditors.

The focus of bankruptcy is the 'class' of creditors, i.e. the creditors of a bankrupt as a whole. This has several important implications:

1. Firstly, the creditor who brings ('presents') the petition is not given any special treatment. If something is in the interests of the creditors as a whole but not in the interests of the petitioning creditor, the court's instinct will be to protect the class.

2. The court will treat all creditors equally, within the statutory scheme. In particular, all the 'unsecured' creditors will be treated the same way. They will each receive a distribution in the bankruptcy which is proportionate to their debt. For example, if one creditor is owed £10,000 and another is owed £5,000, and the Trustee only has £1,500 to distribute, then the proceeds will be split 2:1, and each creditor will receive 10p for every pound owed. 'Secured' creditors are entitled to the proceeds of sale of a particular asset – for example, a bank who provides a mortgage over a house will be repaid from the proceeds once the house is sold. 'Unsecured' creditors are owed money without the benefit of receiving the proceeds of the sale of any

---

[1] *There were also a small number of receiverships which this book does not discuss.*

property in particular.

3. Since the petitioning creditor is not treated differently from the other creditors, the debts owed to the petitioning creditor are not given any priority. This is important: by spending money pursuing a bankruptcy petition, some of which will not be recovered, a creditor is compounding their loss. The primary strategy for settling a bankruptcy petition is simply to say that it is not worth the creditor spending money which it will never recover.

4. The court is more involved in a bankruptcy hearing than in other areas of law. If a creditor sues a debtor for an ordinary debt, there are only two parties to the claim. If they both agree, the court is likely to respect their agreement. Not so for bankruptcy, where the court steps in to protect the interests of the creditors as a whole. For example, having presented a petition, court permission is required to withdraw it in case there is some side-deal which prejudices the class of creditors.

Bankruptcy is something which happens to one individual at a time. If a bankrupt co-owns something with someone else (typically, a family home which belongs to two parents), then only the bankrupt's share is available for the creditors. Put differently; it is not possible to claim a debt against both a bankrupt and their spouse unless the spouse has actively chosen to accept the liability. Chapter 11 deals with guarantees, which is the most common way in which the spouse might be held liable.

Corporate insolvency law is similar. However, a company is a 'legal fiction', i.e. it is recognised by the law but it does not actually exist. As a consequence, the company can be 'wound up' at the end of the insolvency process and then dissolved.

PART 1 BANKRUPTCY

The next few chapters describe the bankruptcy process. A typical bankruptcy looks like the following:

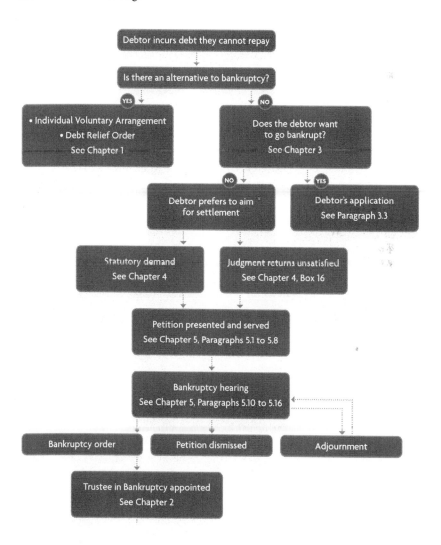

Chapter 1   Alternatives to bankruptcy

Some debtors may wish to go bankrupt for the advantages it brings. Others have an alternative to bankruptcy, for example if the creditors prefer to settle the claim out of court or if they qualify for a niche alternative. Creditors may prefer to settle the bankruptcy claim out of court, frequently because they prefer a smaller sum now to an uncertain sum in the future. Nothing stops a debtor informally agreeing with a creditor to pay less debt, or to have more time to pay. However, the Insolvency Act creates certain structures which can be helpful to give a debtor an alternative to bankruptcy. This chapter discusses these alternatives.

1.1   Individual Voluntary Arrangements

An important alternative to bankruptcy is an 'Individual Voluntary Arrangement' (IVA). An IVA is a type of contract between the debtor and their creditors. If an IVA is passed it binds all known creditors who were entitled to vote in the arrangement, or would have been if they had notice of it. This includes creditors who voted against the arrangement.

BOX 1:   WHO IS BOUND BY AN IVA?

An IVA binds all creditors, except:

- ► Certain family support orders
- ► Student loans
- ► Magistrates' fines
- ► Loans which are secured, e.g. mortgages

An IVA will bind 'contingent' and future creditors, i.e. those whose debts are not currently owed but might be. An example of a future creditor is where a purchaser buys an item and agrees to pay for it in future monthly instalments. A contingent creditor is where the debt depends on an external event, for example if someone is being sued – the potential damages which the court might award is a contingent debt. An IVA does not bind contingent creditors if the debt is wholly prospective, i.e. too unlikely to arise.

Since an IVA binds future creditors, those creditors are likely to take steps to minimise their exposure to the debtor. For example, an individual might be tied into a gym membership for 24 months, and so, in theory, the gym is a future creditor for 24 months' worth of monthly fees. However, the gym is more likely to end the contract and will participate in the IVA only to the extent of the historic unpaid amount.

Typically IVAs are agreements where the creditors agree to receive a smaller sum, and the debtor agrees to pay the creditors the money they are owed. An IVA could include a commitment to sell specific property, or for a connected party like a family member to pay money into the IVA, on the condition that the creditors accept a smaller sum. An authorised professional (a qualified Insolvency Practitioner) supervises the debtor's implementation and compliance with the terms of the IVA.

There are many private providers of IVAs. Some debt charities such as StepChange will also organise an IVA. Insolvency Service statistics show that the most popular provider of IVAs in 2019 was Creditfix, followed by Hanover Insolvency. Providers advertise the ability to write off large proportions of debt. IVA providers will be able to deliver on this promise – but only if the creditors agree.

1.1.1   The IVA process

The IVA process typically goes as follows.

If a debtor is interested in an IVA, they will contact an Insolvency Practitioner, who will likely become the 'supervisor' (monitor) of the IVA. The Insolvency Practitioner will have a standard template for an IVA. They will establish what funds the debtor has, what they are prepared to do as part of the IVA, and who their creditors are. They will contact all the creditors informally and discuss a potential proposal. If there appears to be an informal agreement, the supervisor will hold a creditors' meeting. A creditors' meeting typically is not a physical meeting of creditors, but a 'virtual meeting' where creditors will express their opinions formally and the IP will count votes. If 75% of the creditors, measured by the value of debts, agree, the proposal is passed.

From a debtor's perspective, this means that the majority of creditors have to agree with the proposal. It may appear unusual that creditors routinely agree to accept a reduction (in slang, a 'haircut') on their debts. They are less likely to do so without the structure that an IVA creates. The presence of the supervisor is helpful for both the debtor and the creditors. It is helpful for the debtor because they will have some external assistance in negotiating the settlement. A standard payment structure for IPs is that they only get paid as part of the IVA. Potential supervisors are therefore typically motivated to try as hard as they can to agree a settlement between the creditors and debtor. It is helpful for the creditors because the IP is an independent professional who they are likely to trust more than the debtor, who has already defaulted on the debt. The supervisor can help enforce its terms.

A debtor does not need to prove they are insolvent to pass an IVA, as they need to for a voluntary bankruptcy, but if the debtor has the resources to pay their creditors then the creditors are unlikely to accept any form of reduction or delay. However, a debtor may be able to show that there is a real prospect that they will be unable to pay their debts at the current rate, and it is in the creditors' interests to make a reduction today in order to receive a greater return over time.

Creditors can challenge an IVA by applying to the court. There are two primary grounds for challenging an IVA: firstly, that it is unfairly prejudicial to the creditor, and secondly that it was passed on the basis of a material irregularity. An example of 'unfair prejudice' would be an IVA where 24.9% of creditors received £0 and the remainder received their debts in full: such an IVA would probably get the 75% support in order to be approved, but it would unfairly prejudice the minority. An example of a material irregularity is the failure to assess the level of debt of each creditor accurately. Finally, creditors who were unaware of the vote will be able to challenge it within 28 days of receiving notice on either of the two grounds.

It may appear possible, at first glance, to propose an IVA with a debtor's friendliest creditors and rely on the fact that other creditors would be bound by the agreement. This is unlikely to work. First, the supervisor will try to contact as many creditors as they are aware of, and it is an offence to make a false representation in order to obtain approval to pass an IVA, including lying to the supervisor about the list of creditors. Second, the creditors will be able to challenge the IVA as materially irregular if they were not contacted when they should have been.

A debtor who proposes an IVA can seek an interim order. An interim order operates as a 'moratorium', i.e. it prevents creditors from beginning or continuing any legal process against the debtor without court permission. In particular, it prevents a landlord forfeiting a lease, bailiffs repossessing property, or the presentation of a bankruptcy petition. The moratorium usually lasts for 14 days, but they are routinely extended for longer to allow the potential supervisor of the IVA to prepare their report on how viable the IVA is.

BOX 2: INTERIM ORDER FAQS

Why do they exist? Interim orders exist to make it easier for an IVA to be made. Consider a position where one creditor is in favour of an IVA, but another insists on a bankruptcy petition and yet another is trying to repossess some property. A debtor would have to deal with all creditors at once, and the IVA is likely to be low priority.

Who can get an interim order? The court will only make an interim order if it is satisfied that: a) the debtor intends to make an IVA proposal; b) the debtor would be able to make a bankruptcy application (or is already an undischarged bankrupt); c) no previous application has been made by the debtor in the previous 12 months; and d) there is a prospective IVA supervisor who is willing to act.

How do I get an interim order? The debtor needs to apply to the court and pay the fee, which is currently £180. The potential supervisor is likely to be willing to complete the paperwork on behalf of the debtor. They may even pay the fee upfront in the expectation of being repaid as part of the arrangement.

Overall, if it is possible to enter into an IVA, this will almost certainly lead to a better outcome for the debtor. Notwithstanding any fee the supervisor charges (typically a few thousand pounds), IVAs come with reduced legal fees since no litigation will be necessary. In nearly all IVAs the creditors either agree to accept a lesser sum, or accept it later. There will also be no need to appoint a Trustee in Bankruptcy to realise property: the debtor will be expected to realise it themselves or to give it voluntarily to the supervisor to sell. Not surprisingly, IVAs are extremely popular. Statistics from the Insolvency Service show that there were almost 78,000 IVAs agreed in 2019.

IVAs do, however, share some of the negative features of bankruptcy, including:

- The debtor's name and details of the IVA are publicly listed on the Insolvency Register.

- There are still restrictions on the debtor incurring liabilities (i.e. getting into debt) without permission of the supervisor.

- An IVA still has an impact on credit rating. Since an IVA can last longer, it can remain on the debtor's credit score for longer.

- IVAs typically last for a longer period than bankruptcy. Bankruptcy is over in a year; IVAs are typically several years long.

1.1.2 Failure of the IVA

If a debtor does not comply with the terms of the IVA, the IVA is said to 'fail'. The effect of failure will depend on the terms of the IVA, but usually this results in the supervisor petitioning for the bankruptcy of the debtor. A supervisor can petition for the bankruptcy of the debtor if they can show that the debtor has failed to comply with the IVA's terms; that the debtor submitted misleading or false information in support of the IVA; or that the debtor has not complied with the reasonable requests of the supervisor (s276 of the Act). The creditors' position is also likely to be determined by the terms of the IVA, but the default is usually that they are no longer bound by the IVA.

In exceptional circumstances, the court can order that the IVA should continue despite the debtor's breach. This can be, for example, on the basis that the IVA is still in the best interests of creditors. However, the court's starting point will be that if the debtor agreed to the IVA, and the IVA has specific provisions dealing with its failure, then the debtor should be bound by the agreement. A debtor cannot rely on the court's discretion to dismiss a bankruptcy petition in these circumstances.

If one IVA fails, or if it seems likely to fail, it is possible to pass a second IVA provided creditors vote for it. The rules for a second IVA are the same as the first.

1.1.3 Conclusion

From the perspective of a debtor who cannot pay their debts, an IVA is likely to be the best route out of their financial difficulties. However, it is not within the debtor's power to enter into an IVA by themselves: they need 75% of the creditors by value to agree as well. Most of this book concerns situations where the creditors (or at least more than 25% of them by value) insist on presenting a bankruptcy petition. However, a common litigation tactic for debtors is to make an IVA appear more attractive in order to settle the claim. As will be discussed, a bankruptcy petition must be dismissed by the court or withdrawn by the petitioner if an IVA is agreed. Part of the strategy of a debtor is likely to be to promote an IVA, and so the route should never be closed. It follows that making a threat of the form "*if you do not agree by a certain date, I will withdraw the proposal*" is likely to be counter-productive.

1.2 Debt relief orders

Debt relief orders (DROs) are an administrative scheme which allows debtors with very little money to escape their debts. They can only be made when a debtor has total assets of less than £1,000, unsecured debts of less than £20,000 and a disposable surplus monthly income (after household expenses and taxes) of less than £50 per month.[1] There are complications with the definition of these terms, but if the debtor's financial position is in this range, then a DRO may be an option. A DRO does not involve a Trustee in Bankruptcy selling the estate of the debtor, like an IVA. However, unlike an IVA, a debtor subject to a DRO will not be expected to contribute to repaying the debts. This is because the debtor's estate is of such little value that it would not be worthwhile doing so.

A DRO application must contain a list of liquidated debts, sometimes called a schedule of debts. A DRO removes all debts in that schedule. Not all debts can be included in a schedule to the DRO application: unliquidated debts and the debts in Box 1 on page 7 above cannot be included. A DRO creates restrictions similar to a bankruptcy order, which last a year. For example, debtors subject to a DRO cannot borrow more than £500 without disclosing the existence of the DRO, and similar criminal offences apply to a debtor who makes a gift with an intention to defraud creditors. The DRO does not affect the right of a secured creditor to enforce their security, for example, if the creditor has a log-book loan, they may still be able to repossess the car.

If a debtor makes a DRO and accidentally fails to include a debt, it falls outside of the DRO and a creditor will be able to enforce it.

There are typically more DROs made than bankruptcy orders. There were almost 27,500 DROs made in 2019. The debtor is required to submit a paper application to the Official Receiver via one of six approved bodies. These are Citizens Advice; StepChange; MoneyPlus; Institution of Money Advisers; National Debtline; and Payplan. A DRO currently costs £90, but some providers allow this to be paid in instalments and some charities provide grants to help applicants.

---

[1] *The precise conditions for a DRO are that: a) the debtor is domiciled in England and Wales on the application date, or at any time during the three years before applying the debtor was ordinarily resident or had a place of residence or carried on business in England and Wales; b) the debtor is not an undischarged bankrupt, subject to an interim order or an IVA, or subject to a bankruptcy restrictions order or a debt relief restrictions order; c) a bankruptcy application has not been made, or has been made but was not successful; d) a creditor's petition has not been presented before the determination date, or it had been presented but proceedings had been finally disposed of, or the presenter of the petition has consented to the making of an application for a DRO; e) has not had the benefit of a DRO in the six years before the determination of their application; f) has not given a preference or entered into a transaction at an undervalue within two years ending with the application date.*

BOX 3: WHAT IF THE DEBTOR NEARLY QUALIFIES FOR A DRO?

A debtor with £1,001 of assets cannot apply for a DRO. From the debtor's perspective, this is highly regrettable. If they qualified for the DRO, they would keep up to £1,000. If they do not qualify then they may be made bankrupt and so lose their £1,001 in the various legal fees concerned. What can the debtor do?

It is a criminal offence to make a false representation in the application (s251O of the Act). It is a criminal offence to make a gift or transfer of property within two years of making an application (s251Q). A person is not guilty if they had no intention to defraud or conceal the state of affairs (s251Q(3)). It is likely to be a criminal offence to give the £1 to a friend before applying for a DRO. It is **not** a criminal offence to spend the £1, provided it is not done to defraud the creditors. If the money was spent on something of lasting value, this would remain the property of the debtor and count towards their assets. However, if the purchase was on food or at the cinema, nothing of value would remain afterwards.

The intention of the debtor is critical. It would be a criminal offence to deliberately go to a restaurant so that their creditors do not receive the money. It is not a criminal offence if an individual feels hungry and decides to spend a few extra pounds at a restaurant. The key difference is whether or not the debtor has the motive of defrauding their creditors. The criminal offences applicable to DROs are similar as for bankruptcy, and so see Chapter 7 for more detail.

If a debtor has assets of over £1,000, and debts of over £20,000, it may be possible to repay the debts until the debts fall below the critical level of £20,000. This is a sensible strategy for the debt since it allows them to keep at least £1,000. Care should be taken when repaying debts to ensure it does not constitute a preference. In practice, this means the primary motivation should not be to allow a particular creditor to be in a better position (and certainly not a connected creditor, such as a family member). A debtor who repays their landlord because they are concerned about being evicted would not be giving a preference.

If a debtor increases their assets or income to above the minimum set out above, the Official Receiver can revoke the DRO. This commonly happens because the debtor receives a windfall (say, they receive an inheritance which takes them over the £1,000 limit) or because the debtor starts a new job which increases their disposable monthly income. This creates a perverse incentive not to be promoted (and perhaps, not be employed at all). However, the effect is only a year and a relatively small increase in assets is unlikely to trigger a review by the Official Receiver. If the income arises after the DRO year, then the debtor can keep it without needing to repay their earlier debts.

If a debtor qualifies for a DRO, a DRO is likely to be an even better outcome than an IVA. This is because there is no need to repay the debts: the slate is wiped clean automatically. It is also because a DRO does not require creditor approval. No creditor will choose to approve a DRO: it guarantees zero return and bars them from recovering their debt. A DRO can be challenged, but in practice, unless the creditor believes that the debtor has substantially more than £1,000 of assets, it will not be value for money for them to do so. Note the use of a DRO when negotiating an IVA: if the debtor is in a poor financial position, they may be able to use the threat of a DRO to ensure that they keep at least a few hundred pounds of assets left to themselves.

A debt relief order can lead to a debt relief restriction order or undertaking: these are equivalent to bankruptcy restriction orders, for which see Chapter 9.

The six organisations that can submit DROs all have websites which are written for the ordinary user and can be consulted for more information about the process.

Stop press

There is currently a consultation to raise the thresholds to make it easier to obtain a DRO. This would increase the total amount of debt allowable to £30,000 (from £20,000); increase the value of assets owned by the individual to £2,000 (from £1,000); and increase the level of surplus income to £100 (from £50) per month.

1.3   County Court Administration Orders

A County Court Administration Order (CCAO) is another insolvency procedure where the County Court takes control of the debtor's finances. It is rarely used. There were fewer than 150 of these orders made in 2019.

Under s112 of the County Courts Act 1984, where a debtor is unable to pay a County Court judgment of less than £5,000, the court may make an order providing for the administration of their estate. This typically is the payment of the debt by instalment, or the debt may be written off after a certain time. Since the debt must be less than £5,000, the creditor could not present a bankruptcy petition in any event.

The debtor needs to complete form N92, which can be found at https://www.gov.uk/government/publications/form-n92-application-for-an-administration-order.

The decision is usually made without a hearing. There is space for the debtor to suggest an appropriate repayment amount per week or month, or the court can make its own decision. There is space on the form to state any particular circumstances which the court ought to know about.

If the order is made, the court will send a copy to all the creditors who will be included in a schedule to the order. This procedure is appropriate when the debtor cannot use a DRO because they do not meet the qualifying conditions. They can be used when the debtor has a monthly income above the DRO threshold but the creditors refuse to agree to an IVA. These orders can be made by any County Court.

There are possible changes to this procedure, but since these are on indefinite hold, they are of no current interest to a debtor.

Stop Press: The Debt Respite Scheme (Breathing Space)

The Government is planning on introducing a 'Debt Respite Scheme', also known as 'Breathing Space'. This will allow debtors some protection from enforcement action, including the presentation of a bankruptcy petition, for up to 60 days. For example, creditors will not be able to start a claim against the debtor, send bailiffs, repossess property, or disconnect the gas supply, while the scheme is in place. The Debt Respite Scheme will also freeze most interest and charges on debts. The Debt Respite Scheme is available to every debtor, but there is an extension for individuals who are receiving mental health crisis treatment. Those individuals will be able to access this scheme for as long as their crisis treatment lasts, plus 30 days. The scheme can only be accessed via a debt adviser, and the policy behind the proposal is to encourage debtors to get debt advice at an early stage. The debt adviser will need to be satisfied that the Debt Respite Scheme would be appropriate for their client, and that the debtor cannot, or is unlikely to be able to, repay all their debts.

This scheme is scheduled to commence in May 2021. It appears to be a shortcut to obtaining an interim order and could be used to allow the debtor to enter into an IVA or some other compromise position with their creditors. However, the Debt Respite Scheme as currently drafted appears to only stop bankruptcy proceedings *beginning*, and does not automatically stay bankruptcy proceedings once they have been initiated regardless of whether the debtor is having a mental health crisis. However, a judge would still have discretion to adjourn a hearing if they considered it appropriate during the 'Breathing Space' period.

For more details, see the Government's advice to creditors at https://www.gov.uk/government/publications/debt-respite-scheme-breathing-space-guidance/debt-respite-scheme-breathing-space-guidance-for-creditors.

Chapter 2   Effect of bankruptcy

This chapter is about what happens when someone goes bankrupt. Most of this book assumes the debtor wishes to contest the bankruptcy petition. This, and the next chapter, discuss whether that is a sensible decision or whether bankruptcy is a better outcome.

BOX 4:   PRE-BANKRUPTCY

People are not suddenly made bankrupt. Where an individual is made bankrupt on the request of their creditors, the individual is likely to have had a debt for several months and the creditor would have written to ask for repayment on multiple occasions. Then the creditor will issue a 'statutory demand' (see Chapter 4) which is a formal step demanding repayment within 21 days, and which permits the issuing of a bankruptcy petition. The court will then have a hearing to determine that the conditions for making a bankruptcy order are met (see Chapter 5). If they are, the court will make a bankruptcy order. There is typically at least four months between the statutory demand and the first hearing of the bankruptcy petition.

2.1   Stages of bankruptcy

Shortly after the bankruptcy order is made, the bankrupt will be contacted by their 'Trustee in Bankruptcy'. The Trustee is the person who will be in charge of administrating the bankruptcy. They must be an independent, regulated Insolvency Practitioner. The Trustee will likely be the Official Receiver, a civil servant working for the Department for Business, Energy and Industrial Strategy. However, the bankrupt's creditors will be able to decide whether to appoint a private practitioner to be the Trustee in Bankruptcy to replace the Official Receiver.

The Insolvency Service has an internal target of 20 days to complete the first interview of the bankrupt following a bankruptcy order made by a creditor's petition. In practice, they may be a few days slower.

The role of the Trustee is, under s305 of the Act, to 'get in and realise (i.e. sell) the estate of the bankrupt'. It is helpful to discuss the estate of the bankrupt and the process of 'realising' it separately.

2.2 The estate of the bankrupt

The 'estate' of the bankrupt is the property which a Trustee in Bankruptcy is entitled to sell. The definition of 'property' is very wide, and it includes property held overseas, shares, and goodwill of the bankrupt's business.

The property of the estate automatically 'vests' (i.e. belongs) to the Trustee. The role of the Trustee is to sell that property to distribute the proceeds to the creditors. To give an example: before a debtor becomes bankrupt, they have unrestricted access to their own bank account. After the bankruptcy order is made, the Trustee is entitled to make payments out of that account, and the bankrupt is no longer able to. It is contempt of court not to deliver up to the Trustee all the property, books and records which they are required to take control of: see s312 of the Act. A bankrupt is **not** allowed to sell property they once held without the permission of the Trustee. One of the first acts of the Trustee is likely to be to contact all the bankrupt's banks to request that no further transactions take place from the account without their permission, or to transfer the money into a separate account controlled by the Trustee.

2.2.1 Exceptions

Not all property which belongs to the bankrupt gets automatically transferred to the Trustee. Most of it does. The only property which does not get transferred to the Trustee is set out in s283(2) of the Insolvency Act:

- such tools, books, vehicles and other items of equipment as are necessary to the bankrupt for use personally by them in their employment, business or vocation;

- such clothing, bedding, furniture, household equipment and provisions as are necessary for satisfying the basic domestic needs of the bankrupt and their family.

The first exception means that if the bankrupt is, for example, a builder then they can keep the main items of equipment needed for their job such as a vehicle with a large boot or a valuable collection of drills. This exception is limited because the Trustee has the power to replace an expensive item with a less expensive item which will perform a similar purpose. To give an extreme example, if the Trustee decides that the bankrupt does not need a Jaguar car, but can perform their job with a Skoda, then the Trustee can sell the expensive car, buy the cheaper one, and distribute any profit to the creditors. In practice, a Trustee will only choose to substitute an item if there is a substantial difference between the sale price of the second-hand item and its replacement price. Otherwise, it is not worth the Trustee's time to make the sale.

The second exception means that the bankrupt can keep their bed linen, oven and basic living equipment. Again the exception would allow a Trustee to substitute an expensive bed for a cheaper one if they deemed it fit. Since second-hand domestic goods are of little value, it is rare for the Trustee to sell them unless they are almost new.

2.2.2   Legal claims

The bankrupt's 'property' includes any potential legal claims the bankrupt could make. Only the Trustee in Bankruptcy can sue third parties; the bankrupt cannot do so themselves. The bankrupt cannot even act as a litigant in person even if this comes at no direct cost to the bankrupt's estate. This is because if the bankrupt brought a claim and lost, the estate would probably be held liable for the costs to the defendant. The Trustee is in charge of making all claims on behalf of the bankrupt. They can abandon an active case, or settle a claim instead of taking it to court.

There are two exceptions to this rule. Firstly, a bankrupt can appeal against their own bankruptcy order. Secondly, the bankrupt can bring a claim where the claim is personal to the bankrupt – for example, a personal injury claim, a defamation claim or a claim for unfair dismissal. Where a claim is a 'hybrid' of both types, such as a personal injury claim where the claimant's car was also damaged, the claim can only be made by the Trustee. If the Trustee makes a recovery, they will recover the personal element on behalf of the bankrupt and will have to give it back to them and not the creditors. The bankrupt should tell the Trustee about all the possible claims they could make, as part of describing all of the assets in the estate.

If the Trustee does not want to go ahead with a case, the bankrupt will need to ask the Trustee to transfer ('assign') them the claim if they wish to do so themselves. A Trustee would be unlikely to allow a bankrupt to commence litigation while their bankruptcy was undischarged, but they might consider it afterwards. A solicitor will be cautious about accepting instructions from an undischarged bankrupt to ensure that the individual has the right to litigate the claim, rather than their Trustee.

It frequently happens that a bankruptcy order is made on a judgment debt. Once the bankruptcy order is made, the bankrupt would have no standing to even challenge this debt, except with the permission of the Trustee or an order of the court.

2.2.3   Trusts

If the bankrupt is the beneficiary under a discretionary trust, the bankrupt would not have the right to any trust property unless and until the individuals controlling the trust make a distribution. It follows that nothing would fall into the bankrupt's estate. However, if the assets are held on a 'bare trust', i.e. if the bankrupt can insist on being given the assets, then this will be property of the estate.

2.2.4   Pensions

'Property' also includes certain pension rights, but the Trustee is restricted from accessing this money. A Trustee in Bankruptcy cannot compel the bankrupt to draw down a pension, and most pension income is excluded from the estate. The capital sum of an individual's pension is also excluded from the definition of 'estate' out of a concern that if individuals lose their pensions their only form of support later in life will be from the state. However, pension income is considered 'income' for an income payments order, and so can be recovered that way (see Paragraph 2.13). A Trustee can also recover excessive pension contributions made historically (see Paragraph 2.6).

2.2.5   Jointly held property

Only property which belongs to the bankrupt falls into their estate. A common situation is that the bankrupt is married, and they jointly own the house they live in with their spouse. The Trustee is only entitled to the bankrupt's share of the assets. This means that if, for example, after considering the mortgage, a house is worth £100,000 and it is shared equally between a bankrupt and her husband, then the Trustee will own the bankrupt's £50,000 share. The Trustee would have a duty to sell the house for the highest possible price, and then transfer half the proceeds to the non-bankrupt husband. The Trustee is entitled to take the bankrupt's share. More information on house repossessions is set out in Chapter 6.

A Trustee in Bankruptcy has to decide what property this is. It is difficult, sometimes impossible, to determine who owns what contents of a household. Unless there is evidence which proves that a certain item belongs to the bankrupt as opposed to their spouse, the Trustee is likely to take a pragmatic approach and be content provided roughly half the valuable items fall into the estate.

BOX 5:   HOW MUCH OF THE HOUSE DOES THE BANKRUPT OWN?

The starting point for a Trustee in Bankruptcy is that the Land Registry should say who owns what percentage of a house: for example, whether a husband and wife own the property 50:50, or if there is some other division of interest. Unless the bankrupt and their family can produce evidence to the contrary, this will be the end of the analysis.

However, it is possible that the Land Registry, which only reports the 'legal interest', does not represent the beneficial interest. This would happen when the legal owner holds part of the house on trust for someone else. This could be through some express declaration of trust; or when one party made a contribution to some or all of the purchase price, or payments towards the mortgage or upkeep of the house. The non-bankrupt partner should present a schedule of all the payments they have made in relation to the house to claim as large a proportion of the property as possible. They may need separate legal advice to help them demonstrate what their true entitlement is. In practice, a Trustee is likely to want to come to a settlement rather than litigate.

2.3   Sale of the estate

Under s306 of the Act, the bankrupt's estate vests in the Trustee automatically, without any further formalities. This means that the Trustee can control the balance in the bank account, and has the power to sell property belonging to the bankrupt such as any valuable items like a television or car. If necessary, the Trustee can issue a warrant authorising the seizure of property, to break open premises, or to allow a police constable or officer of the court to search property not belonging to the bankrupt, but which contains important documents (s365 of the Act).

The sale of assets is one of the most important aspects of bankruptcy. Other than the exceptions discussed above, all property which the bankrupt owns is transferred to the Trustee in Bankruptcy to sell. This means that the Trustee has the right to physically remove property which the bankrupt otherwise has in their possession. The Trustee may decide that certain items are not worth the sales value. For example, they are unlikely to sell a collection of photo frames. However, this decision is for the Trustee to make, and the bankrupt has no direct say in the matter. Applications to challenge decisions of Trustees are set out in Chapter 8.

A Trustee can use whatever means of selling the property they consider best. They frequently use auctions as a way of selling something quickly and to the highest bidder on the day. There is sometimes a trade-off between obtaining the highest price and making a quick sale. The Trustee is likely to make this decision based only on the views of the creditors. A Trustee owes limited duties to the bankrupt, discussed in Chapter 8. The Trustee will be responsible for paying taxes, like capital gains tax, which are payable as expenses of the bankruptcy.

2.3.1   Sale of shares

If the bankrupt owned shares in a private company, the Trustee will be likely to negotiate the sale of the bankrupt's shares with the other shareholders. The Trustee cannot compel the shareholders to purchase the shares. Since it is unlikely to be useful to the creditors to be given a share in a private company, the Trustee is in a weak negotiating position. By virtue of s771(5)(b) of the Companies Act 2006, the company cannot refuse to register the Trustee in Bankruptcy as the holder of the shares in place of the bankrupt. However, the company might have restrictions around the transfer of shares to a potential external purchaser. The Trustee can use their shares to vote in company meetings if this would be in the interest of creditors. The Trustee would be bound by a shareholders agreement or articles of association. They would probably also be bound if the agreement provides that upon bankruptcy, the shareholder must sell shares to a particular person and at a particular price.

2.3.2   Sale of house

There are special rules around the sale of the house in which the bankrupt lives (see Chapter 6). The Trustee has the power to apply to the court for the bankrupt's post to be redirected elsewhere for up to three months, although this is not routinely used.

2.4   Disclaimer of property

By virtue of s315 of the Act, the Trustee has the general power to disclaim 'onerous property': i.e. it is not obliged to keep property or commitments which burdens the estate. In particular, the Trustee has the power to breach contracts, and let the other party claim ('prove') for compensation as an unsecured creditor for any loss and damage they suffered. If the bankrupt holds property which carries with it some liability to pay money – such as freehold land which incurs tax liability, or a lease with monthly rent – the Trustee can unilaterally decide to 'disclaim' it, such that it has no owner.

The Trustee can use the power to disclaim property without requiring permission of the court. An exception is for after-acquired property or property which the Trustee has replaced (see s315(4) of the Act). A Trustee disclaims property by giving notice to the bankrupt and to anyone else with an interest in the property and the court.

Property which has been disclaimed does not go back to the bankrupt. Since the Trustee gets nothing from a disclaimer (they merely avoid a liability) it may be possible to persuade a Trustee to sell the property to a friend of the bankrupt for a token amount.

BOX 6:   RELATIONSHIP WITH THE TRUSTEE

The Trustee plays a crucial part in the life of the bankrupt. They can decide what the bankrupt can spend money on, what items they can keep and what is to be sold. They can apply for the bankruptcy to be extended beyond its usual length of a year. They decide whether they believe that the bankrupt has committed any misconduct. If the Trustee thinks the bankrupt has, the Trustee will be responsible for what happens next. If the Trustee feels they can rely on the bankrupt, they are less likely to dispute what the bankrupt tells them. For example, if the bankrupt has a good relationship with the Trustee, the Trustee will not be suspicious if the bankrupt says that an item is owned by the spouse of the bankrupt rather than the bankrupt themselves and so does not fall into their estate. It follows that it is vital for the bankrupt to get on with the Trustee at a personal level. A strong working relationship can be achieved by: 1) being open and cooperative when asked questions; 2) being realistic about what the bankrupt will be allowed to keep and not keep; and 3) not making any attempts to hide assets. If the Trustee is the Official Receiver, they are unlikely to care that the bankrupt opposed the bankruptcy petition, provided they acted honesty during the process.

It is difficult for the bankrupt to keep calm when a stranger has so much control over their life. A Trustee should do their best to explain what they are doing and why. Not all Trustees are diligent. However, although it will take a large amount of effort to be polite and courteous to the Trustee, the effort will be rewarded. Put differently: there can be serious consequences of the relationship breaking down. Chapter 8 discusses ways in which a bankrupt can control the Trustee's actions. These are challenging applications to make.

2.5   Review of the conduct of the bankrupt

Another aspect of the Trustee's role is to examine the conduct of the bankrupt and see if they have committed any bankruptcy offences. These relate to deliberately defrauding creditors and are examined in more detail in Chapter 7.

The Trustee is likely to review the bank accounts of the bankrupt to look for unusual transactions, and they are likely to interview the bankrupt again if they find anything suspicious. It is a criminal offence for the bankrupt to lie to the Trustee. The Trustee can also apply to the court to summon the bankrupt's spouse or business partners to give them evidence about the bankrupt's affairs. A Trustee is likely to contact any lawyers instructed by the bankrupt to be able to understand their affairs properly. Trustees are entitled to read private legal documents which no other person would be entitled to read. The only documents they do not have access to would relate to a claim the bankrupt might make against the Trustee themselves. Examinations are discussed in Paragraph 2.16.1.

If the Trustee believes that the bankrupt has absconded or is about to, or is likely to remove or conceal important property or documents, the court may issue a warrant for the bankrupt's arrest (s364 of the Act). The purpose is not to punish the bankrupt, but to compel them to comply with their obligations as a bankrupt.

2.6   Increasing the asset pool

A Trustee will have all the powers of the bankrupt to sue for debts owed to the bankrupt. If the bankrupt were themselves owed money by some third party, the Trustee would demand that it gets repaid. Creditors of the bankrupt will not escape paying because of the bankruptcy order, although the Trustee may strike a deal to ensure prompt payment of the debts owed.

However, the powers of a Trustee go much further than those of the bankrupt. A Trustee can apply to the court to undo certain transactions. The two most common are:

1. **Transactions at an undervalue**: s339 of the Act. Where the bankrupt has 'at a relevant time' entered into a transaction at an undervalue, the Trustee can apply for an order for the court to restore the position to what it would have been had the transaction not happened. A transaction at an undervalue includes a gift, or when the amount received is significantly less than the value given by the bankrupt. An example of a transaction at an undervalue is when a car with a street value of £10,000 is sold for £5,000.

    The 'value' of an object is, in practice, subjective. A car may achieve £10,000 if the seller is diligent in finding a purchaser, but only £5,000 if the seller goes to the first car dealership they know about. Transactions at an undervalue are usually only identified in extreme cases, where the best explanation for why the item was sold at that value is the desire for the purchaser to make a profit at the expense of the soon-to-be bankrupt. This desire is not a requirement of a s339 transaction.

2. **Preferences**: s340 of the Act. Where a bankrupt has 'at a relevant time' given a preference to any person, the Trustee can apply for an order for the court to restore the position to what it would have been had the individual not given that preference. A 'preference' is given where one creditor (or a guarantor of the bankrupt's debts) is deliberately put in the position where they are better off. It will be assumed that the preference was deliberately given if it was received by an 'associate' of the bankrupt. Outside of an associate, it is often difficult for a Trustee to show that a preference was given with the wrong intention. An example of a preference is when a bankrupt repays her parents' loan in full. Even though the money was owed to the parents, the parents would be in a better position than had they received the same treatment as their daughter's other unsecured creditors.

'Associate' is defined in s435 of the Act, but it commonly refers to a relative or a spouse. It excludes best friends, perhaps because it would be difficult to demonstrate that two people were sufficiently friendly. This does not mean it is acceptable to grant a preference to a best friend – this could be a criminal offence if the intention was to defraud creditors – but only to note that it is more difficult for the Trustee to undo the preference. An associate includes an employer or employee. A company is an associate of another person if that person has control of it, or if that person or their other associates together have control of it. Merely because someone is a 'business associate' of the bankrupt does not mean that they are an associate for the purposes of s435 of the Act, although the two might be associates through joint control of a company.

Although a transaction at an undervalue does not need to be to an associate, in practice a Trustee will most likely suspect a transaction has been made at an undervalue when it was made to someone connected with the bankrupt in some way. It would be peculiar for a bankrupt to make a transaction at an undervalue with a stranger: there would be no reason not to obtain full value.

The 'relevant time' is defined in three ways,

- For a transaction at an undervalue, it is five years before the day when the bankruptcy petition was presented.

- For a preference which is not a transaction at an undervalue but is given to an associate, it is two years ending with the presentation of the bankruptcy petition.

- Finally, for a preference which is not a transaction at an undervalue and not given to an associate, it is six months ending with the day the petition is presented.

If the Trustee's application is successful, the court will "*make such order as it thinks fit for restoring the position to what it would have been if that individual had not entered into that transaction*". The order the Trustee typically applies for is an order to undo the transaction or preference. For example, it would be to reclaim the money paid to the parents, who would then be repaid at the same proportion as all of the other creditors. However, the court has wide powers to make the appropriate order to undo the transaction. In the example of the car sold at an undervalue, the Trustee might ask simply for the excess £5,000 to be repaid rather than undoing the whole transaction and receiving a £10,000 car.

There is some protection given for third parties who are affected by transactions at an undervalue or preferences where they can show that they acquired the property in good faith and for value under s342 of the Act. Where the person did not deal directly with the bankrupt, they cannot be required to pay any money back or undo the transaction. Even where they did deal directly, the order will not undo the transaction. An example where this matters is where there is a transfer of shares which are later worth more: the Trustee cannot ask for a return of the shares.

However, if the third party was aware that the individual was likely to go bankrupt and that the property was at an undervalue, or if they were an associate of that individual, then it will be presumed that they were not acting in good faith. The third party will be able to bring evidence to rebut this presumption.

It is a defence to a claim under these sections if it can be shown that the bankrupt was solvent at the time and did not become insolvent as a consequence of the transaction. If that was the case, then the creditors were not prejudiced by the transaction or preference, since (at that time) they could still be repaid by the bankrupt. The bankrupt's insolvency is presumed if the transaction was to an associate.

These claims can be brought even after the bankruptcy is discharged. The money returned by the claim will be distributed to the creditors as if it was an asset of the estate during the bankruptcy. A Trustee has six years to bring a claim for the return of money and 12 years for any other remedy.

The court has discretion to make the order it thinks fit. This includes making no order at all. In *Bucknall v Wilson* [2020] EWHC 1200 (Ch) the bankrupt instructed his stepdaughter to provide accountancy services for which he owed her £99,330. The bankrupt paid his stepdaughter and all his other creditors rather than repay a judgment debtor against whom he had a personal grudge.

The judge held that this repayment to the stepdaughter was a preference. The stepdaughter, who was a litigant in person, relied on her personal circumstances and said that the only way she could repay the preference would be to sell her house where she lived with her two children. The court declined to order her to repay the preference. It placed weight on its finding that the debt arose from a commercial relationship and represented a fair amount for the work done, the stepdaughter had acted in good faith, and she would face wholly disproportionate consequences should an order be made.

The next most common forms of transaction review in descending order of importance are:

3. **Avoiding dispositions made after the presentation of the bankruptcy petition**: s284 of the Act. Due to this section, all 'dispositions' of property made by the bankrupt after the presentation of the bankruptcy petition are void unless ratified by the court. The disposition is void even if it is otherwise a harmless transaction. However, the Trustee may decide not to take any steps to reclaim property if it would not be cost-effective. 'Disposition' refers to all the ways a bankrupt can transfer property, including a sale, a gift, a loan, etc. There is protection in s284(4) of the Act for a third party who received property in good faith, for value and without notice of the bankruptcy petition. The practical point for the bankrupt is that someone aware of the petition may refuse to trade with them or even accept part payment of a debt, out of concern that any transaction will be void under this section. If the bankrupt wishes to continue to trade, for example, then they will need to seek a 'validation order' from the court permitting the disposition.

This section has a far reaching legal effect. In theory, a debtor's purchase of a sandwich from a shop is a void disposition, albeit one where no claim is possible against the shop. In practice, s284 only matters for particularly large transactions (including a series of small transactions), transactions with a counterparty who is aware of the bankruptcy petition (for example, a bank), and as a means of short-cutting the process for proving a particular transaction was at an undervalue. It can be difficult to prove a disposition was at an undervalue, but it is usually simple to prove that it was made after the presentation of the bankruptcy petition.

BOX 7: VALIDATION ORDERS

In virtue of s284 of the Act, after a bankruptcy petition has been presented all dispositions of property are void unless they were made with the consent of the court, either before or after the disposition. This does not allow any claim against a third party who received property for its fair price ('for value') and without notice that the petition had been presented. However, if a third party does have notice then it is not safe for them to trade with the debtor because the Trustee can claim against them. The section therefore creates a problem for the debtor if they need to sell property or grant a charge over property in order to raise money to pay their debts.

The solution is to apply to the court for permission to make the sale, known as a 'validation order'. The debtor should give notice of the application to the petitioning creditor. A petitioning creditor is likely to agree to this application, if they think that the transaction is legitimate. The rules for the application are found in paragraph 12.8 of the PDIP. The court will make the order if it is satisfied that either the debtor is solvent and able to pay their debts, or that the transaction will be beneficial to and not prejudice the unsecured creditors of the debtor as a whole.

The selling of an asset for value will not usually prejudice the unsecured creditors. For example, imagine the debtor owns a car worth £10,000. Before the sale, the debtor held an asset, the car. After the sale, the debtor holds £10,000. The unsecured creditors are no worse off: if anything, their position has been improved since the debtor is now able to pay the creditors more easily.

An example application for a validation order for a company is at Annex 1.

4. **Transactions defrauding creditors**: s423 of the Act. This applies even when the individual has not gone bankrupt, but where they entered into a transaction at an undervalue and the purpose of the transaction was to defraud the creditors, i.e. to put assets outside of their reach. Where there are multiple purposes, the court will apply a 'substantial purpose' test, i.e. that one important result which the debtor <u>intended</u> to achieve by the transaction was that creditors would be put in a worse position. In general, Trustees will prefer to use the standard 'transaction at an undervalue' approach where it would not be necessary to demonstrate that the bankrupt had a particular intention.

Finally, the following claims are theoretically possible but they are almost never used:

5. **Assignment of book debts**: s344 of the Act. When someone trades, they are likely to have a list of debtors who owe them money. It is possible to assign the debtors to a third party so that the third party can collect the money. Such an assignment would not bind the Trustee unless the assignment has been registered under the Bill of Sales Act 1878. Such registration requires an application to the Queen's Bench Division of the High Court. It is not common to have such a general assignment of debts.

6. **Excessive pension contributions**: s342A of the Act. Where an individual has made 'excessive' contributions to their pension which has unfairly prejudiced the creditors, these can be claimed back by the Trustee. This rarely applies due to the difficulty in showing that the payments were indeed excessive. It is often easier to show that the pension payments were made to remove the assets from the estate, i.e. to bring a s423 claim.

7. **Extortionate credit transactions**: s343 of the Act. If the bankrupt takes out a loan with 'grossly exorbitant' repayments or otherwise 'grossly contravenes ordinary principles of fair dealing' then this can be undone. An exaggerated example would be where the bankrupt took out a loan of £100 for a month, and then had to repay £10,000 30 days later. This is rarely applied due to the difficulty in showing that the loan was extortionate. If the loan is so extreme, the Trustee may be suspicious it was a transaction at an undervalue.

2.7 Calculating the debts of the bankrupt

The Trustee will compile a list of the debts of the bankrupt. Potential creditors will be asked to 'prove' their debt, i.e. demonstrate that the bankrupt owed them a certain sum of money. Creditors owed debts of less than £1,000 will not need to submit formal proof but will be believed automatically unless there is some reason to challenge the debt: r14.1(3) and para 18A of Sch 9 of the Act.

The making of a bankruptcy order stops the clock on interest accruing under a debt. Creditors will prove for the amount owed as of the date of the bankruptcy order. After then, all interest on debts will accrue at the statutory rate of 8% p a

BOX 8: PROOF OF DEBT

Due to r14.2(1) all claims by creditors are provable as debts against the bankrupt, whether they are present or future, certain or contingent, and regardless of whether they have an ascertained value. The Trustee in Bankruptcy will decide what value to give to a proof of debt. The exceptions to this rule are fines, or claims for child support or family law proceedings. The significance of a proof of debt is that a non-provable debt will not be written off when the bankruptcy is discharged.

A bankrupt might dispute the existence or size of the debt with a potential creditor. A Trustee is unlikely to continue this dispute because, unlike the bankrupt, they have no personal interest in the matter. From their perspective, a Trustee can either admit the debt upon seeing the evidence the creditor wishes to provide, refuse to admit the debt and see if the creditor wishes to sue them, or settle the claim with the creditor. Most potential creditors are unlikely to want to take a bankrupt to court because such action is expensive, and they know that there is little prospect of recovering the money.

As part of this process, the Trustee will ask the bankrupt's creditors whether any of them hold security. A debt secured on property is one where the creditor is entitled to the proceeds of sale of that property (or the property itself) if the debt is not repaid. This increases their chance of recovering their money.

The Trustee will establish whether the bankrupt holds any property which does not belong to him. For example, if the bankrupt had a dispute about who owned particular property, the Trustee will decide who (in their opinion) the property belongs to. If the property belongs to the bankrupt, it will likely fall into the estate, be sold, and used to repay the creditors as a whole. If it belongs to the other individual, the Trustee will return it and that individual will be 'repaid' in full. If the potential owner does not agree with the Trustee's decision, they are entitled to claim against the estate and the court will decide.

2.8 Effect on the bankrupt's career and business

An undischarged bankrupt:

• Cannot be a director of a company without the permission of the court. Even if the company is solvent, a bankrupt who is a director will have to change their role within the company fundamentally. It could be that the company simply asks the bankrupt to be an employee. However, it is a criminal offence for the bankrupt to serve as a director under s11 of the Company Disqualification of Directors Act 1986. A bankrupt may need to have an awkward conversation with the other directors. It may be that the bankrupt owns the company: if so, ownership of the company (i.e. its shares) would also transfer to the Trustee in Bankruptcy. The Trustee might be happy to continue to let the bankrupt work as an employee, although this is a matter for the Trustee to decide. This rule applies to 'shadow' directors, i.e. it stops someone controlling a company even if they do not formally hold the position of director.

- Cannot be an active member of a limited liability partnership: s7 of the Limited Liability Partnership Act 2000. This does not affect their entitlement to a payment from the partnership (see s7(3)).

- Cannot trade under a different name from the one in which the bankruptcy order was made: s360(1)(b) of the Act. Breach of this is also a criminal offence.

- Cannot be a solicitor without permission of the Solicitors' Regulatory Authority.

- Will be automatically expelled from any partnerships, unless the partnership agreement provides otherwise.

The restriction on acting as a director applies under English law and to an English company. The rules of acting as a director of a non-English company may be different.

BOX 9:   BANKRUPTCY AND EMPLOYMENT

As a general rule, most bankrupts do **not** automatically lose their jobs if they are employed. If the bankrupt is a regulated professional – for example, an accountant or an architect – it may be necessary for the bankrupt to tell their regulator of the bankruptcy order, and their regulator would decide what happens next. Some employment contracts have a clause which says that the employee going bankrupt is a ground for automatic dismissal, although the employer is likely to have discretion about whether to use this right. In general, if an employee is dismissed automatically because they go bankrupt, this may be a ground for a claim for unfair dismissal in the Employment Tribunal. The reader is directed to David Curwen's *Employment Claims Without a Lawyer* for more information.

Most bankrupts do not have to tell their employer about their bankruptcy, but this will depend on the terms of the employment contract.

In general, the Trustee in Bankruptcy will want the bankrupt to keep working. The bankrupt will sign an 'income payment agreement' (see below), and the bankrupt will need a job in order to be able to make the payments. A Trustee might even be prepared to write a reference to reassure a nervous employer or prospective employer.

If the bankrupt themselves had employees, then those contracts will also not automatically end. If the Trustee in Bankruptcy decides to keep them, this counts as continuity of employment for various employment rights. However, the Trustee would be entitled to dismiss the employees – for example, for re-dundancy - and the employees can seek their redundancy payment from the National Insurance Fund. This becomes a preferential debt and the Trustee will repay the sum to the fund before the other unpaid creditors.

There is also no restriction on a bankrupt opening a new bank account, although most banks will not offer this service to an undischarged bankrupt. Those that do are unlikely to offer any credit facilities whatsoever, i.e. to offer a current account with no overdraft.

2.9   Inability to obtain credit

It is a criminal offence for a bankrupt to borrow more than £500 without first disclosing their status as an undischarged bankrupt (s360(1)(a) of the Act). This would include a hire-purchase agreement or an agreement where the bankrupt takes the goods early and pays in instalments over time. The criminal offence applies regardless of the lender, and so it includes personal contacts. However, the offence is only borrowing money without disclosing the status. It is not an offence for a bankrupt to borrow money from a friend if that friend is aware that they are an undischarged bankrupt.

Credit rating agencies (and so credit suppliers, like credit card companies and payday lenders) will be aware of the bankrupt's credit history. Professional lend-ers are unlikely to lend during the bankruptcy at all. Even after the bankruptcy is discharged lenders are unlikely to make a loan to a former bankrupt, and if they do the loan will be at a higher interest rate to reflect the higher risk. Credit rating agencies will keep a record of the bankruptcy for around six years. One of the effects of bankruptcy in practice is that it will be a long time until an individual can borrow money as freely as they did before.

The impact on an individual's credit rating is mitigated by the fact that an indi-vidual with high levels of debt is likely to have a low credit rating anyway. The marginal effect of going bankrupt is likely to be small.

2.10 Running the bankrupt's business

The bankrupt's business, although not any tools of trade, will fall into the estate. A Trustee might decide that it is in the best interests of the creditors for the bankrupt's business to be sold to a third party. This might happen if, for example, the business is incorporated and it is possible to sell the shares of the company. However, the Trustee is also able to run the business themselves, or appoint a manager (including the bankrupt) to do so on their behalf. This creates an opportunity for the bankrupt to offer their services running the business as they were doing previously. However, since the bankrupt was not so successful at running the business, otherwise they would not be made bankrupt, a Trustee may be cautious before agreeing to this proposal.

A bankrupt is not prohibited from starting a new business in the same industry provided they can do so within the constraints of bankruptcy, including a) not being able to act as the director of a company, b) restrictions on the ability to borrow as above, and c) many of the assets of the previous business will now vest in the Trustee. The Trustee in Bankruptcy cannot compel the previous customers to trade with them and not the bankrupt. The rules on after-acquired property (to be discussed below) do not apply to property acquired by the bankrupt in the ordinary course of their business (r10.125(4)), but the bankrupt must share accounting and profit information with the Trustee.

If the bankrupt engages in business, they must trade under the name in which they were made bankrupt (s360(1)(b) of the Act). This is similar to the restriction on obtaining credit: it only imposes the obligation to disclose relevant information.

2.11 Effect on immigration status

Due to s41A of the British Nationality Act 1981, in most circumstances, a person applying for British citizenship must meet a 'good character' requirement. This includes 'consideration of financial soundness'. The Home Office guidance on this requirement can be found at https://assets.publishing.service.gov.uk/government/uploads/system/uploads/attachment_data/file/770960/good-character-guidance.pdf.

An application will not usually be refused simply because the person is in debt. However, the application form, Form AN, asks at question 3.14 "*Have you ever been declared bankrupt?*". The guidance explains that if the bankruptcy was discharged over ten years ago, annulled or if the individual was the director of a company that went into liquidation (presumably when insolvent) over ten years ago, the application can be granted. Otherwise, the Home Office reviewer will take into account the scale of the bankruptcy, the economic circumstances at the time of the application, and make a judgement about whether the person was at fault. The guidance recognises that a person may be made bankrupt through little or no fault of their own if they were the victim of the poor business decisions of others.

The guidance and the form are not clear on how the Home Office treats other forms of insolvency procedure other than bankruptcy, such as entering into an Individual Voluntary Arrangement. Since individuals who sign an IVA will be on the public insolvency register alongside bankrupts, the Home Office is likely to notice. The Secretary of State has wide discretion when applying the good character test, and would be entitled to consider the effect of an IVA. However, the accurate answer to question 3.14 is 'no'.

For more information on applying for citizenship, the reader is directed to the CLP Legal Practice Guides on Immigration Law.

2.12 After-acquired property

While a debtor is still an undischarged bankrupt, they must notify the Trustee if they acquire any additional property or if there is an increase in their income within 21 days of receiving it (r10.125(1)). They cannot dispose of it without the Trustee's consent until 42 days after giving notice, and if they do they have a duty to disclose the name to whom they disposed of the property, for the Trustee to decide whether to attempt to recover it. Failure to comply with this section without a reasonable excuse is contempt of court (s333(4) of the Act).

This provision is intended to capture cases where the bankrupt receives a windfall: for example, they win the lottery or receive an inheritance. If the amount is substantial (in practice, more than a few hundred pounds) the Trustee is likely to distribute it to the creditors rather than allow the bankrupt to keep it for themselves. The Trustee cannot acquire any income of the bankrupt which they earned following the bankruptcy order by notice (s307(5)). Instead, the Trustee will have to apply for an income payment order or make an income payment agreement with the bankrupt.

2.13 Income payments orders

Only property which falls within the bankrupt's estate gets transferred to the Trustee. The bankrupt's estate is defined in terms of property belonging to the bankrupt when the bankruptcy order is made (s283(1)). This means that future income does not automatically belong to the Trustee.

However, the Trustee has the power to apply for an income payments order (IPO) under s310 of the Act. This is an order which claims any income received by the bankrupt beyond the amount needed to satisfy their reasonable domestic needs and the needs of their family. 'Income' here includes business income, although it is in the interest of both the Trustee and the bankrupt for the bankrupt to continue to trade. An application for an IPO can only be made before the bankruptcy is discharged. An IPO can last up to three years from when it is made (s310(6)).

'Reasonable domestic needs' will depend on the circumstances of each individual. It has been held that private school fees were a reasonable domestic need, where removal from school would be detrimental to the children. In general, the Trustee (and the court) will be more favourable to the needs of the bankrupt's family than the bankrupt themselves. The bankrupt should estimate what their typical monthly expenditure is. If the bankrupt routinely earns enough to have savings for the future, the bankrupt should anticipate losing these savings in an IPO. This is an area where the Trustee has a large amount of discretion, and so a good working relationship is likely to lead to a more favourable outcome for the bankrupt.

If the bankrupt and their family are renting property, an often contentious topic is whether they should be forced to move to cheaper accommodation. The Trustee should consider the impact on the bankrupt's family, for example, whether the home has special features to accommodate a disability.

The Insolvency Service has published guidance which can be found at https://www.insolvencydirect.bis.gov.uk/technicalmanual/Ch25-36/Chapter31/part7/Introduction.htm. It says its Official Receivers will seek to use the Office for National Statistics data on the national average outgoings. However, there is no fixed rule. The OR will not seek to collect surplus income if the surplus is too small, e.g. less than £20 per month. In general, the bankrupt will not be allowed luxuries at the expense of the creditors. For example, the Insolvency Service guide says at paragraph 31.7.113 that "*No allowance should be included for social and entertainment expenses (e.g. cigarettes, alcohol, betting etc.)*" and at paragraph 31.7.114 "*In normal circumstances membership of a sporting club, gym, golf club, stables etc. is not considered an essential day-to-day living requirement*". At paragraph 31.7.116, the guide says there should be an allowance of only £10 a month for the bankrupt and for each dependant household member for 'sundries and emergencies'. The guidance was published in 2010. A bankrupt could reasonably ask for more today.

An IPO can also be an order that a bankrupt's employer or other source of income makes a payment directly to the Trustee instead of to the bankrupt (s310(3)(b)). The usual practice is for the order to be that the bankrupt makes payments to the Trustee rather than make any order to a third party. However, if the bankrupt does not meet the payments in the order themselves, the Trustee can apply to vary the IPO for the sum to be paid by a third party.

In order to avoid an IPO, the Trustee is likely to offer an income payments agreement (IPA) under s310A of the Act. The Trustee can send a draft to the bankrupt, who will have 14 days to decide whether to approve it or state the reasons why they do not approve: typically because it does not allow expenditure on an item the bankrupt considers reasonable. This is a binding agreement, but it does not require court approval. It typically takes the form where the bankrupt agrees to pay the Trustee £x a month for Y months. The IPA is likely to have provision for variation, in case the bankrupt gets a promotion or loses their job. An IPA is likely to lead to a better outcome for both the Trustee and the bankrupt. The Trustee will avoid the additional expense of going to court, and is likely to make a more generous offer in order to do so. As a policy, the OR allows a 14 day 'cooling off' period following an IPA to give the bankrupt time to reflect on whether they are happy with the agreement. An IPA, once it has been agreed, can be enforced as if it was a court order (s310A(2)).

Both IPAs and IPOs can only last for three years beginning with the date of the order or the agreement. It is common to last the full three years. There is therefore an advantage to the bankrupt of agreeing the IPA as quickly as possible. The sooner it is agreed, the sooner it will be over.

The court is not sympathetic to Trustees who apply for IPOs in order to recover funds for the creditors when the sum of money requested is disproportionate to the cost of the application itself. Given that a contested application will cost (say) £4,000 at 2021 rates and an IPO will last at most 36 months, the court will be unimpressed if the difference between the Trustee's demand and the bankrupt's offer is less than £100 per month. This factor is a useful point for negotiation: provided the bankrupt makes a reasonable offer, even if it is at the lower end of reasonable offers, the Trustee will feel pressure to accept it rather than make a costly application for an order. See Chapter 18 on settlement for further information.

In practice, the Trustee will give the bankrupt an allowance which they consider reasonable. The Trustee is likely to have a conversation with the bankrupt about what the bankrupt needs to spend money on, for example on fuel for the car, or clothing for children. The bankrupt may need to rely on social security for housing support or to supplement their income. This book does not describe the process for relying on support from the local authority or Universal Credit: see https://www.gov.uk/browse/benefits for more information. The aim of a Trustee in Bankruptcy is not to let the bankrupt starve, but the Trustee will expect outgoings to be at a minimum to collect the extra money to distribute to the creditors.

If the bankrupt suffers a loss in income or enjoys an increase, both an IPO and an IPA can be varied to change the amount to be paid. An IPA can be varied either voluntarily with written agreement of the bankrupt and the Trustee/OR, or by order of the court (s310A(6)).

2.14 Distribution to creditors

Once the Trustee has gathered funds, they will then make a distribution to creditors. The distribution must follow the statutory regime, which in outline is:

- First, secured creditors will be paid. This includes mortgages, which are loans secured on the house. If the sale of the security does not cover the whole amount owed to the creditor, the remaining part is treated like an unsecured debt.

- Second, bankruptcy expenses of the Trustee in Bankruptcy (see r10.149). This includes the Trustee's fees; any expenses they spent on contesting debts; the costs of running the bankrupt's business if the Trustee chooses to do so; and the costs of the petitioner's petition which the court allowed. The significance of this, from the bankrupt's perspective, is that the Trustee is likely to be relatively assured of having their fees paid and so, unlike unsecured creditors, is unlikely to be put off from lengthy negotiation and correspondence.

- Third, preferential debts, which typically refers to unpaid wages, redundancy pay if the bankrupt had employees and certain taxes to HMRC.

- Fourth, ordinary unsecured creditors.

- Fifth, interest on any debt, which will accrue at 8% since the date of the bankruptcy order.

- Sixth, debts to the bankrupt's spouse.

- Finally, any surplus remaining will go to the bankrupt themselves.

If there is not enough to pay all the debts in the category, the amount which remains will be divided equally within the category. For example, if the estate is worth £10,000, the Trustee's expenses come to £5,000, there are no preferential debts and there are unsecured debts of £50,000, the Trustee would be paid in full, and the unsecured creditors would each share the remaining £5,000: i.e. for each £1 of debt they are owed, they would receive 10p. A Trustee may discover that the individual has so few assets that it is not worth making a distribution at all.

A bankrupt may have borrowed money from their own family. Family members will be treated as unsecured creditors – in particular, the family members will receive the same proportion of their loan as the other unsecured creditors. However, one notable exception is the spouse of the bankrupt. Spouses are demoted in the ordinary order since they are only repaid after the interest on debts is paid (s329 of the Act). To re-use the above example, if the unsecured debts can be broken into £30,000 from a bank, £10,000 from the bankrupt's parents and £10,000 from the bankrupt's spouse, the bank and the parents would share the £5,000 and would receive £3,750 and £1,250 respectively (they would each receive 12.5p in the pound). The spouse would receive nothing.

The consequence of this order of distribution is that family members should be aware of the risk of lending money to someone who might go bankrupt: they are likely to receive the same return as the other creditors which is typically a few pennies in the pound. If the bankrupt did repay their family shortly before bankruptcy, the payment is likely to be undone as a preference (see Paragraph 2.6 above). If a generous family member wishes to make a gift to the bankrupt, they are unlikely to want to pay the debts of the bankrupt. The family member, presumably, would want the bankrupt to have the money for themselves. However, such a gift would be 'after-acquired property', and the bankrupt would need to notify their Trustee of the payment under s333 of the Act. A Trustee in Bankruptcy could claim a gift for the estate under s307 of the Act (see below). The best way to help the bankrupt, therefore, is to purchase items for them which the Trustee in Bankruptcy will not want to resell, for example, to do the shopping for them, rather than give them the money to shop themselves. The alternative would be to agree the terms of the gift with the Trustee in Bankruptcy before it is made.

If all the bankrupt's creditors are paid, the bankruptcy will be annulled (see Paragraph 9.2).

This distribution is the only amount creditors will receive. Creditors are not able to demand repayment through other routes, like sending in bailiffs, by virtue of s285 of the Act.

2.15 Publicity of bankruptcy

The name of the bankrupt, their address and their occupations are published on the public Insolvency Register. The register can be found at https://www.insolvencydirect.bis.gov.uk/eiir/. In practice, it is unusual for members of the public to check the Insolvency Register. However, it remains a matter of public record and it is routinely relied on by banks and potential lenders. There will also be a notice with similar information made in the London Gazette, which is at https://www.thegazette.co.uk/.

2.16 Investigations by the Trustee in Bankruptcy

A few days after the making of a bankruptcy order, the Insolvency Service will contact the bankrupt to organise an interview with their Trustee in Bankruptcy. From the bankrupt's perspective, all the details of the bankruptcy are sorted out by the Trustee in Bankruptcy. Most of a Trustee's time is spent understanding the assets and liabilities of the estate. They have powers under the Act which help them to do this.

2.16.1 Investigation powers

The bankrupt is under a duty to cooperate with the Trustee in Bankruptcy under s333 of the Act. This includes giving information to the Trustee about his affairs, meeting the Trustee in person ('attend on the Trustee'), and *"do all such things as the Trustee may for the purpose of carrying out his functions reasonably require"*. This includes giving information about property acquired while still an undischarged bankrupt even after the bankruptcy has been discharged. Failure to cooperate with the Trustee without a reasonable excuse is contempt of court.

At first, the Trustee will speak to the bankrupt informally, perhaps at the debtor's home or at the office of the Trustee. If the Trustee is the Official Receiver (the 'OR'), they will usually require the bankrupt to fill in a 'Bankruptcy Preliminary Information Questionnaire' prior to the face to face interview. A copy of this form can be found at https://www.nationalbailiffadvice.uk/img/PIQB.pdf. If the interviewee is unable to complete the questionnaire, for example, because they are unable to read, the Official Receiver will ensure that the form is read to them.

The Trustee will ask the bankrupt to set out all the property they are aware of, all their debts and the details of all major transactions undergone in the last few years. This will not be done under oath, but it remains a criminal offence to conceal property or to lie to the Trustee in Bankruptcy: see the full list of offences in Chapter 7. Without giving the full list of offences, it is generally the case that any scheme which the bankrupt may think of in order to avoid paying creditors (admitting a false debt; concealing information; transferring property away in advance of bankruptcy; etc.) is a criminal offence.

If the Trustee does not think this response is adequate, they can apply for a public or private examination of the bankrupt. This is a formal hearing where the Trustee will ask the bankrupt questions under oath. It is substantially easier for the bankrupt and the Trustee not to use the examination process. In practice, it is only likely to happen when the Trustee suspects that the bankrupt is hiding something important.

The court has discretion about whether or not to make the order for examination. However, unless it is wholly unreasonable, unnecessary or oppressive the court is likely to accede to the Trustee's request. The mere fact that the examination is inconvenient or involves a lot of preparatory work does not make it unreasonable. It would potentially be unreasonable if the examination was to take place after a significant and unexplained delay, or if there is no real prospect of a recovery for the bankrupt's estate. The court is likely to start with the premise that the OR or the Trustee is not going to waste their time for nothing.

The OR must seek a **public examination** if creditors of more than half of the value of the bankrupt's debts require them to (s290(2) of the Act). The creditors will need to give a reason why they require a public examination. If the OR thinks the request is unreasonable, they may apply to the court for an order to be relieved from making the application (see r10.101).

The court will fix a date for the public examination of the bankrupt. Failure to attend is contempt of court (s290(5)).

The examination itself is similar to a cross-examination of a witness in a usual civil trial. The OR and any creditors have the right to use a barrister to put questions to the bankrupt, and the bankrupt has the right to instruct a barrister for the purpose of putting any questions required to explain or qualify any answers given (r10.103), if they can afford it. The main difference from a civil trial is that the record may be used as evidence in any further proceedings under r10.103(5). In particular, it can be relied on in criminal proceedings. However, if there are existing criminal proceedings, the court may decide to adjourn the hearing if it is of the opinion that the examination might prejudice a fair trial (r10.103(6)). In practice, a public examination typically precedes criminal proceedings and it is not common to have both in parallel.

A **private examination** is slightly different. As the name suggests, it is held in private. Only the bankrupt can be subject to a public examination under s290, but under s366(1) the court can also summon the bankrupt's spouse or former spouse, anyone known to possess any property in the bankrupt's estate or who is indebted to the bankrupt, or anyone who may be able to give information concerning the bankruptcy. The consequence is that the bankrupt cannot hide behind their ignorance of their own financial affairs: the Trustee is likely to ask them who does know the answers to their questions, and then examine them under s366.

However, despite being held in private, it is an equally serious affair. The court has the power to issue an arrest warrant to support the private examination. A private examination does not need to take place in court itself, or even in the UK (s367(3)).

Typically someone who receives legal advice is able to refuse to disclose it. This rule is known as 'legal professional privilege', and the advice is said to be 'privileged'. The protection of privileged material applies to the spouse of the bankrupt, or anyone else who is required to undergo a private examination. It does not apply to the bankrupt when asked a question by the Trustee or for documents they possess. However, the Trustee cannot then disclose the privileged information to third parties. Two exceptions to the rule that the Trustee is entitled to know the bankrupt's privileged information are where a) the advice has no relevance to the bankrupt's estate (for example, it relates to custody of children), or b) the advice is about a possible claim against the Trustee themselves.

Under either examination, the court can order HMRC to disclose their tax records or correspondence with the bankrupt under s369 for the purposes of the examination. This is another blocked avenue for a bankrupt who wishes to hide behind their ignorance of their financial affairs.

BOX 10:   BANKRUPTCY OFFENCES

A Trustee in Bankruptcy may find evidence that the bankrupt has committed a criminal offence. For details, see Chapter 7. The Trustee in Bankruptcy will not be the prosecutor. Instead, if the Trustee suspects an offence has been committed, they will report it to the Insolvency Service. The Insolvency Service will decide whether to forward the case onto prosecutors.

A Trustee who considers that the bankrupt has not been forthcoming with information is likely to apply for a suspension of the automatic discharge of the bankruptcy: see Chapter 9. This will allow them more time to complete their investigation.

2.17 Length of bankruptcy and effect of discharge

The typical length of bankruptcy is a year from the date where the order was made (s279 of the Act). Discharge will happen automatically unless the bankruptcy has been extended (see Paragraph 9.1 for when that can happen). After the bankruptcy is discharged, in most cases the individual is released from the bankruptcy restrictions and is not obliged to pay any debt which they owed before the bankruptcy. The slate is wiped clean. Discharge also removes future debts which the bankrupt was going to owe at the date of the presentation of the petition, and contingent debts which they might have owed if certain other events occurred. It also includes potential claims which could have been brought before the bankruptcy order, but were not.

However, the discharge does not release the bankrupt from:

- Money owed under family proceedings – for example, child maintenance awards

- Student loans accrued after September 2004

- Court fines

- Debts created after the bankruptcy order.

These debts are not provable in the bankruptcy (see Box 8 on page 26). This means that the Trustee will not include them when making a distribution to creditors.

A discharged bankrupt still has obligations to assist their Trustee in Bankruptcy in relation to their estate (s333(3) of the Act). A Trustee may continue working after the bankruptcy has discharged, for example, if they decide to let the bankrupt live in their family home for a year and sell it afterwards, or if they have started a claim in order to recover property for the estate.

Discharge does not release the bankrupt from any debt which arose as a result of fraud, or a liability to pay damages for personal injury although these debts are provable in the bankruptcy (see s281(3) and (5) of the Act). An example of where this mattered is *Jones & Pyle Developments v Rymell* [2021] EWHC 385 (Ch): an individual was ordered to pay a claimant £50,723 in 2013 after they made fraudulent misrepresentations when they sold the claimant land. The individual went voluntarily bankrupt shortly afterwards and his bankruptcy was discharged in 2014. Several years later, the individual retired and had access to his pension fund and so had the means to repay his debt. Since the original claim was based on fraud, discharge did not release the bankrupt from the judgment debt, and so the creditor was still able to enforce the judgment. If the original claim had been for innocent or negligent misrepresentations, or for breach of contract, the debt would have been released.

See Chapter 9 for more details on the conclusion of bankruptcy, and when restrictions can continue on the bankrupt after a year.

Chapter 3   Should a debtor go bankrupt?

A summary of the previous chapter is that bankruptcy radically changes the bankrupt's life for (in most cases) a year. A Trustee in Bankruptcy sells most of their property, including potentially the house they live in. On the positive side, their creditors can no longer chase them for pre-bankruptcy debt. The day after the bankruptcy order is made, a former bankrupt cannot receive a threatening letter from a creditor who previously they needed to repay. The threatening letter can be handed straight over to the Trustee to deal with. The aim of bankruptcy is, at least in part, to allow the debtor to start life again.

This book offers a debtor guidance on how to contest a bankruptcy petition.[2] However, it is important to decide whether to contest the petition at all. There is also a process for voluntarily becoming bankrupt, and so there is no need to wait for a creditor to present a petition if bankruptcy seems to be a positive outcome.

This chapter should be read by both litigants in person and those able to afford legal advice. Even a debtor who can afford legal advice should think carefully about their strategy since their own legal fees are likely to accrue very quickly if they decide to contest the bankruptcy proceedings.

This chapter assumes that the debtor admits that at least £5,000 debt is due to the creditor and remains unpaid. If the debtor disputes this, then there are strong grounds for opposing the petition (see Chapter 5). Note that if a debtor does owe a debt, even if a bankruptcy petition is successfully defeated, the debt will still be due.

3.1   Is the debtor solvent on the 'balance sheet' basis?

In my opinion, the most important factor to consider before opposing a bankruptcy petition is whether or not the debtor has more assets than they have

---

[2] *This chapter is framed in terms of contesting a bankruptcy petition, but this should be understood as shorthand for contesting the whole process, for example, whether to make an application to set aside a statutory demand. It is usually better to contest the proceedings as early as possible (see Paragraph 4.12).*

debts. This is known as 'balance sheet' solvency. A bankruptcy petition can only be made if the debtor has not paid a particular debt (see Chapter 5) of over £5,000. However, this does not mean that the debtor cannot afford to pay. For example, the debtor may have the money to pay, but cannot access it easily, and so they are only cashflow insolvent.

An example is where a debtor has a house which is worth £100,000 and debts of £50,000. Because it is not easy to sell the house, the debtor cannot pay their debt. An impatient creditor can issue a bankruptcy petition against the debtor, and the debtor will need to decide whether or not to contest it.

If the debtor has the money to pay their admitted debts, they should not contest the bankruptcy petition, except perhaps to ask for an adjournment to find time to pay. It will be preferable to have as few court processes involved as possible. It is expensive to go to court, and an unsuccessful debtor will be expected to pay the legal fees of the other side. To return to the example of the house, if the debtor has debts of £50,000 but an asset worth £100,000, the best possible outcome would be to sell the house and still have £50,000. The worst possible outcome is to be ordered to pay the legal expenses of the petitioning creditor and Trustee in Bankruptcy of over £50,000, and have nothing left once the house is eventually sold.

To decide whether the debtor is solvent on the balance sheet basis:

1. Firstly, calculate how much money they admit that they owe. Gather together all the bills they are aware of, including those which are not chasing for money, but the debtor knows that they should be paid within the next few months. Include the unpaid interest and any fines for late payment.

2. Next, calculate the total value of the property of the debtor. Look at how much money the debtor has in their bank account(s), the value of their house after accounting for the mortgage and co-ownership (if any), and any non-pension savings. Include the debtor's potential income over the next year, if any, including the possibility of an inheritance.

If the figure of (1) is greater than (2), or if (1) is less than £10,000 more than (2) (to include legal and administration fees), then the debtor is insolvent and the debtor could consider contesting the bankruptcy petition. However, if (2) is substantially greater than (1), then the debtor would probably gain little from contesting the bankruptcy petition and would be likely to increase costs which ultimately they are likely to pay.

This exercise is challenging: it involves collecting a lot of information which may be scattered in different places, and it requires planning for an uncomfortable situation. Some people are not confident with the mathematics, and they may need help from a friend. Know that a Trustee in Bankruptcy will do precisely the same thing, and so it is worthwhile doing the exercise sooner rather than later.

3.2   Other factors

These are other considerations which may affect the decision whether or not to contest the petition in roughly descending order of importance:

1.   **The strength of the case against the petition.** This is discussed in Chapter 5. It is difficult to oppose a petition based on an undisputed debt but it is not impossible.

2.   **Likelihood of settlement.** It is likely to be better for all parties to settle, and it is usually possible to find a position short of a bankruptcy order which the creditor is comfortable with. This will be discussed more in Chapter 18. For present purposes, it is enough to comment that it can take time to settle. This can be because it takes time for a debtor to gather the funds to make a proper settlement offer; or because it takes time for the creditor to realise that settlement is in their interest. It is also important to note that merely threatening to contest a bankruptcy petition can lead to settlement if the creditor can be persuaded that the bankruptcy process will lead to increased legal costs and a reduced prospect of recovery, provided there is some basis for opposition. In general, if the debtor genuinely is insolvent, then it will be in the creditor's interest to accept an IVA rather than face a contested bankruptcy.

3.   **Whether the debtor has made any transactions which could be reviewed.** As set out in Paragraph 2.5, after a bankruptcy order is made the Trustee will review the affairs of the debtor. They can apply to undo certain transactions. The time limits for this review differ depending on the transaction. However, critically, they are periods going back from when the bankruptcy petition was presented. This means that challenging a statutory demand will nearly always result in the bankruptcy petition being later. This will typically be a delay of around six months, which might put an otherwise voidable transaction out of time. The creditor may suspect that there are transactions worth reviewing, but there are more limited options for presenting a bankruptcy petition without a statutory demand.

4.   **How easily stressed the debtor gets in adversarial situations.** Even if the debtor can afford some legal advice, litigation is a stressful business. The litigation process works by demonstrating to the judge the correctness of one's own position, and the problems with the other. The petitioning creditor will inevitably position themselves as entirely correct and justified while casting aspersions on the debtor's behaviour. The debtor will make sensible, reasonable arguments to protect their position, and a professional

lawyer will try their best to undermine them. If a debtor does not have legal advice, they will receive several official letters with serious legal consequences, which they might find stressful. As much as this book will try to make this less stressful, if the debtor gets easily stressed through conflict then they should consider the effect on them of contesting the petition.

5. **Future cashflow.** A debtor can be made bankrupt on the basis that they cannot pay their present debts, and it is not relevant whether the debtor will be able to pay their debts in the future, due to some large payment which is expected. It may be the case that if the debt can be delayed just a few weeks or months, avoiding bankruptcy will justify the additional costs of contesting the bankruptcy. This is partly a question of when and how the money will arrive: if the money will arrive regardless then it might be worth allowing a bankruptcy order to be made knowing that it will be annulled once the money arrives and all the debts are paid. However, if this is the situation then the best approach is to act consensually: share the evidence that the money will arrive with the creditor, and seek an adjournment with their consent for the appropriate time. The creditor should also be concerned about wasting costs. If the creditor refuses, the court is likely to grant an adjournment for this purpose for at least a few months (see Paragraph 5.12.3 below).

6. **How bankruptcy would affect the debtor's job.** As described in Chapter 2, certain professionals are not able to work if they are made bankrupt. On the other hand, it may be better to face the inevitable sooner rather than later.

7. **Ability to move.** If a bankruptcy order is made against the debtor and they own at least part of a house or flat, they will likely be forced to move. They may have a bespoke element of their house, for example, it may be a ground floor flat, and the debtor may have mobility issues. This is discussed further in Chapter 6 on possession hearings, but it may be worth the costs of contesting a petition if it gives the debtor more time to organise their affairs.

8. **Country in which the individual wishes to be made bankrupt.** Someone can only be made bankrupt in England if they have a sufficient connection to the country (see Paragraph 5.2). This is assessed from the presentation of the bankruptcy petition. If someone prefers not to be made bankrupt in England, contesting a statutory demand allows time to pass for their new location to be the determinative one.

> **BOX 11:   IMMIGRATION REASONS**
>
> As discussed in Paragraph 2.11 above, going bankrupt is likely to lead to a citizenship application being declined. However, citizenship applications take roughly two to six months. If an individual was considering applying for citizenship and receives a statutory demand, they may consider applying to set it aside primarily to gain time if they have grounds to do so.

In my opinion, the following factors are less important:

9. **Effect on credit score.** If the debtor becomes bankrupt, they are unlikely to be able to borrow money while the bankruptcy is undischarged, and potentially for several years afterwards. However, if the debtor is in a position where they cannot pay their debts, they are likely to be a high credit risk already. For example, credit rating agencies are aware of court judgments made against a debtor, which are a matter of public record. More importantly, if the debtor is in a position where they can pay their creditors, the rate of interest is likely to be high and it would be prudent to pay off the debts sooner rather than later.

10. **The social embarrassment of going bankrupt.** As described in the Introduction, tens of thousands of bankruptcy orders are made each year. It is not a pleasant experience, but neither is being chased for debt. One might feel that the short term embarrassment of being made bankrupt is not worse than a longer term embarrassment of having regular visits from bailiffs. Furthermore, if the bankrupt has more assets than debts, then the bankruptcy will be annulled early (see Chapter 9).

11. **Stubbornness.** It is tempting for a debtor to respond to someone threatening them with a bankruptcy petition aggressively and fighting back on principle. This is understandable given the emotional situation a debtor is in, but it can be an expensive response. A debtor should consider carefully how much they are prepared to pay for the contest.

3.3   Voluntary bankruptcy

An individual can voluntarily apply to an adjudicator to have themselves made bankrupt. A voluntary bankruptcy leads to the same outcome as being made bankrupt on a creditor's petition. It is quicker and so cheaper for the individual.

A debtor interested in this voluntary bankruptcy must fill in the form on the Online Debt Solutions website run by the Insolvency Service: https://

apply-for-bankruptcy.service.gov.uk/ and pay an adjudication fee of £130 and a deposit of £550. The website is clear and easy to use. The debtor must provide evidence of their insolvency to an adjudicator, who is an official employed by the Insolvency Service. The adjudicator makes a single decision: whether they satisfied that the debtor cannot pay their debts.

It is a criminal offence to knowingly or recklessly make a false representation or omission in a bankruptcy application, for example, not disclosing an extra bank account. Note that making a false representation is a particularly bad idea given that the OR is going to review the debtor's paperwork and is likely to find the relevant undisclosed or misleading evidence. The OR is a professional who is used to looking at financial information and identifying irregularities.

An adjudicator must make a bankruptcy order within 28 days of the debtor making the application (r10.40) unless they request further information, in which case they have 42 days from receipt. If the adjudicator refuses to make the order, a debtor has 14 days to request a review. If the review is unsuccessful, the adjudicator will give their reasons, and the debtor has 28 days to appeal to the court. In all instances, the deposit money, but not the adjudication fee, is returned if the application is unsuccessful.

The vast majority of applications are successful: it is not difficult to demonstrate insolvency. The main reasons why applications are declined are technical ones, such as failure to pay the deposit correctly. In practice, debtors who wish to use this route can do so quickly and efficiently. There are roughly 12,000 applications for bankruptcy each year.

Chapter 4   Statutory demands and unsuccessful execution of judgments

A bankruptcy petition must be preceded by either a statutory demand or 'judgment returning unsatisfied'. Statutory demands are the more conventional route. This chapter sets out what a statutory demand is, and how to successfully conduct an application to set aside a statutory demand.

4.1   Types of debt

The starting point for all petitions is that the debtor incurs a debt: usually either a loan, or a tax liability, or a judgment debt. However, only certain types of debt can be the basis of a bankruptcy petition. The following conditions in s267 of the Act must be satisfied at the time when the petition is presented:

1. The debt which the creditor's petition is based on must equal or exceed the minimum bankruptcy level of £5,000. If a creditor is owed less than £5,000, they cannot by themselves present a bankruptcy petition. However, multiple creditors can jointly present a petition and sum the debts together for these purposes.[3] The £5,000 threshold must apply at the time of the presentation of the petition. If, perhaps following a statutory demand, the debtor paid the debt to below the £5,000 level, the petition **must** be dismissed.

2. The debt must be (a) a liquidated sum, (b) payable to the petitioning creditor, (c) either immediately or at some certain future time, and (d) be unsecured. These conditions each require explanation:

    a)   A 'liquidated' debt is one which is for a fixed, quantifiable sum. It is easiest to see what a liquidated debt is by comparison to what is <u>not</u> a liquidated debt. If someone takes out a loan, then that debt can be

---

[3] *This means that a debtor cannot avoid bankruptcy by paying off their creditors until they have £4,999 remaining each.*

quantified and it is a liquidated debt. Similarly, if the court orders an individual to pay money, the debt will be quantified and so liquidated. By contrast, a claim for particular property (a 'proprietary' claim) is not a liquidated debt. Neither is a claim for compensation (for example, damages caused by poor service) or a potential application for legal costs, until the court makes an order that the debtor pays a certain amount.

b) The presenter(s) of the petition must themselves be owed a debt worth £5,000 or more. It is not enough that the debtor owes money to someone else.

c) In practice, it is rare to present a bankruptcy petition in respect of a future debt. This is because it is difficult to prove that the debtor will be unable to pay it. It is easier for a creditor to wait and see what happens.

d) A secured debt is one where the creditor has the right to be paid from the sale of a particular asset if the debtor does not pay the debt. If there is a surplus from the sale, the creditor must return that surplus to the debtor. If there is a deficit, then the creditor would be unsecured for that remaining sum. A creditor has the option of voluntarily releasing their security and becoming an unsecured creditor. s269 of the Act provides that a secured debtor can still present a petition if the petition contains a statement that the person is willing to give up their security for the benefit of all creditors. It is unlikely that a secured creditor would wish to give up on their security, especially if there are other unsecured creditors.

3. The debt, or each of the debts, is a debt which the debtor is unable to pay or has no reasonable prospect of being able to pay. 'Inability to pay' is a defined legal concept and does not relate to the practicalities of whether a particular debtor can or cannot pay the debt. The definition of 'inability to pay' is set out in s268 of the Act. It can only apply when either a) a petitioning creditor has served a statutory demand and at least three weeks have elapsed, or b) execution of a judgment debt has been unsuccessful. In either case, it is irrelevant if the debtor has the funds but refuses to pay for other reasons: in law, they will be considered unable to pay their debts. Statutory demands are the more usual route, and both routes will be discussed in the next chapter.

4. There is no outstanding application to set aside a statutory demand: if there is an outstanding application, the court cannot be sure that the debtor is unable to pay, because this inability depends on the statutory demand being valid. Applications to set aside statutory demands are discussed in

Paragraph 4.6.

If these conditions apply, the creditor is entitled to seek a bankruptcy order.

4.2   What is a statutory demand?

A statutory demand is a formal request for money. There is an example of a statutory demand at the end of this chapter.

A statutory demand must satisfy the rules in r10.1 of the Insolvency Rules 2016. There are templates which are frequently used; they are also routinely used incorrectly. The rules which are most often broken are:

- **r10.1(1)(c)**: The demand must state the name and address of the creditor. A statutory demand should use the <u>creditor's</u> name and address, rather than the name and address of the representative of the creditor (for example, their solicitor). This may sound obvious, but it is often mistaken.

- **r10.1(1)(l)**: The demand must name the court to which, according to the present information, the debtor must make an application to set aside the demand (i.e. the High Court, the County Court at Central London or a named hearing centre of the County Court as the case may be). Demands often name the wrong court. The correct court is typically the nearest hearing centre to the debtor, but see Paragraph 4.6.1 below.

- **r10.1(7)**: If a statutory demand includes additional charges such as overdue fees, or interest, then the demand must be clear about what was the initial debt and what was the subsequent debt. Frequently statutory demands bundle the sum together into one single amount. This is incorrect.

- **r10.1(8)**: The amount claimed for such charges must be limited to that which has accrued at the date of the demand. It is incorrect to include expected future charges.

- **r10.1(10)**: Where the statutory demand is to be served outside of England and Wales, different time limits apply. The statutory demand must be amended to show the correct time limits. For details, see Box 12 on page 49.

If the statutory demand does not comply with these rules, it is 'defective'. The implication of a defective statutory demand is discussed in Paragraph 4.6.2 in the context of when the court will set aside the statutory demand. A statutory demand is not itself a court document and so there is no form creditors must use. Any document can be a statutory demand, provided the Insolvency Rules at r10.1 are satisfied. It is quick to prepare a statutory demand since it does not require involvement from the court. There are no statistics on how many statutory demands are made because it is, at least initially, a private matter between the creditor and the debtor.

4.3   Service of a statutory demand

r10.2 of the Insolvency Rules 2016 says that "*A creditor must do all that is reasonable to bring the statutory demand to the debtor's attention and, if practicable in the particular circumstances, serve the demand personally*". 'Personal service' means that the creditor must employ someone (often a 'process server') who will find the debtor, and personally hand them the paper. The debtor must either receive the paper themselves, or, if they will not accept it, the debtor must be told what the document contains and the document be left with or near them. A process server is someone whose job it is to serve documents. Although the creditor could, in theory, hand the paper to the debtor themselves, there is an advantage of paying a stranger who knows the rules to do it for them.

Sometimes personal service is not practicable. This is typically because the debtor is actively running away from the creditor to avoid service, but it may also be because the debtor has no fixed address and the creditor cannot find them. In these circumstances, it might be appropriate use 'alternative' or 'substituted' service, which typically is sending the demand by email, first class post, or hand-delivering it to the person's residence. The process for service if personal service is not practical is set out in PDIP para 12.7:

- The creditor must make one personal call at the residence and at the place of business of the debtor. If the debtor has multiple addresses, a personal call must be made at each address.

- Then the creditor must write a letter referring to the visit, its purpose, and propose a further visit on a specified place, time and date with at least two business days' notice. The appointment letter must set out that if the proposed time is not convenient, the debtor should propose some other time and place.

- When attending the appointment made by letter, the server should inquire as to whether the debtor is still resident at the address, or frequents the address, and if they are aware whether or when the debtor will be returning. If they do frequent the address, this might justify a further visit at the appropriate time. Similarly, if the server is given a new address, the creditor should serve the demand there. However, if the server is told that the debtor has left the country (for example) then this will be grounds to justify substituted service of the demand and later the bankruptcy petition.

- If the debtor is represented by a solicitor, the creditor should attempt to arrange an appointment for personal service through them.

Proper service of the statutory demand is important: failure to serve the statutory demand properly can lead to the entire bankruptcy petition being dismissed (see Paragraph 5.13.1 below). Unlike a bankruptcy petition, the court does not need to authorise alternative service of a statutory demand. The court may decline to file the petition if not satisfied that the creditor has done all that was reasonable to bring the demand to the debtor's attention (r10.9(4)).

4.4 Consequences of a statutory demand

A debtor has 21 days to pay the sum specified in the statutory demand. If they do not, the debtor will be deemed to be insolvent and the creditor will be able to present a bankruptcy petition on that basis. Alternatively, the debtor has 18 days to apply to set it aside. The fact that a debtor is able to pay the statutory demand but chooses not to is irrelevant. They will still be deemed to be insolvent regardless of their actual financial state.

BOX 12:   TIME LIMITS IF THE DEBTOR IS OUTSIDE ENGLAND AND WALES

The main text refers to a debtor who is served a statutory demand within England and Wales, who has 18 days to make an application to set aside the demand, or 21 days to pay. If they are served outside, the time limits are longer. The length of time depends on which country they are in. The starting point is the number of days in the table at CPR Practice Direction 6B, which can be found at http://www.justice.gov.uk/courts/procedure-rules/civil/rules/part06/pd_part06b. The debtor has this number plus four days to set aside the statutory demand, and this number plus seven days to pay before the bankruptcy petition can be presented. For example, if the debtor is in France, they have 25 days (21 + 4) to set aside the demand, or 28 days (21 + 7) to pay. Only people with a connection to England and Wales can be made bankrupt here: see Paragraph 5.2 below.

4.5 Expedited demand

If there is a serious possibility that the debtor's property or the value of the property will be significantly diminished following the presentation of a statutory demand, a petition may be presented before the end of three weeks (s270 of the Act). This occurs where the creditor has good reason to believe that the debtor is likely to irrevocably move assets away from the estate, or perhaps deliberately destroy them. This procedure can occur even where the debtor applies to set aside the statutory demand. However, it is an exceptional procedure and not often used. It cannot justify presenting a petition without serving a statutory demand. Instead, it can only reduce the three weeks a debtor otherwise has to pay the amount demanded.

4.6 Application to set aside the statutory demand

4.6.1 How to make the application

An application to set aside a statutory demand is made using the 'IAA' form which can be found at https://www.gov.uk/government/publications/apply-to-the-court-about-an-insolvency-issue-form-iaa. There is an example application to set aside a statutory demand in Annex 1.

The application should usually be sent to the debtor's own closest hearing centre (see r10.48). An exception is where the creditor is a Government Department or a minister, the debt is the subject of a judgment, and the demand indicates the creditor's intention to present the eventual bankruptcy petition in the High Court (r10.4(4)). Unusually, there is no court fee when applying for setting aside a statutory demand. This is because the applicant, by definition, is likely to have difficulty paying debts. Once the application has been filed at court, the time for compliance with the demand ceases to run and that creditor cannot present a bankruptcy petition (r10.4(5)). This does not stop the accrual of interest on the demand or stop other creditors presenting a statutory demand in respect of a debt owed to them.

4.6.2 Contents of application

The application must contain a copy of the statutory demand itself if it is in the debtor's possession (r10.4(6)). It must also contain a witness statement with the date on which the debtor became aware of the statutory demand, the grounds on which it should be set aside, and any evidence in support. Even though the court requires the debtor to outline their case in their application, it can admit evidence submitted at a later date. If there is some reason why it is not possible to include particular information in the witness statement accompanying the application to set aside the statutory demand, the debtor should say so in the witness statement and seek permission to rely on further evidence at the first hearing of the application.

There are four grounds for setting aside the statutory demand, which can be found in r10.5(5). They will be discussed in turn, but the common theme is that the creditor must genuinely be owed the demanded debt, and that the statutory demand must be properly made:

1. r10.5(5)(a): The debtor appears to have a counterclaim, set-off or cross demand which equals or exceeds the amount of the debt specified in the statutory demand

Even if the debtor agrees they owe a certain sum to the creditor, the demand can be set aside if the creditor appears to owe the same amount or more to the debtor. This 'counterclaim' does not need to be agreed by the creditor. The court will decide at the hearing to set aside the statutory demand whether the debtor raises a 'genuine triable issue'. It means that it is possible that the debtor will succeed based on the law, and on the facts that the debtor says is the case. The debtor does <u>not</u> need to show that they will definitely succeed or even that it is more likely than not that they will succeed. The court will not conduct a mini-trial, but if the debtor's story is unrealistic based on the available documents it will not set aside the statutory demand.

For example, if two people, A and B, often do business together, A might agree that he owes B a certain sum of money – over £5,000. However, A also says that B owes A the same amount of money, or more. The court will hear the reason A states that B owes him money, and decide whether that is sufficient to set aside the statutory demand.

Note that if A owes B £10,000 but A says that B owes him £7,000 this ground cannot be relied upon because the cross-demand does not equal the amount of debt specified in the statutory demand. However, the difference between the two sums – the undisputed net debt – is £3,000, which is less than the bankruptcy limit. This means that B cannot bring a bankruptcy petition. In this circumstance, A could argue that the fourth ground applies, which is that the court has a general discretion to set aside a statutory demand. However, the court is not required to do this and typically the policy is not to. For a full discussion, see *Howell v Lerwick Commercial Mortgage Corporation Ltd* [2015] EWHC 1177 (Ch).

The reason this ground exists is because, according to the debtor, the counterclaim means that there is some asset which properly belongs to the debtor. If the creditor paid this asset, the debt would be extinguished. It is not fair to progress to a bankruptcy petition if the reason the debtor cannot pay the debt is due to some fault with the creditor. Although the creditor does not admit the counterclaim, provided that the court finds that there is a genuine triable issue, the debtor has the benefit of the doubt.

2. **r10.5(5)(b): The debt is disputed on grounds which appear to the court to be substantial**

This is the most common ground. Again, the test is whether there is a genuine dispute on substantive grounds. If there is a genuine triable issue with a real prospect of success, then the application to set aside the demand will be successful.

The debtor must present evidence that the debtor does not owe the money at all. Although this is specific to each debt, some examples may be useful:

- The debt is for car repairs. However, the debtor says the car mechanic did a poor job and also overcharged. The debtor will need to provide a witness statement giving information on the state of the car beforehand, afterwards, and details of what the proper charge should have been.

- The debt is owed under a guarantee, but the debtor says the guarantee is invalid: see Chapter 11 for more details.

- The debt is for a loan which the debtor says was repaid. The debtor will need to provide a witness statement giving details of any payment, and associated bank statements.

Note that although it is not impossible to challenge a judgment debt, i.e. a debt which the court has ordered an individual to pay, it is difficult. It is not enough to apply to appeal the judgment for the statutory demand application. This is because as a general rule the court will not adjourn an application pending the outcome of the appeal: PDIP para 11.4.4. If necessary the possible challenge to the debt will be dealt with at the hearing of the bankruptcy petition. However, the court does have discretion (rarely used) to dismiss a statutory demand based on an unchallenged judgment debt.

Also under PDIP para 11.4.4 is the rule that the court typically will not inquire into the validity of a tax assessment at this stage. This means HMRC can present a statutory demand in respect of a tax debt even while the debtor seeks to appeal it, provided that the tax is owing at the time of the statutory demand and the set aside hearing.

BOX 13: CHALLENGING HMRC TAX ASSESSMENTS

This book cannot give any detail about challenging HMRC's tax assessments. The reader is directed to Keith Gordon's book 'Tax Appeals and Discovery Assessments: How to challenge them'. In outline, the rules are as follows. First, taxpayers must give notice of an appeal to HMRC. There are strict time limits for doing so. Typically the taxpayer has 30 days, but this depends on the tax. After giving notice, the taxpayer can either notify the appeal to the tax tribunal or request an internal review by HMRC. HMRC may offer an internal review proactively, and the taxpayer must respond to either accept the offer or to notify the Tribunal. In some taxes, the taxpayer may need to pay the tax in advance of the appeal. There is the possibility of making a 'hardship application' which would be relevant to a debtor facing bankruptcy proceedings. The precise rules of challenging HMRC depend on which tax is owed.

In general, the author's experience is that HMRC will only commence bankruptcy proceedings if they consider that the appeal against the tax assessment is, or will be, meritless. This includes where the appeal is out of time. Where there is more doubt, HMRC's preference appears to be to exhaust the avenue of appeal before going down the bankruptcy route.

The test which the debtor needs to meet to set aside a statutory demand because the debt is disputed is relatively low. The Insolvency Court is not the place to determine the merits of the disputed debt or a possible counterclaim. Instead, the Insolvency Court acts as a filter. Any claims with the potential of being successful – i.e. they are legally consistent, and it is possible that the facts alleged will be established – will be heard elsewhere. If a debtor can show that the debt is disputed, the statutory demand will be set aside. However, the creditor can still bring a separate claim to prove that the debt is owed.

3. **r10.5(5)(c): The creditor holds security, and either did not properly represent this in the statutory demand, or the security equals or exceeds the full amount of the debt**

Paragraph 4.1 above sets out that a bankruptcy petition and a statutory demand must be for unsecured debt. A creditor with security must put a value on it (r10.1(9)).

If the value is equal to or more than the debt, this ground prevents a creditor from issuing a statutory demand. It is possible to issue a demand if the creditor holds security and they value it at less than the debt, provided that their statutory demand specifies the nature and value of the creditor's security, and that the demand is for the part of the debt which would be unsecured. Failure to properly describe the security is grounds for setting aside the demand.

An example would be where a bank has a mortgage over a property and the debtor has not made the proper mortgage repayments. If the value of the property is equal to or more than the outstanding mortgage, the court will set aside the bank's statutory demand. The court could be asked to determine the value of the property at the hearing to set aside the statutory demand, if the bank disagrees with the debtor about its value.

This ground is rarely relied on. Typically a creditor who has a secured debt will realise the security, i.e. sell the underlying secured asset. This is a more direct way of recovering the debt. If the sale does not cover the entirety of the debt, then the creditor will become wholly unsecured. If the sale does cover the debt, then they can no longer make a statutory demand. In the example, the bank would typically repossess the property and sell it. If there is still a shortfall, r10.5(5)(c) would no longer be a ground for disputing the statutory demand.

4.   r10.5(5)(d): The court is satisfied, on other grounds, that the demand ought to be set aside

This ground gives the court wide powers to dismiss a statutory demand, for two main reasons: (a) the demand is defective and (b) the demand has been served incorrectly. The general approach of the court is that these are circumstances where it would be unjust to allow the creditor to present a bankruptcy petition.

a)   **Defective demand**. The fact that a demand contains an error is not of itself a sufficient reason to set it aside (see *Coulter v Chief Constable of Dorset Police* [2004] EWCA Civ 1259). Instead, the debtor will need to argue that they were *prejudiced* by the mistake. In general, this will be when the demand was so defective as to be unfair, or where there was evidence that the debt would have been paid immediately but for the mistake. For example, if the size of the debt was <u>understated</u>, this may be a technical defect, but causes no prejudice to the debtor. However, if the debtor can show that the debt was for too large an amount, and they would have paid the correct amount had they not needed to apply to set aside the statutory demand, then the debtor has a reasonable argument.

In *Coulter v Chief Constable of Dorset Police*, the statutory demand was made in the name of the Chief of Dorset Police, but the underlying judgment debt was owed to someone who was once the Chief Constable but had subsequently retired. In turn, the former Chief Constable would have to pay any sums received to the Dorset Police Authority. In his judgment, the judge stated the rule that the court would set aside a demand where there are defects which make it sufficiently confusing as to make it unjust for the debtor to comply, or where the document is so defective it cannot be regarded as a statutory demand at all. The court will have regard to the circumstances at the time of the hearing and not just when the demand was served. For example, where the amount of debt and the interest calculations are wrong, that may not be enough to be sufficiently confusing. Where a debtor is unable to pay a debt, the court will be aware that the only practical consequence of setting aside a demand is that the creditor will serve another demand which will inevitably not be complied with. In *Coulter*, although the situation with the name of the creditor was confusing since the underlying position was an unchallenged judgment debt and whoever the Chief Constable was would have to pay the Dorset Police Authority, the court refused to set aside the demand.

The court's approach is not usually overly technical. It will not be enough for the debtor to show that the technicalities of Part 10 of the Insolvency Rules were not satisfied. In particular, the result of the most common errors set out in Paragraph 4.2 above is unlikely to prejudice the debtor. However, certain judges place greater weight on the significance of following the Insolvency Rules than others – or, perhaps, certain judges are more open to the idea that the breach of the rules is prejudicial to the debtors. Furthermore, even if a judge is not minded to set aside a statutory demand on the grounds of its defects, it is still worth briefly bringing the defects to the court's attention because every successful argument made helps the debtor when it comes to a final costs order.

b) **Incorrect service**. The rules for proper service are set out above at Paragraph 4.3. If the creditor does not 'do all that is reasonable to bring the statutory demand to the debtor's attention', it will be set aside. There is something of a paradox here: if the creditor does not bring the demand to the debtor's attention, then the debtor would have no notice of the demand and so cannot apply to set it aside. Service is more important for bankruptcy petitions rather than statutory demands. The court repeatedly stresses that the service requirements should be strictly observed: see *Bush v Bank Mandiri (Europe) Ltd* [2011] BPIR 19. However, in practice the court does not always enforce the requirements strictly.

In *Bush v Bank Mandiri*, for example, the demand was not served upon Mr Bush at his place of residence in Switzerland, which the creditor was aware of and had been using for other correspondence, but rather left at the UK address of his girlfriend. No explanation was given for the mode of service used. Nonetheless, the judge held that since the debtor did receive the demand, and was able to secure an extension of time, he was not prejudiced by the breach and so it would be disproportionate to set it aside. Mr Bush argued that he was forced to rush his application to set aside the statutory demand as a consequence, but the judge placed weight on the fact that he had received an extension of time to do so. This case illustrates the difficulty a debtor will have on dismissing a demand through improper service.

In the case of incorrect service, the debtor should file a witness statement setting out their version of events. No witness statement is needed for a misleading demand if it is merely to point out errors, but it may be needed if the debtor wishes to rely on other facts such as their willingness to pay the correct amount.

It is also possible to argue under r10.5(5)(d) that the statutory demand is an abuse of process. This argument is more commonly made for the bankruptcy petition, and the judge hearing the application to set aside the statutory demand may prefer not to decide this question until the petition is presented. If so, they will dismiss the application to set aside the statutory demand. For this reason, this argument is discussed in Paragraph 5.13.7 below with reference to a bankruptcy petition.

It is also possible to argue that the statutory demand should be dismissed because the debtor does not fall into the jurisdiction of the English court – it should be dealt with in a different country. However, the rule from *O'Donnell v Bank of Ireland* [2012] EWHC 3749 (Ch) is that the relevant date for deciding which country the debtor lives in for the purposes of bankruptcy law is the date of the presentation of the bankruptcy petition. As such, a jurisdictional argument should usually also be dealt with on the hearing of the bankruptcy petition and so it is discussed in Paragraph 5.2.

BOX 14: APPLICATIONS OUT OF TIME

An application to set aside a statutory demand can be made after the 18 day time period (see PDIP para 11.4.2). The application should be made as soon as possible: further delay affects whether the court will allow a late application, even if it does not affect the merits of the application itself. The debtor must give a witness statement in support of the extension i.e. explaining why the application was delayed, and why it should be allowed. The witness statement must state that to the best of the debtor's knowledge and belief the creditor(s) named in the statutory demand has/have not presented a bankruptcy petition. In practice, if the application is a few days late, and the debtor can give a good reason like difficulty obtaining legal advice, but that they gave informal notice to the creditor, then the time limit is unlikely to be a problem.

If the bankruptcy petition has been presented by the time the debtor would like to make a set aside application, then the arguments for why the demand should be set aside are likely to become arguments for why the petition should be dismissed. These can be heard at the hearing of the petition. This is the risk of a late application. Conversely, if the application to set aside a statutory demand is made, even if late, a bankruptcy petition cannot be presented (s267(2)(d) of the Act).

4.7 Statutory demands in respect of debts not immediately payable

A statutory demand can be made even if the debt is not payable immediately (s268(2) of the Act). If so, the statutory demand must require the debtor to establish to the satisfaction of the creditor that there is a reasonable prospect that the debtor will be able to pay the debt when it falls due. It is rare for a statutory demand to be presented in respect of future debts because it is difficult to prove either way whether a debtor will or will not be able to pay a future debt.

However, if a debtor does receive such a statutory demand, they should still apply to set it aside. This is because after three weeks they will be deemed to be insolvent as if it were a demand in respect of an immediately payable debt.

It is less common for statutory demands to be presented in respect of future debts. The court will be sympathetic to the debtor who offers an optimistic outlook for their future ability to pay. The debtor may also argue that presenting a bankruptcy petition (which would involve informing the world that the creditor considers that the debtor will be insolvent) will have an adverse effect of their future ability to pay. These are both reasons for the court to set aside the demand on the catch-all ground of r10.5(5)(d).

Note that a statutory demand should not be presented based on a contingent debt, i.e. one that may or may not arise. For example, if the court has ordered the debtor to pay the creditor, but the order is stayed pending appeal, the debt is a contingent one. A demand based on this debt must be set aside. Unlike a future debt, a bankruptcy order cannot be made on a contingent debt.

4.8 Initial review by the court

The court has the power to review an application to set aside a statutory demand and dismiss it without a hearing, without even informing the creditor of the application (r10.5(1)). This will be used only in truly hopeless cases. Most of the time a judge will assume that an applicant lacks legal training and has a sensible case which was poorly expressed on paper and so it is more common for even hopeless cases to proceed to a hearing in person. The only positive outcome for a debtor whose application is dismissed is that the time for complying with a statutory demand runs again from the date of dismissal of the application (r10.5(2)).

Where the court thinks there is a possibility that the debtor might succeed on the face of the application, the court will fix a venue and give at least five business days' notice to the parties (r10.5(3)). In practice the courts are busy and it would be unusual to have only five days' notice of the hearing to set aside the statutory demand. The standard time is two to three months.

BOX 15:   COURT DELAYS

The court process is slow, partly because it takes the court time to process all the relevant paperwork and to find space in the court's diary ('the cause list' or 'the list') to have a free hearing room with a judge available for the case. It is common to wait several months between applying to set aside a statutory demand, and the hearing itself. The longer the hearing is, the more difficult it is to find time in the cause list, and so inevitably a longer hearing will be listed later in the year than a shorter hearing. Court delays are a mixed blessing for the debtor. Often a debtor is simply seeking time to pay, and any event which delays the bankruptcy process is welcome. A debtor who considers they have a strong case may feel differently.

4.9   The first hearing

In practice the first hearing of an application to set aside a statutory demand is usually treated as a 'directions' hearing. A directions hearing is where both the creditor and the debtor are given orders about the preparation of evidence for a later 'substantive' hearing where the court will make a decision on the application itself. It follows that at the first hearing the debtor should expect the judge to ask them and the creditor how long it will take to determine the main application, how long they need to provide evidence and roughly what evidence will be relied on. It is unusual, unless it is unopposed, to determine the application the first time around. This is because the creditor is unlikely to fully understand the debtor's application, and to have submitted all the evidence that they intend to rely on.

The debtor should come prepared with a time estimate for how long the substantive hearing will take. The debtor should be realistic about this, but they have an incentive to give an estimate on the higher end. This is because the longer the hearing lasts, the more difficult it is for the court listings office to find a time, and so inevitably a longer hearing will be heard later in the year (see Box 15 on page 58). If a debtor is a litigant in person, they can submit that it would be sensible for the court to allot more time, given that (with the best will in the world) it will be harder for the court to determine the issues at stake when the debtor will often not be able to put their case as clearly as a professional can.

The usual direction would allow the creditor to put in evidence to support the demand, and then allow the applicant debtor to put in evidence 'in reply'. 'Reply evidence' strictly should be evidence which responds to the creditor's evidence, rather than additional evidence which does not relate to it. However, in practice the courts do not police the scope of the evidence in reply, since to do so would be to increase the number of issues which the judge has to determine, for relatively little gain.

This description of a first hearing is the one which is likely to happen if the hearing is listed for less than 30 minutes, or if the parties have not had the opportunity to put in evidence. If the creditor has put in evidence, and if the hearing is listed for more than 30 minutes, the judge would be likely to want to give judgment on the application or petition, which is sometimes described as determining the matter 'substantively'. It is still possible to argue that the original hearing time is not enough and the application should be adjourned, particularly if the debtor can say that they expected it to be a directions hearing as this is the first time it has come before the judge.

4.10 The substantive hearing

Following a directions hearing, the application will be listed for at least half an hour, but probably longer. See Paragraph 18.4 for a description of how court hearings usually operate.

4.11 Orders at the hearing

Regardless of the type of hearing, the court will make at least one of the following orders:

1. **The statutory demand is set aside.** If so, the debtor is successful and will expect to receive their costs of the hearing (see Chapter 16). If the demand is set aside due to it being a disputed debt, or a set off by a cross-claim, the next stage may be to have the creditor issue a claim to determine what the true position is.

2. **The application is dismissed.** If so, the creditor is successful, and will expect to receive their costs. The court must then make an order authorising the creditor to present a bankruptcy petition either as soon as

reasonably practicable, or on or after a specified date (r10.5(8)).

3. **The application is adjourned (delayed) to be relisted with a time estimate of a particular length.** This will be the order where the court is not able to determine the application properly, either because there is not enough time due to the parties not being ready or because there is not enough evidence. A typical example of an adjournment would be five weeks for the creditor to prepare a witness statement giving details of the manner of service. There would then be another hearing as soon as the court can list it, in at least five weeks. Another example would be an adjournment for the debtor to try to secure pro bono advice or representation.

4. **An order for a Pre-Trial Review (PTR).** A PTR is a hearing which precedes the main trial in order to make decisions about matters such as how long each witness should speak for. PTRs are routinely 'non-attendance', or 'on the papers', which means that the judge will review written submissions on what the parties say should happen in the trial without the parties being present in court. It is not common to have a PTR for a trial which is less than three days – this covers the majority of all insolvency hearings.

5. **An order for costs.** This is dealt with in more detail in Chapter 16. If the demand is set aside the creditor will ordinarily be liable for the debtor's costs. If it is set aside because the debt itself is disputed (ground 2) in Paragraph 4.6.2 above) then this may be considered an abuse of process and justify indemnity costs. The order at a directions hearing will probably be 'costs in the application', which adjourns the costs decision to the substantive hearing.

4.12 Challenging the statutory demand

In many ways an application to set aside a statutory demand is like a bankruptcy petition. A demand and a petition need to be served in similar ways, and are dismissed on similar grounds. If the debtor chooses not to apply to set aside the statutory demand, they are not prevented from disputing the debt at the hearing of a bankruptcy petition. However, in order to prevent the court's time being wasted, a debtor who unsuccessfully made an argument on an application to set aside a statutory demand cannot reuse that argument at the hearing of the bankruptcy petition unless there has been a change of circumstance or some other special reason. What counts as a change of circumstance will be for the judge to decide. There is no rule, for example, that a debtor who has obtained legal advice is allowed to make the same arguments twice.

This puts the debtor in a difficult tactical position. Do they dispute the statutory demand, or do they wait and dispute a possible bankruptcy petition? The advantages of disputing the demand early is that:

a) Although the application to set aside the demand will be heard in public, it is less public than a hearing of a bankruptcy petition. This is because notice of the petition must be given to the Land Registry, and it will be readily accessed by other creditors. Applications to set aside statutory demands are more private. If the creditors realise that the debtor is facing a bankruptcy petition, then they will treat the debtor differently: refusing to extend further credit, and more likely to enforce debts while they are still able to.

b) There are additional arguments which can be made about a bankruptcy petition which cannot be made about a statutory demand. A debtor may dispute both.

c) There is an advantage to delaying the date a bankruptcy petition is presented. This time is relevant for reviewing the transactions of the debtor as discussed in Chapter 2. If a bankruptcy petition is presented later, more historic transactions will fall outside of the scope of review.

d) Dispositions of property after the presentation of the bankruptcy petition are void unless the court orders otherwise (s284 of the Act). This means that if the bankrupt needs to sell property in order to pay the petitioning creditor, they require permission of the court: see Box 7 on page 24.

e) If an application to set aside a statutory demand is unsuccessful, the creditor will be awarded (most) of their legal costs. However, this costs order will not receive any priority in the bankruptcy, and so it will be paid at the same rate as the debtor's other unsecured debts: see Chapter 16. By contrast, the petitioning creditor's costs in the bankruptcy have a higher priority and so are more likely to be paid. It follows that by contesting the statutory demand, a debtor is more likely to reach a favourable settlement, because a creditor will be concerned about throwing good money after bad.

On the other hand:

a) An application to set aside a statutory demand has slightly lower stakes. A dismissed application does not lead to a bankruptcy order directly. This means that a judge may be more generous to the debtor and so resolve any doubt in their favour on the petition, rather than at the set aside hearing. This is particularly true for technical details like problems with service or mistakes on the form. Indeed, if the debtor makes technical arguments at the application to set aside the statutory demand, it is likely that the creditor will ensure that their bankruptcy petition is technically flawless. The reverse of this is that if the debtor chooses not to raise these defects initially, there is a chance that the bankruptcy petition would also be defective. This would put the debtor in a stronger position for the hearing of the petition.

b) A debtor has 18 days to submit their application to set aside a statutory demand. If it is difficult to gather together evidence (and in particular, if the debtor requires pro bono legal advice) then this timeline might cause a problem. The debtor might be better off preparing a robust opposition to the petition rather than sending a rushed and inadequate set aside application. If the debtor repeats an argument at the petition which they made to set aside the statutory demand, even if it is more developed and better evidenced, the creditor is inevitably going to argue that this was determined at the earlier application and cannot be disputed again. A late and rushed application to set aside can be remedied by the debtor with a request to submit further evidence at the first directions hearing, but in general it is better to present arguments properly the first time.

c) If the statutory demand has been improperly served, it may make more sense to raise this argument at the hearing of the petition. If it is made earlier, then the demand may simply be re-served.

Overall, whilst there are reasons to make arguments before the bankruptcy hearing, my advice is to make them early.

BOX 16: EXECUTION OF JUDGMENT

A less commonly used alternative to serving a statutory demand is proving that the creditor has a judgment in their favour and execution of that judgment has returned unsatisfied in whole or in part. It is common for creditors to have judgments in their favour. These creditors are also likely to try to enforce their debt, for example by sending round a bailiff (or a High Court Enforcement Officer) whose role is to seize goods or repossess property. If the bailiff is successful, they will be able to sell these goods on to satisfy the debt. If the bailiff is unsuccessful, either because there is nothing to take, or because the assets were not worth the full amount, then they can provide a witness statement to that effect and this proves the insolvency of the debtor under s268(1)(b) of the Act.

This route has the advantage to the creditor of cutting through the need to issue a statutory demand and risk a set aside application. Nonetheless, this route is less commonly relied on by creditors in insolvency proceedings. This is partly due to the speed and ease of using a statutory demand. It is also because a mere visit by a sheriff and a report of their inability to gain access is insufficient: the sheriff must make a serious attempt to execute the debt. The court treats this process extremely cautiously and is reluctant to waive mistakes ('cure defects').

For an illustration, in *Re Debtor (No. 340 of 1992)* [1996] 2 All E.R. 211 the debtor owed the creditors £910,071. A sheriff twice visited the debtor's home, but he found no one at home and so he was unable to gain access. The sheriff certified that his writ was unsatisfied in whole, but the sheriff had failed to 'levy execution', i.e. to see if there were any goods which could be sold, and if there were then to sell them. It was not said that the debtor had any goods of that high a value sitting in his house. This means that it was not disputed that, if the sheriff had managed to access the property, he would have been unable to levy execution. Nonetheless, since the sheriff had not gained access, the statutory condition was not met. However, the court held that it had no power to waive the failure to meet the requirements of the Act. As a result of failing to gain entry, there was no presumption that the debtor was unable to pay their debts.

Rule 10.1
Form SD 2

Statutory Demand under Section 268(1)(a) of the Insolvency Act 1986. Debt for Liquidated Sum Payable Immediately

Consequences of a statutory demand: see Paragraph 4.4 ↓

Warning

- This is an **important** document. You should refer to the notes below entitled "How to comply with a statutory demand or have it set aside."

- If you wish to have this demand set aside you must make application to do so **within 18 days** from its service on you.

- If you do not apply to set aside **within 18 days** or otherwise deal with this demand as set out in the notes **within 21 days** after its service on you, you could be made bankrupt and your property and goods taken away from you.

- Please read the demand and notes very carefully. If you are in doubt about your position you should seek advice **immediately** from a solicitor, a Citizen Advice Bureau or a licensed insolvency practitioner.

Notes for Creditor

- If the Creditor is entitled to the debt by way of assignment, details of the original creditor and any **intermediary** assignees should be given in part B on page 3.
- If the amount of debt includes interest not previously notified to the company as included in its liability, details should be given, including the grounds upon which interest is charged. The amount of interest must be shown separately.
- Any other charge accruing due from time to time may be claimed. The amount **or** rate of the charge must be identified and the grounds on which it is claimed must be stated.
- In either case the amount claimed must be limited to that which has accrued due at the date of the demand.
- If signatory of the demand is a solicitor or other agent of the creditor the name of his/her firm should be given

-

Demand   ← *Service: see Paragraph 4.3*

To _____

_____

Address _____

_____

This demand is served on you by the creditor:

Name _____   *Claim for a 'liquidated debt': see Paragraph 4.1*

Address _____

_____

The creditor claims that you owe the sum of £ _____, full particulars of which are set out on page 2, and that

SD2 - Statutory Demand under Section 268(1)(a) of the Insolvency Act 1986. Debt for Liquidated Sum Payable Immediately (04.17)

Statutory demand: page 1

Statutory Demands And Unsuccessful Execution Of Judgments

it is payable immediately and, to the extent of the sum demanded, is unsecured.

The creditor demands that you pay the above debt or secure or compound for it to the creditor's satisfaction.

[The creditor making this demand is a Minister of the Crown or a Government Department, and it is intended to present a bankruptcy petition in the [High Court][County Court at Central London] [Delete as appropriate].

Signature of individual _____

Name _____
      BLOCK LETTERS

*Delete if
signed by
the creditor
himself.

Date _____

*Position with or relationship to creditor _____

* I am authorised to make this demand on the creditor's behalf.

N.B. The person making this demand must complete the whole of pages 1, 2 and parts A, B and C (as applicable) on page 3

* This is the
address to
which the
court or the
creditor will
send any
documents
relating to
this
demand

Address _____

_____

Tel. Nº _____

Ref. _____

Details of Debt
(These details must include (a) when the debt was incurred, (b) the consideration for the debt (or if there is no consideration the way in which it arose) and (c) the amount due as at the date of this demand.)

SD2 - Statutory Demand under Section 268(1)(a) of the Insolvency Act 1986. Debt for Liquidated Sum Payable Immediately (04.17)

Statutory demand: page 2

Insolvency Law Made Clear – A Guide For Debtors

Note: If there is insufficient space, please continue on a separate sheet and clearly indicate on this page that you are doing so.

Part A
Appropriate Court for Setting Aside Demand

Rule 10.4(4) and 10.48 of the Insolvency Rules 2016 states that the appropriate court is the court to which you would have to present your own bankruptcy petition in accordance with Rule 10.11. In accordance with those rules on present information the appropriate court is [the High Court] [the County Court at Central London] [or] [County Court Hearing Centre] (address)

Setting aside a ← *statutory demand:*

Any application by you to set aside this demand should be made to that court.

see Paragraph 4.6

Part B

The individual or individuals to whom any communication regarding this demand may be addressed is/are:

Name _____
    (BLOCK LETTERS)
Address _____

_____

Telephone Number _____

Reference _____

Part C
For completion if the creditor is entitled to the debt by way of assignment.

	Name	Date(s) of Assignment
Original Creditor		
Assignees		

How to comply with a statutory demand or have it set aside (ACT WITHIN 18 DAYS)

If you wish to avoid a bankruptcy petition being presented against you, you must pay the debt shown on page 1, details of which are set out on page 2 of this notice, with the period of **21 days** after its service upon you. Alternatively, you can attempt to come to a settlement with the creditor. To do this you should:

- Inform the individual (or one of the individuals) named in Part B above immediately, that you are willing and able to offer security for the debt to the creditor's satisfaction; or
- Inform the individual (or one of the individuals) named in Part B immediately that you are will and able to compound for the debt to the creditor's satisfaction.

If you dispute the demand in whole or in part you should:

SD2 - Statutory Demand under Section 268(1)(a) of the Insolvency Act 1986. Debt for Liquidated Sum Payable Immediately (04.17)

Statutory demand: page 3

- Contact the individual (or one of the individuals) named in Part B immediately.

If you consider that you have grounds to have this demand set aside or you do not quickly receive a satisfactory written reply from the individual named in Part B whom you have contacted, you should **apply within 18 days** from the date of service of this demand on you to the appropriate court shown in Part A above to have the demand set aside.

Any application to set aside the demand should be made within 18 days from the date of service upon you and be supported by a witness statement stating the grounds on which the demand be set aside. The forms may be obtained from the appropriate court when you attend to make the application.

REMEMBER! From the date of service on you of this document
  (a) you have only 18 days to apply to this court to have the demand set aside, and
  (b) you have only 21 days before the creditor may present a bankruptcy petition

SD2 - Statutory Demand under Section 268(1)(a) of the Insolvency Act 1986. Debt for Liquidated Sum Payable Immediately (04.17)

Statutory demand: page 4

Chapter 5   Bankruptcy petitions and bankruptcy hearings

If 21 days pass from the service of a statutory demand, a creditor is entitled to present a bankruptcy petition. This chapter sets out what a bankruptcy petition is and how to contest a petition presented by a creditor.

5.1   What is a bankruptcy petition?

A bankruptcy petition is a form which typically looks as reproduced on the following pages. Problematic areas are shown in grey and discussed further below.

5.2   Jurisdiction

'Jurisdiction' is about the extent of the power of the court. There must be a geographic connection between the debtor and the English courts: a foreign debtor, even if they have English debts, should be made bankrupt by their home courts and not in England. The court has no 'jurisdiction' to make a foreign debtor bankrupt. Most debtors facing bankruptcy petitions live and work in England and Wales. The rules concerning jurisdiction are only relevant where the debtor has a connection to a foreign country. This section can be skipped for all other debtors.

Jurisdiction is a technical point, which at the very least is likely to delay a bankruptcy petition and it can easily lead to it being dismissed.

This section was written based on the rules at the time of writing. These rules have not substantially changed from the pre-Brexit rules as the Government tries to minimise disruption from the UK exiting the European Union. It is possible that the rules will change post-Brexit, if the Government decides to use its new powers to change English insolvency law. In particular, the Government may make it possible for a debtor who would otherwise have to be made bankrupt in Europe to be made bankrupt in England. If England does choose to differ from the European regulations, it is likely to apply the non-European rules to European countries rather than create a bespoke regime.

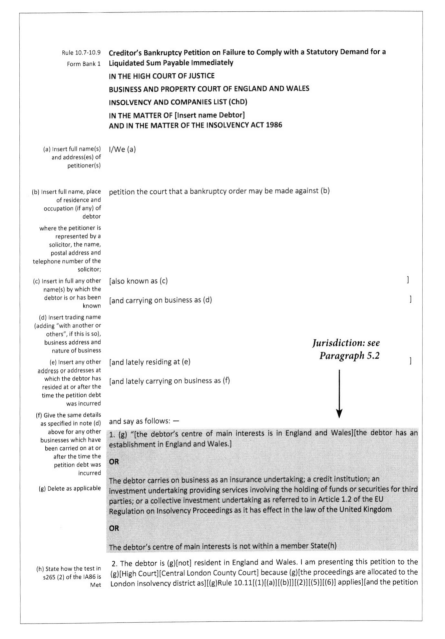

Rule 10.7-10.9   **Creditor's Bankruptcy Petition on Failure to Comply with a Statutory Demand for a**
Form Bank 1   **Liquidated Sum Payable Immediately**

IN THE HIGH COURT OF JUSTICE

BUSINESS AND PROPERTY COURT OF ENGLAND AND WALES

INSOLVENCY AND COMPANIES LIST (ChD)

IN THE MATTER OF [Insert name Debtor]

AND IN THE MATTER OF THE INSOLVENCY ACT 1986

(a) Insert full name(s)   I/We (a)
and address(es) of
petitioner(s)

(b) Insert full name, place   petition the court that a bankruptcy order may be made against (b)
of residence and
occupation (if any) of
debtor

where the petitioner is
represented by a
solicitor, the name,
postal address and
telephone number of the
solicitor;

(c) Insert in full any other   [also known as (c)   ]
name(s) by which the
debtor is or has been   [and carrying on business as (d)   ]
known

(d) Insert trading name
(adding "with another or
others", if this is so),
business address and   *Jurisdiction: see*
nature of business

(e) Insert any other   [and lately residing at (e)   *Paragraph 5.2*   ]
address or addresses at
which the debtor has   [and lately carrying on business as (f)
resided at or after the
time the petition debt
was incurred

(f) Give the same details
as specified in note (d)   and say as follows: —
above for any other
businesses which have   1. (g) "[the debtor's centre of main interests is in England and Wales][the debtor has an
been carried on at or   establishment in England and Wales.]
after the time the
petition debt was   **OR**
incurred

(g) Delete as applicable   The debtor carries on business as an insurance undertaking; a credit institution; an
investment undertaking providing services involving the holding of funds or securities for third
parties; or a collective investment undertaking as referred to in Article 1.2 of the EU
Regulation on Insolvency Proceedings as it has effect in the law of the United Kingdom

OR

The debtor's centre of main interests is not within a member State(h)

(h) State how the test in   2. The debtor is (g)[not] resident in England and Wales. I am presenting this petition to the
s265 (2) of the IA86 is   (g)[High Court][Central London County Court] because (g)[the proceedings are allocated to the
Met   London insolvency district as][(g)Rule 10.11[(1)[(a)][(b)]][(2)][(5)][(6)] applies][and the petition

Bankruptcy petition: page 1

debt is (g)[£50,000 or more][less than £50,000]][and within the 6 months immediately preceding its presentation (g)[the debtor carried on business in England and Wales and the debtor carried on business within the area of the London insolvency district (g)[for the greater part of that period of 6 months][for a longer period than in any other insolvency district]][the debtor has not carried on business in England and Wales but has resided in England and Wales and the debtor resided within the area of the London insolvency district (g)[for the greater part of that period of 6 months][for a longer period than in any other insolvency district]].

OR

The debtor is (g)[not] resident in England and Wales. I am presenting this petition to this county court because (g)Rule 10.11[(3)][(4)][(a)][(b)] applies [and within the 6 months immediately preceding its presentation (g)[the debtor has carried on business in England and Wales and for the longest part of the period during which the debtor carried on business within that period of 6 months, the [principal] place of business has been situated in the district of this county court][the debtor has not carried on business in England and Wales, but has resided in England and Wales and for the longest part of the period during which the debtor was resident in England and Wales within that period of 6 months, the debtor resided in the Insolvency district of this county court]].

Debt: see
Paragraph 5.3

(j) Please give the amount of debt(s), what they relate to and when they were incurred. Please show separately the amount or rate of any interest or other charge not previously notified to the debtor and the reasons why you are claiming it

(k) Insert date of service of a statutory demand

(l) State manner of service of demand and date

(m) If 3 weeks have not elapsed since service of statutory demand give reasons for earlier presentation of petition

3. The debtor is justly and truly indebted to us in the aggregate sum of £(j)

4. The above-mentioned debt is for a liquidated sum payable immediately and the debtor appears to be unable to pay it.

5. On (k) a statutory demand was served upon the debtor by (l) in respect of the above-mentioned debt. To the best of my knowledge and belief the demand has neither been complied with nor set aside in accordance with the Insolvency Rules and no application to set it aside is outstanding

(m)

Statutory demand: see
Paragraph 5.4

6. I/We do not, nor does any person on our behalf, hold any security on the debtor's estate, or any part thereof, for the payment of the above-mentioned sum

OR

I/We hold security for the payment of (g) [part of] the above-mentioned sum.
I/We will give up such security for the benefit of all the creditors in the event of a bankruptcy order being made.

OR

I/We hold security for the payment of part of the above-mentioned sum and we estimate the value of such security to be £ . This petition is not made in respect of the secured part of our debt.

Bankruptcy petition: page 2

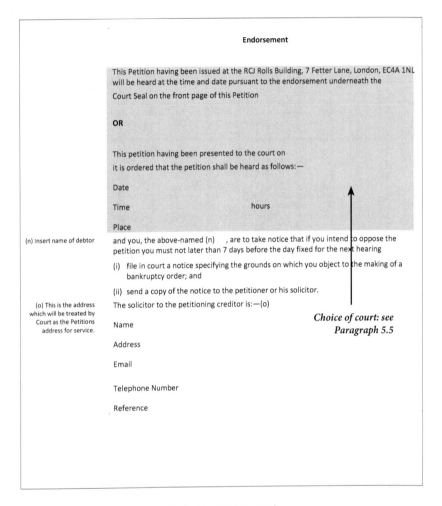

Bankruptcy petition: page 3

The rules determining jurisdiction are set out in s265 of the Act. A bankruptcy petition can only be presented in respect of a debtor if:

a) Their 'centre of main interests' is in England and Wales, or

b) Their 'centre of main interests is in a member state (other than Denmark) and the debtor has an establishment in England and Wales, or

c) Their 'centre of main interests' is outside of the EU, and they are either:

a.   'Domiciled' in England and Wales, or

b.   Within three years of the presentation of the petition they either:

    i.   Were resident or had a place of residence in England and Wales, or

    ii.   Carried on business in England and Wales, including via an agent or manager

The 'centre of main interests' (known as the COMI, pronounced '*coe-mee*') test is a question of where the debtor accrues their debts on a regular basis. English law has the same meaning for COMI as in the EU Recast Insolvency Regulation it was based on (s265(4)). For an individual running an independent business, the COMI is presumed to be where the individual's principal place of business is, unless it has moved within three months of the bankruptcy petition (see Article 3(1) of the Recast Insolvency Regulation (Insolvency Regulation (Regulation (EU) No. 2015/848)). For all others, the COMI is presumed to be the habitual residence of the debtor, unless this has moved within six months of the bankruptcy petition: also Article 3(1). For many debtors this is easy to establish. Someone who lives and works in England will have their COMI in England. Similarly, it is obvious that a French tourist with no English connection cannot be made bankrupt in England. An 'establishment' is any place of operations where a debtor has carried out a three month 'non-transitory economic activity': in practice, where they have a permanent business in England or Wales.

Problems arise when the debtor lives and works in different places. It is worth analysing European countries separately from non-European.

In Europe, the COMI is determined by where the person does business, unless they are employed by a company they do not control, in which case it would be their residence. If someone had a house and family in France, but works for a large international company and is posted to England, they will have a strong argument that their COMI is in France and their role was too transitory for this to constitute an establishment. However, if someone ran their own business (perhaps importing and selling French wines) with their primary shop in London, their COMI is likely to be in England or, at the least, they have an English 'establishment'. A small exception to the rule about European countries is Denmark, which has not subscribed to the European regulations on insolvency, and so will be treated as non-European.

However, if someone's COMI is outside of Europe, the rules change. The three tests are based on (1) domicile, (2) residence, (3) carrying on business.

Domicile is, in short, something inherited at birth as the 'domicile of origin'. Subsequently a debtor can acquire a 'domicile of choice' by moving permanently (i.e. having their permanent home and residence) to another country. Whether the debtor **resides** in England is a factual matter without clear rules, but in general it is a question of the degree of permanence. If a debtor owns a house and spends time in England they are likely to reside in England. The court will consider evidence such as how many days a debtor spends in England, as against other countries. It is possible to be ordinarily resident in England as well as another country. **Carrying on a business** must have a degree of continuity or regularity, and it must be the debtor's business rather than that of their company: to merely own shares in a company with a business in England is not sufficient. A bankruptcy petition can be presented if any of these tests are met.

Note that there is no requirement that the law governing the debt be English law, or be in pounds sterling. If the court is satisfied that the debtor falls within the jurisdiction of English bankruptcy law, they can be made bankrupt on a debt governed by foreign law. However, if the debt is disputed (or if the debt is close to £5,000 but may fall below due to a change in the exchange rate), the court is more likely to dismiss the petition on other grounds.

In practice, a debtor who thinks their COMI is not in England or Wales is well advised to seek an adjournment in order to obtain proper legal advice. The court is likely to grant it, at least at the first hearing, unless the jurisdiction argument seems hopeless.

BOX 17:   FORUM SHOPPING

There is a phenomenon known as 'forum shopping' where people come to England with a view to being made bankrupt here rather than some other country. The English regime can be seen as debtor friendly, for example because the bankruptcy is usually discharged after only a year. The comparison between English and foreign bankruptcy regimes is beyond the scope of this book, but there are useful resources online, such as a 2018 OECD report: http://www.oecd.org/officialdocuments/publicdisplaydocumentpdf/?cote=ECO/WK-P(2018)52&docLanguage=En.

Alternatively, a debtor may wish to move abroad to avoid being made bankrupt in the UK. Note that it is a criminal offence for someone in the six months before the presentation of a bankruptcy petition to leave England and Wales with any property which will fall into the estate worth more than £1,000 (s358 of the Act). This would include driving a car to a different country, if that car has a sufficiently high second-hand value. There is a defence that the removal was done without the intention of defrauding creditors and it is unlikely that a debtor will be prosecuted under this section unless they were aware that they were potentially facing bankruptcy proceedings.

There may be other reasons why a debtor would prefer to leave England – for example, a debtor might want to be nearer their families for support. Even after the bankruptcy order is made, it is not an offence to leave the country provided that the bankrupt leaves with less than £1,000 in value. It would be prudent to inform the Trustee in Bankruptcy of the move so they do not get suspicious. If the Trustee thinks a bankrupt is absconding with a view to avoiding debts, they can apply for an arrest warrant under s364 of the Act.

5.3   Debts

The bankruptcy debt must meet the same conditions as a statutory demand: it must be an unsecured, liquidated (quantified) sum of £5,000 or more which the debtor does not dispute. See Paragraph 4.1 above for a discussion.

The bankruptcy petition must identify the debt, and whether it is presented because the debtor has not complied with a statutory demand or because execution of a judgment debt was returned unsatisfied (r10.9).

If a debtor has paid or secured part of the statutory demand, the creditor is still allowed to present a bankruptcy petition unless the remaining unpaid or unsecured part is less than £5,000. However, once the petition has been properly presented, paying the debt until it falls to less than £5,000 will not invalidate the petition or be automatic grounds for its dismissal. Instead, it will be a factor which the court could consider in its discretion as to whether or not to make a bankruptcy order. It will be a persuasive factor, but the court may decide to make the bankruptcy order anyway, for example because the amount falls only just below the limit or because the debtor has other debts which render bankruptcy inevitable. The court cannot take into account the costs of the petition to bring the 'petition debt' above the bankruptcy level. In *Lilley v American Express Europe Ltd* [2000] BPIR 70, the judge made the order even after part payment on the petition debt due to the history of non-payment by the debtor.

5.4   Statutory demand

In most cases, the petition should be presented between three weeks and four months after service of the statutory demand.

A bankruptcy order cannot be made less than three weeks after the statutory demand has been served (s271(2) of the Act), even under the expedited process described in Paragraph 4.5. In practice this is rarely an issue, and nor will it grant the debtor much time. If the bankruptcy petition is presented less than three weeks after the statutory demand and the test for the expedited process is not met, the petition should be dismissed. This is because s267 of the Act provides that the debtor must be unable to pay their debts at the time the petition was presented. The debtor is not deemed to be unable to pay their debts under s268 unless three weeks have elapsed.

If the debt is presented based on a statutory demand served more than four months before the presentation of the petition, the creditor must state the reason for the delay (r10.7(2)). This delay is not necessarily grounds to dismiss the petition, but the court will be concerned about a possible abuse of process, and what prejudice is caused to the debtor by the delay. A debtor can argue that they relied on the fact that no bankruptcy petition was commenced within four months, and so it would be unfair for the creditor to rely on the historical demand. This might happen if, for example, the debtor spends money which they otherwise say they held to pay the debt in the demand. The time limit restarts if an application is made to set aside the statutory demand, which typically takes more than four months to resolve.

A creditor will need proof that they served the statutory demand. This is called a 'certificate of service' and it will usually be signed by the person who served the statutory demand and verified by a 'statement of truth' (a formal declaration that the contents are true). Without these documents, a court will have no evidence that the demand was properly served, and the court may assume that it has not been.

5.5   Court choice

The petition must contain sufficient information to establish that it is presented in the appropriate court. If the petition is presented in the County Court then it must contain sufficient information to establish it was presented in the appropriate hearing centre (r10.11(7)). If the petition was presented in the wrong court, the debtor should ask for it to be transferred.

The rules determining which court to present a bankruptcy petition are different from the rules determining which court to apply to set aside statutory demands. The complete rules can be found in r10.11, r12.5 and in the PDIP para 3. The locations are determined by where the debtor did business or, if no business was done, where the debtor resided within the six months preceding the presentation of the petition.

If the debtor resides or did business within the London Insolvency District, or if the petition is presented by a minister of the Crown or government department (typically HMRC) then the petition must be presented in the High Court if the debt is more than £50,000 and the County Court at Central London where the debt is less than £50,000. The scope of the London Insolvency District is set out in the London Insolvency District (County Court at Central London) Order 2014 and it includes most of London within the North Circular road.

Otherwise, the petition must be presented to the debtor's own hearing centre, i.e. the hearing centre for the insolvency district where the debtor carried on business: either the principal place of business, or where they resided. The Insolvency Districts are found in Schedule 6 of the Insolvency (England and Wales) Rules 2016: the smaller courts have no jurisdiction to even receive bankruptcy petitions.

The county courts are grouped into six geographic clusters called 'circuits'.

The circuits of England and Wales

After the petition is presented in the proper County Court, once the petition is disputed it <u>must</u> then be transferred to either the circuit's County Court with insolvency jurisdiction (which is Birmingham, Bristol, Leeds, Liverpool, Manchester, Newcastle, Cardiff or Central London County Court), or one of the specialist centres (currently Brighton, Croydon, Medway, Preston, or Romford). Broadly speaking, it is likely that the case will be heard at whichever of the above courts is closest, although an individual may live on the border of a different circuit and so even if another of the acceptable courts is closer, the petition will be heard at the circuit court. This means that it is common that the first hearing of the petition will only be to decide that the petition is being heard in the wrong court and it will need to be transferred. After the petition has moved to the more specialist court, it may be transferred back to the debtor's local court under PDIP para 3.8. A debtor may want to rely on this section if the travel to the specialist centre is highly inconvenient, but in general the court would prefer that the more experienced judges hear the petition and transfer back rarely happens.

Although it is possible for the court to strike out proceedings which are commenced in the wrong court or hearing centre under r12.31, it is likely to assume the creditor was incompetent rather than crooked and so it will order the transfer to the correct court or hearing centre. This will delay the hearing of the petition a further few months. A debtor who turns up to court who has already given proper notice of their opposition to the petition only for it to be transferred to the correct hearing centre can ask for their costs.

It is important that the petition is heard in the correct court. In *Crabbe v Day* [2020] EWHC 222 (Ch) the petition was presented to Winchester County Court and it was opposed. Even though Winchester County Court is not able to hear opposed bankruptcy petitions, a bankruptcy order was made. This order was set aside on appeal as a serious procedural irregularity.

Debtors whose place of business or residence is unknown are deemed to fall within the London Insolvency District. Where the debtor has an IVA and the supervisor has reported to the court, the petition must usually be presented to the court who received this report (r10.11(6)).

5.6 Additional steps

The creditor must also:

- File a statement of truth supporting the petition, to confirm that the contents of the petition are true. This is a serious procedural step because in order to make the bankruptcy order, the court has to be satisfied that the statements in the bankruptcy petition are true (r10.24(1)). The statement of truth turns the bankruptcy petition from merely being assertion to it being evidence which the court can rely upon. Where the creditor has failed to do so and has also made other contentious points (for example, where the debtor disputes that the debt is due) the court is likely to view a failure to file a statement of truth as a serious procedural breach and dismiss the petition. However, where the creditor merely omits the statement of truth, the court is likely to adjourn the petition and order the creditor to remedy the breach. The court will not automatically dismiss the petition.

- Conduct a search to see if there are already bankruptcy proceedings against that debtor (PDIP para 12.3.1). There is no automatic bar on presenting a second petition if a petition has been presented already.

- On the day of the substantive hearing, file a 'certificate of continuing debt' (this is a statement that the debt remains owing) (PDIP para 12.5.1). In London this is done in the sign-in sheet outside of court. They are commonly filed for every bankruptcy hearing, even if the court is only going to give directions.

5.7   Withdrawal of petition

By virtue of s266(2) of the Act, a creditor cannot withdraw a bankruptcy petition once it has been presented without the leave of the court. This is because bankruptcy is a class process (see the Introduction) with the aim of treating similar creditors in the same manner. This rule makes it more challenging to have a side deal with the creditor who presented the bankruptcy petition at the expense of other creditors. The court will consider whether other creditors could be substituted in to control ('take carriage') of the petition (see Paragraph 5.15 below). A creditor needs permission to withdraw a petition even if the petition was never served on the debtor: in practice it will be granted unless another creditor objects.

5.8   Service of the petition

Like a statutory demand, the sealed bankruptcy petition must be personally served onto the debtor. The rules are similar, but they are applied more strictly because a petition has more serious consequences than a statutory demand. Although the rules for service of a demand have been set out in Paragraph 4.3 above, it is worth providing more detail in the context of a petition.

The petitioning creditor has to arrange for the papers to be physically handed to the debtor. The creditor will then have to certify when service was affected. Process servers are typically used (as mentioned earlier, a process server is someone whose job it is to serve documents). Where applicable, the petition must also be served on the supervisor of the debtor's IVA (r10.14(2)). If the debtor physically refuses to take the papers given to him, the server must tell the debtor what the documents are, and the document must be left with or near the debtor. Anything less than this is not personal service. A solicitor cannot accept personal service of a bankruptcy petition, although they can for a statutory demand (PDIP para 12.7.1(4)).

The court has broad discretion to waive defects or irregularities in insolvency proceedings under r12.64. Where an attempt to personally serve the debtor has been made, the court may waive this as a defect. However, if there was a complete failure to attempt personal service this is a fundamental error: see *Gate Gourmet Luxembourg IV SARL v Morby* [2016] EWHC 74 (Ch) at [55]. In *Gate Gourmet*, the debtor was accompanied by a friend and the process server gave the paperwork to the friend. The friend and the debtor discussed the petition, tried to return it to the process server, then put it in the rubbish bin. This was held to be sufficient service, since the debtor was personally made aware of what the paperwork contained. However, the judge held that even if he was wrong about that, he would waive the error using his discretion.

If the creditor is unable to serve the petition personally, the creditor must apply to the court for an alternative form of service (often known as 'substituted service'). This is a key difference with the service of a statutory demand, where the creditor can take the view independently that personal service is not practicable. The creditor must file evidence which sets out what steps have been taken to serve the petition. The court will order substituted service if it is satisfied that the debtor was keeping out of the way to avoid service of the petition: i.e. that the debtor was deliberately evading service. The court will then permit or direct alternative forms. The court probably can allow an alternative means of service retroactively.[4] If the court does permit alternative service, the certificate of service must be accompanied by the sealed copy of the order permitting it (para 6(3) of Sch 4 to the Insolvency Rules). The usual order for substituted service is service by post – or potentially email – with the deemed date of service seven days later.

The court will only hear an application for substituted service if service has been properly attempted. It will expect the steps set out in PDIP para 12.7.1 to have been followed:

Where personal service of the bankruptcy petition is not practicable, service by other means may be permitted. In most cases, evidence that the steps set out in the following paragraphs have been taken will suffice to

---

[4] *Under the old Insolvency Rules, it was commonly thought that the court had no jurisdiction to retroactively allow alternative service: see Ardawa v Uppal [2019] EWHC 456 (Ch). However, when the new Insolvency Rules 2016 came into force on 1 January 2019, the wording was slightly different. The old position was then doubted in Yu (also known as Lau) v Cowley [2020] EWHC 2429 (Ch) which permitted alternative service retroactively. Yu was not about service of a bankruptcy petition, but the underlying principles would apply to bankruptcy petitions as well.*

justify an order for service of a bankruptcy petition other than by personal service:

(1) One personal call at the residence and place of business of the debtor. Where it is known that the debtor has more than one residential or business addresses, personal calls should be made at all the addresses.

(2) Should the creditor fail to effect personal service, a letter should be written to the debtor referring to the call(s), the purpose of the same, and the failure to meet the debtor, adding that a further call will be made for the same purpose on the [day] of [month] 20[ ] at [ ] hours at [place]. Such letter may be sent by first class prepaid post or left at or delivered to the debtor's address in such a way as it is reasonably likely to come to the debtor's attention. At least two business days' notice should be given of the appointment and copies of the letter sent to or left at all known addresses of the debtor. The appointment letter should also state that:

(a) in the event of the time and place not being convenient, the debtor should propose some other time and place reasonably convenient for the purpose;

(b) in the case of a statutory demand as suggested in paragraph 11.2 above, reference is being made to this paragraph for the purpose of service of a statutory demand, the appointment letter should state that if the debtor fails to keep the appointment the creditor proposes to serve the demand by advertisement/ post/ insertion through a letterbox as the case may be, and that, in the event of a bankruptcy petition being presented, the court will be asked to treat such service as service of the demand on the debtor;

(c) (in the case of a petition) if the debtor fails to keep the appointment, an application will be made to the court for an order that service be effected either by advertisement or in such other manner as the court may think fit.

(3) when attending any appointment made by letter, inquiry should be made as to whether the debtor is still resident at the address or still frequents the address, and/or other enquiries should be made to ascertain receipt of all letters left for them. If the debtor is away, inquiry should also be made as to when they are returning and whether the letters are being forwarded to an address within the jurisdiction (England and Wales) or elsewhere.

Failure to follow these steps means that the court will not grant permission, prospectively or retrospectively, for substituted service.

A debtor might be tempted to try to avoid service by (for example) refusing to open a door to a process server and pretending they are not in. This is unlikely to help the debtor in the long term. A petitioning creditor will, with relatively little inconvenience, be able to obtain an order permitting substituted service. However, there is the risk that the judge will view an order for substituted service as an indicator that the debtor is unreliable, and discount their future arguments accordingly.

The petition may not be heard until at least 14 days have elapsed after service, and so the petition must be served at least 14 days before the dated listed for the hearing (r10.21).

5.9 Timing of the hearing

A petitioner may need to apply for the bankruptcy hearing date to be moved back. This is most commonly done when they wish to apply to use alternative service, or when service is late and so there is not 14 days between the service of the petition and the hearing of the petition. However, if the court considers that the debtor has absconded or there are other reasons for an expedited hearing, the court may hear the petition notwithstanding these problems on such terms as it thinks fit.

5.10 The hearing of the petition

Bankruptcy hearings, like most court hearings, are usually held in public. This means members of the public are able to sit and watch from the back rows. However, the hearings are also typically held in small rooms and it is rare for a member of the public to actually attend unless the debtor is particularly famous.

In theory, a debtor who opposes the petition is required to file a notice of opposition to the court and deliver a copy to the petitioner not less than five business days before the hearing (r10.18(1)). This is a short form which can be found at https://www.gov.uk/government/publications/give-notice-of-opposition-to-a-bankruptcy-order-form-bank-6. In practice, if the debtor turns up and objects the court will almost certainly waive this requirement, because it would be extremely unfair to make a bankruptcy order on the basis of a procedural mistake.

BOX 18: WHEN TO FILE A NOTICE OF OPPOSITION

In general, if the debtor has a strong case for dismissing the petition, it is sensible to let the creditors know as soon as possible to encourage them not to proceed and to avoid an adverse costs order for failing to notify the creditor in good time. Similarly, if the debtor requires time to seek legal advice, it is sensible to communicate this with the other side and agree an adjournment.

5.11 Outcomes of the hearing

There are three main outcomes of a bankruptcy hearing: it can be a) adjourned, which means 'postponed', b) the petition can be dismissed, or c) the bankruptcy order can be made.

The standard structure for a debtor's argument is to argue both that the petition should be dismissed, and (if the court does not agree) then the petition should be adjourned.

5.12 Adjournment of the petition

The court has general discretion to adjourn a petition, and can do so for any reason it sees fit. However, in general an adjournment is only granted in three circumstances: firstly to enable any **technicalities** to be dealt with; secondly to enable the **evidence** on either side to be fully heard; and thirdly to enable the debtor to satisfy the court of their power to **pay their debts** in full.

5.12.1 Technicalities

This book has described many technical rules concerning bankruptcy petitions and statutory demands. A complete list of rules is at Annex 12. A judge facing a technical defect has three choices. Either they can waive it; or they can dismiss it; or they can order the party in default to remedy the change. This last option will often come with an adjournment for the party to have time to remedy the change.

An example of a technical defect is failure to file a certificate of service. The debtor would be unaffected by this defect, which is between the petitioner and the court, and so in the absence of other serious failures, the court is unlikely to dismiss the petition entirely as a consequence. Neither is the court likely to waive the defect: the petitioner may have correctly served the petition, but the court does not have evidence that this has been done. Instead, the court is likely to refuse to make the bankruptcy order on the say-so of the barrister for the petitioner, but rather adjourn for the petitioner to file this document.

5.12.2 Enable evidence to be fully heard

As will be explored in Paragraph 5.13 below, there are ways for a debtor to argue that the petition should be dismissed. However, they each require evidence to be submitted. The court will be concerned that the debtor has the right to have their case heard. This means allowing an adjournment for the debtor to a) seek legal advice (including pro bono legal advice) and b) to file and serve appropriate evidence. At the first hearing, if the debtor appears in person or if their barrister has recently been instructed, a court will be likely to adjourn the hearing at the debtor's request for this to happen. A typical adjournment at first hearing will be of four to eight weeks, but in practice the length of the adjournment will depend on when the court next has time in its diary to hear the case and so it may be substantially longer. At the second hearing, the debtor may again ask for an adjournment, but the court will be more reluctant to grant it. A debtor is more likely to succeed if they can show that progress has been made during the first adjournment, and that further progress is likely by the next hearing. This argument gets progressively weaker as the number of hearings and the total time elapsed since the original petition date increase.

A court is likely to adjourn the hearing on this ground if the debtor suffers some personal tragedy, including a medical condition. The court will be reluctant to make a bankruptcy order against the wishes of the debtor if the debtor is in hospital, or if they are mourning or caring for a close relative who has suddenly been taken ill, because they would not have had time to prepare. In practice, some debtors do pretend to be in worse situations than they really are. The court will lose patience by the second or third occasion, particularly if no evidence has been filed to support the debtor's assertions. On the other hand, if a debtor files a note from the doctor saying that their patient is ill – and ideally, a formal witness statement from them – the debtor can reasonably ask for an adjournment of a month or two. If the debtor falls ill, they may wish to draw the court's attention to the decision of Warby J in *Decker v Hopcraft* [2015] EWHC 1170 (QB) at paragraph 22: "*A court faced with an application to adjourn on medical grounds made for the first time by a litigant in person should be hesitant to refuse the application*". A judge has discretion to decide whether or not to adjourn a hearing: they do not have to adjourn even if the debtor can prove that they are ill.

A recent authority which discusses when to adjourn a trial on the basis that a defendant is ill is *Financial Conduct Authority v Avacade Ltd* [2020] EWHC 26 (Ch). This is not a bankruptcy case, but the judge is likely to follow the same principles. The Defendant submitted medical evidence that a) he was undergoing treatment for a disorder induced by the litigation, and b) he was potentially suicidal. It was said it had become more difficult (but not impossible) to conduct his case. The judge held that this was a case management decision, and so one to be taken looking at all the factors in the round. At paragraph 94, he considered it important that the suggested delay was six months for respite and then recovery would be within 10 to 12 months of starting treatment. However, since the defendant was facing other proceedings he would, presumably, still be under pressure, and so the likely delay could have been even longer. The judge declined to adjourn the trial.

5.12.3 Enable debtor to satisfy the court of their power to pay debts

Judges are aware that bankruptcy is a serious, potentially life-changing matter. Even where a debtor has an undisputed debt, where the debtor can show that they are likely to be in a position to pay it in the short term (rarely longer than three months), a judge is likely to give the debtor the benefit of the doubt and adjourn proceedings.

Ideally at the first hearing and certainly afterwards, the court will expect to see evidence that:

a) the funds to be received are likely to be sufficient to pay the petitioned debt (including the accumulated interest and the petitioner's legal costs), or to bring the debt to below the bankruptcy level of £5,000; and

b) the funds are likely to be received speedily and with a degree of certainty.

Since bankruptcy is a 'class' remedy, the court will also consider whether there are other supporting creditors. The court will be hesitant to adjourn a bankruptcy petition to pay the petitioning creditor if there are other supporting creditors. Even if the petitioner gets paid, bankruptcy may be inevitable and the other creditors will be left unpaid. However, unless the supporting creditors turn up to the hearing to make this argument, the court is likely to focus only on the petitioning creditor before them. The court will not ignore the interests of the remaining creditors, but it will assume that they are indifferent as to whether or not the debtor is made bankrupt, i.e. that they are content to wait for payment or use other routes.

Commonly seen examples where the debtor asks for an adjournment to repay the creditor are:

1. **Re-mortgaging**. It takes time to re-mortgage a property: the court will expect this to be around eight weeks. If the debtor can say that they have contacted a bank or a mortgage broker and present evidence that the remaining equity in the house is worth more than the petitioned debt, they are likely to obtain an adjournment. If the debtor has a letter from a mortgage broker saying they expect the process will take longer, the court is

likely to grant the adjournment necessary.

2. **Sale of property.** This includes a house or flat, but also any other item of value. Again, the court will expect evidence as to the value of the sale. However, it can take several months to sell a house. The court may decide that it would be in the creditors' interests for the Trustee in Bankruptcy to make the sale rather than the debtor, since the Trustee is likely to use an auction which is substantially quicker. Purely from the perspective of obtaining an adjournment, it may be better to seek a mortgage over a sale, because the court will not have as much patience for waiting for a higher-value house-purchaser.

3. **Unsecured lending or gifts.** Those who lend to a debtor facing a bankruptcy petition are likely to be aware that their chances of recovery are limited. In particular, if the debtor decides to repay one particular creditor over another, that transaction can be challenged as a voidable preference: see Paragraph 2.6 above. In practice, an unsecured loan to a debtor facing bankruptcy proceedings is more like a gift, because the chances of recovery are low. However, it is common for family members to help each other out in difficult times, and some debtors are lucky enough to have this support. If a debtor can submit evidence that a wealthier relative is going to support them, perhaps once they, in turn, sell or mortgage an asset, then the court is likely to adjourn proceedings for this to happen.

4. **Repayment of a third party's debt to the debtor.** The debtor may be expecting a third party to pay them, for example to repay a loan the debtor himself made as lender, or for services rendered. Unscrupulous third parties may try to take advantage of the debtor's financial difficulties, reasoning that they might be able to avoid making payment as a result of the bankruptcy order; or that the debtor does not have the means to enforce any payment due. From the debtor's perspective, this seems unfair: they are being made bankrupt due to the fault of some third party who has not paid their debts. However, from the petitioning creditor's perspective, this is not their concern. The creditor has the absolute right to repayment from the debtor. The creditor is unlikely to accept the transfer of the right to seek repayment from the third party instead.

In these situations, the court may grant a short adjournment to allow the debtor to seek repayment of their debt. However, overall it will recognise the right of the petitioning creditor to seek a bankruptcy order. The debtor's argument is more persuasive if they can show that they have a better means of recovering the debt than the Trustee in Bankruptcy would and so creditors would be better off if the bankruptcy order were delayed. This is a difficult argument to make because the Trustee is a professional who would be able to take the same steps as the debtor, such as commence litigation. A debtor might fairly argue that the petitioned debt is small and the costs of enforcement for a Trustee would be great, and so it is impractical for the Trustee to recover the sum. Another potential argument is that the debtor has a personal relationship with the third party and so is more likely to recover the amount. The court is likely to be sceptical of this argument because if indeed the debt is legally enforceable, it will assume that the usual processes for debt collection will be sufficient.

The court is also likely to adjourn a hearing if it considers that an IVA could be made. The court will want to know that the debtor has contacted an Insolvency Practitioner who has agreed to take on the case. The IP will be able to offer further guidance on what evidence to then present to the court to support the adjournment; for example a witness statement from the IP, a draft IVA proposal, and evidence of support from some creditors. The court will also want to know whether the petitioning creditor holds more than 25% of the debt – if so, they will be able to block the passage of an IVA and there is no point adjourning.

As discussed above in Paragraph 1.1, IVAs frequently contain a payment from a third party: someone who is generous enough to donate funds to prevent the debtor from becoming bankrupt. If this happens, it may be sufficient for the debtor to show only that the funds are likely to be received, and so the IVA is likely to be approved. The fact that the money coming in will only cover a fraction of the debtor's debts is irrelevant, provided that the proposal has support from 75% of the creditors by value.

Finally, the court might adjourn or stay a petition if there is an appeal of the underlying petition debt, or relatedly, an appeal of a tax assessment. As discussed in Paragraph 4.6.2 above, this is not enough to adjourn an application to set aside a statutory demand. However, the court may decide that the appeal has no reasonable prospect of success.

In *Gravesham Borough Council v Titilayo Orebanwo* [2020] EWHC 107 (Ch) a deputy district judge adjourned a bankruptcy petition where the debtor had offered to pay £150 monthly until the debt was cleared. The petition debt was £5,712.59, and so it would have taken about three years to be paid in full. Gravesham Council successfully appealed this decision, and the court held that the local authority had a prima facie right to a bankruptcy order, and in any event, three years was not a reasonable length of time. This case illustrates the 'rough justice' of the County Court. Firstly, the judge made a lenient decision towards the debtor not on strict legal principles, but because the judge thought it was fair. One might speculate that the judge might have been less generous had the petition debt not been so close to the £5,000 threshold. Secondly, it was possible that the debtor would have succeeded, had the local authority decided not to spend the money on an appeal. Perhaps had it been repayments of £300 a month, they would not have done so. Thirdly, it is a demonstration of the wide degree of discretion a judge has, even if this particular judge may have gone too far.

BOX 19: STAYING THE PETITION

Where there is cause for an adjournment, but there is no specific point in time to adjourn the hearing to, the court will 'stay' the petition. There is not much difference between the two from the debtor's perspective, except that a stay will be of an indefinite length of time.

5.12.4 Running multiple arguments

To some extent these three arguments can be run consecutively: first a debtor can say that the petition must be corrected, and then evidence must be gathered in their favour, and if there is then an opportunity to pay off the petitioned debt, the court might decide on a further adjournment. In general, a first adjournment is routine – almost to be expected. After then, a second adjournment is common, a third adjournment is rarer etc. There are cases where the debtor has an undisputed debt and the case is adjourned successively over multiple years.

For a recent, high profile example: in *Re: Kevin Stanford* [2019] EWHC 595 (Ch) the first petition was presented on 6 April 2017, the debt was undisputed, but the debtor was only made bankrupt on 22 February 2019. The case illustrates how all these reasons for an adjournment can be deployed:

1. Mr Stanford argued that one of the petitioners who was relying on a judgment debt where execution had returned unsatisfied (see Box 16 on page 62) had made a procedural error.

2. Mr Stanford argued that he was undergoing litigation in Luxembourg which was (he said) likely to lead to a large award which would enable him to pay his debts. Mr Stanford sought an adjournment for him to succeed in the litigation and pay off his creditors.

3. Mr Stanford argued that he had a conditional loan agreement with a third party, who would loan him money to pay one of the creditors.

There were other arguments run, but the bankruptcy order was eventually made. However, if the objective was to buy time then it succeeded.

If a debtor thinks that they are likely to be able to sign an IVA or have funds to pay the petitioned debt, or if they require more time to obtain evidence, then they should present this evidence to the petitioning creditor and ask for a voluntary adjournment. They should do this even if it is likely that the creditor will say no, because if the court agrees with the debtor they can legitimately seek their costs, or at least avoid an adverse cost judgment: see Chapter 16.

It can be a tactical mistake to point out serious errors in the bankruptcy petition in correspondence before the hearing if any errors can be corrected by the petitioning creditor in advance of the hearing, or prior notice supports the argument that there was no prejudice made to the debtor of any error. If the petitioning creditor says that the debtor deliberately waited before raising concerns and this unnecessarily increased their costs, a strong response is that the creditor should be responsible for their own errors. The debtor is under no obligation to do the work for them.

5.13 Grounds to oppose a bankruptcy petition

By virtue of s266(3) of the Act, the court has the power to dismiss a bankruptcy petition. This power is 'quite unfettered', i.e. there is no single list of reasons why the court may dismiss a petition. However, typically the power is exercised on one or more of the following grounds:

1. A serious procedural irregularity which prejudices the debtor

2. The debtor has no assets

3. Bankruptcy would be disproportionate

4. The debt is not for a liquidated sum

5. The debt is disputed

6. The debtor is able to pay their debts or has made an offer to secure or compound for a debt which was unreasonably refused

7. The petition is an abuse of process

8. The creditors are guilty of improper behaviour

9. Bankruptcy would have a serious psychological effect on the debtor

10. The petitioner does not attend the hearing

11. An IVA has been agreed

12. The court has no jurisdiction to make the bankruptcy order

13. The debtor lacks capacity

5.13.1 Serious procedural irregularities

The precise wording of s266(3) of the Act is: "The court has a general power, if it appears to it appropriate to do so on the grounds that there has been a **contravention of the rules** or for any other reason, to dismiss a bankruptcy petition..." Contravention of (i.e. breaking) the rules is the only specified reason why a court might exercise its discretion under this section to dismiss a petition. The insolvency rules must be respected. Where a petitioning creditor has broken the rules, and particularly when it has done so deliberately or the breach prejudiced the debtor, the court will dismiss the petition and award costs to the debtor. The creditor will need to start again.

This typically happens for:

- **Failure to serve a statutory demand or to prove that execution of judgment has returned unsatisfied**. If the demand itself was defective (i.e. contained typos, or omitted a phrase which was implied), the court might be prepared to waive the defects. However, if the debtor has not received a statutory demand – i.e. the demands the creditor made, if any, are so far removed from the rules relating to statutory demands that they cannot be properly said to qualify – the debtor is not unable to pay their debts for the purposes of s267(2)(c) of the Act (see s268) and so the creditor cannot present a petition.

- **Mistakes with service: where a creditor did not effect personal service, or did not follow the court's directions regarding substituted service**. If almost no attempt has been made to personally serve the petition, the most likely outcome is that the petition will be dismissed. However, as discussed in Paragraph 5.8, the court probably can waive this mistake retroactively. The court may take the middle approach and adjourn the hearing to allow re-service.

- **A stale statutory demand**. A creditor who presents a bankruptcy petition more than four months after serving the statutory demand must give a reason why it was delayed (r10.7(2)). Where this explanation is inadequate, and if the delay is substantially longer than four months, the court may dismiss the petition. The court will consider whether the debtor has been prejudiced by the delay, for example whether they have been lulled into a false sense of security.

5.13.2   The debtor has no assets

There is a special mechanism for debtors with assets of less than £1,000 and debts of less than £20,000: see the debt relief order section in Paragraph 1.2 above. This mechanism is recognition that bankruptcy is an expensive process, and where the debtor has no assets it is a waste of resources. The same principle applies to bankruptcy proper.

There is naturally a high burden for a debtor to demonstrate that they have no assets: debtors have an incentive to conceal assets in order to avoid paying their debts. However, where the debtor can show that the bankruptcy order would serve no useful purpose the court may refuse to make the order.

A recent case which illustrates this argument is *Lock v Aylesbury Vale District Council* [2018] EWHC 2015 (Ch). A bankruptcy petition was founded on a statutory demand in respect of £8,067 of unpaid council tax. The debtor was living in social housing and dependant on her daughter, who was the only person in the household to be earning any money. The Council had thoroughly investigated the debtor's financial affairs and were aware of this. Originally a Deputy District Judge made a bankruptcy order, but this was set aside on appeal for his failure to consider whether the order would serve a purpose.[5]

There is some suggestion in the judgment that the argument applies primarily to public authorities, like local authorities or HMRC: see paragraph 36 of the judgment. However, where the debtor genuinely has no assets, there is a good argument that it should be applied more widely.

This argument is a flexible one, and it is difficult to say precisely how little 'no assets' is meant to be. In my view, there is a good case that where the costs of the bankruptcy process are greater than the size of the estate, the order should not be made. This would, at a minimum, be the £990 for the bankruptcy deposit, plus £280 for court fees. As set out in Chapter 16, the Official Receiver charges a fixed fee of £6,000 plus 15% of the proceeds to act as Trustee in Bankruptcy. In practice, the argument can be credibly made whenever the estate is worth less than £10,000.

In *Edgeworth Capital v Maud* [2020] EWHC 974 (Ch), it was said that:

1.   the court has a discretion not to make an order if to do so would be completely pointless;

2.   the test is whether there is no possibility of any benefit to creditors;

---

[5] *For appeals, see Chapter 15.*

3. the impossibility of benefit must be obvious at the petition hearing without any detailed investigation;

4. the concept of benefit includes a reasonable desire on the part of creditors that there should be an investigation by the Trustee in Bankruptcy. A creditor may argue that the order should be made to allow the Official Receiver to investigate the debtor's affairs, potentially with a view to a director's disqualification hearing or criminal proceedings. The creditor would need to show why they believe the debtor had committed some misconduct, and also that it is likely that this misconduct would be investigated;

5. the evidence of the debtor is potentially relevant, but they will need to explain why the bankruptcy order would serve no purpose.

In that case the court held that creditors could not trust what the debtor said, and so further examination was required. The court made a bankruptcy order.

5.13.3 Bankruptcy would be disproportionate

A bankruptcy order can be made when the debt is as low as £5,000. There are other, less draconian measures of enforcing a debt. In particular, many debtors have equity in their houses, and a creditor can enforce their debt by putting a charge over the property. The argument here is not that bankruptcy would serve no purpose, but rather that the same goal can be achieved more efficiently using other tools. In practice this ground overlaps with the argument that the creditor has unreasonably refused to accept an offer to secure the debt, which is described in Paragraph 5.13.6 below. It may be sensible to run both arguments in parallel, in case the judge prefers one formulation to the other, although acknowledging that there is an overlap.

This is also a ground most likely to succeed when the petitioning creditor is a public body like HMRC or a local authority. It is a relatively weak argument, since even where the petitioner is a public body, it is entitled to consider its own interests first, and presumably the authority has a reason for choosing to issue bankruptcy proceedings.

5.13.4 The debt is not for a liquidated sum

As set out in Paragraph 5.3 above, a debtor can only be made bankrupt if they owe a quantified sum of money. It follows that they cannot be made bankrupt if the petitioner says they owe them something other than a quantified sum of money. Examples include where the petitioning creditor says:

*   The debtor has taken their car and not returned it. This is a claim for the return of the car, which is not for a particular amount.

- The debtor delivered defective goods. This would be a claim for damages, which is not yet liquidated.

- The debtor owes them compensation rather than a sum of money, such as for a personal injury or for causing damage to property. Until the court makes an order, it is not clear what compensation this would be for.

A bankruptcy petition rarely makes this mistake, but it does happen. It is more likely to occur where the petitioning creditor does not have legal advice themselves, or the legal advice they receive is not from an experienced solicitor.

5.13.5 The debt is disputed

A debtor who can show that the petitioned debt is disputed will be able to get the petition dismissed and costs awarded in their favour on a favourable basis (for details of costs, see Chapter 16).

This ground was covered in respect of a statutory demand, and the reader is directed to Paragraph 4.6.2 above.

After a certain period (usually six years), a debt can become too old to be enforceable. This is known as 'statute-barred' because it is barred by the Limitation Act 1980. The Limitation Act 1980 provides a complete defence to the debt. One difference between a statutory demand and a bankruptcy petition is that even if the court does not set aside a statutory demand in respect of such an old debt, it will dismiss a bankruptcy petition.

5.13.6 The debtor has made an offer to settle

This is a ground which is commonly argued, but rarely won. Under s271(3) of the Act:

> (3) The court may dismiss the petition if it is satisfied that the debtor is able to pay all his debts or is satisfied –
>
> (a) that the debtor has made an offer to secure or compound for a debt in respect of which the petition is presented,
>
> (b) that the acceptance of that offer would have required the dismissal of the petition, and
>
> (c) that the offer has been unreasonably refused;
>
> and, in determining for the purposes of this subsection whether the debtor is able to pay all his debts, the court shall take into account his contingent

and prospective liabilities.

This can be analysed as two sub-grounds. The court may dismiss the petition if it is satisfied that the debtor is able to pay all their debts, i.e. they are not insolvent. The court can also dismiss the petition if the debtor has made such a good offer to pay the debt that the petitioner has unreasonably refused.

Able to pay all their debts

A debtor who is able to pay their debts in full and who does not contest the petitioned debt would be well advised to pay the petitioning creditor's debt and seek dismissal of the petition afterwards, rather than the other way around. This is particularly true since the debtor would need to be able to pay <u>all</u> their debts, including contingent and future debts. Someone who can do that should not be wasting money on insolvency litigation. One situation where this does occur is when the statutory demand is made in respect of a future debt: if the court is satisfied that this debt will be paid, the petition will be dismissed.

Note that a solvent debtor, i.e. someone who can pay their debts but simply refuses to, can be made bankrupt notwithstanding this section. A debtor is deemed to be insolvent under the statutory demand/execution of judgment process described in Chapter 4 and merely proving that the debtor can pay their debts does not guarantee that the court will dismiss the petition.

Offers unreasonably rejected

It is worth discussing this second argument in three stages: first, the debtor has made an offer to secure or compound the debts; second, acceptance would require dismissal of the petition; and third, the offer is unreasonably refused.

Making an offer to secure or compound the debt. An offer to 'secure' the debt is an offer to give security, such as a charge over a house. An offer to 'compound' is an offer to pay less than the full amount, or to make the payments spread out over time, or both.

Acceptance would require dismissal of the petition. This would be the case if, for example, acceptance would extinguish the debt, or if acceptance would mean that the debt is not immediately payable and there is a good prospect that the debtor will be able to pay the debt when it does fall due.

The offer is unreasonably refused. This is the most important and contentious part. In general the court will approach the matter from the position that the petitioning creditor is entitled to be paid their debt in full and on time. In the event that payment in full will shortly be forthcoming, the court's approach will be to adjourn the petition rather than dismiss it: see Paragraph 5.12.3 above.

The test for 'unreasonableness' is "beyond the range of possible reasonable responses in the circumstances". This may appear circular. It means that the petitioner will argue that just because it may be reasonable to accept the offer, does not mean that it is unreasonable to refuse it. Acting reasonably does not mean acting kindly, or justly or fairly: the creditor is allowed to prioritise their own interests. The leading case which summarises the court's approach is *Revenue and Customs Commissioners v Garwood* [2012] BPIR 575.[6] The judge said at [23]:

1. The starting point is to ask whether a reasonable hypothetical creditor in the position of the petitioning creditor would accept or refuse the offer, bearing in mind, however, that there could be a range of reasonable positions which such a creditor could adopt.

2. The test is objective. This means that it does not matter that a particular creditor had in fact made an irrational decision to reject the offer for a bizarre and irrational reason: provided a reasonable person would make the same decision, the offer was reasonably rejected.

3. It is necessary to consider the extent to which the reasonably hypothetical creditor may be taken to have the characteristics of the petitioning creditor.

4. The court must look at the position at the date of the hearing.

5. The court is not limited to considering the matters taken into account by the petitioning creditor when the offer of security was refused; it must look at all the relevant factors and their impact on the reasonable hypothetical creditor.

6. That includes the history.

7. The debtor must be full, frank and open in providing the necessary information to enable the creditor to make an informed decision.

8. A rigid institutional policy of rejecting offers to secure could be a relevant consideration, since the reasonable hypothetical creditor was obliged to consider an offer on its merits; 'coherent in-house policies', however, are not necessarily wrong.

9. A creditor is entitled to have regard to their own interests and is not obliged

---

[6] *This case unfortunately has no neutral citation number and is not (at present) available on BAILII. If a litigant in person wants to rely on it, they may wish to ask the other side for a copy. If the other side fails to provide a copy, the court is unlikely to order them to share it, but the creditor will appear unhelpful because they would be exploiting the lack of legal representation on the part of the debtor. This is discussed more at Box 57 on page 238.*

to 'take a chance' or to show patience or generosity.

10. The cost and resources implications for the creditor are a 'highly material consideration'.

It can be seen that the test is set relatively high, and the court will consider matters like the behaviour of the debtor and their financial record of repaying debts. The fact that the offer is as much as the bankrupt can afford does not necessarily mean that its rejection is unreasonable. However, if the debtor has genuinely offered to pay 100% of their assets, the court might wonder what purpose would be served by the bankruptcy order, and be suspicious that there is some underlying collateral purpose behind the petition.

In *Garwood* itself, the argument was successful. The debtor had a jointly owned property, which he offered to sell and had received an offer which would complete within two months and make enough money to cover the petition debt. The debtor made an offer of security over the property while he went through this process. HMRC refused the offer, and the court held that this refusal was unreasonable. An alternative approach for the court would have been to adjourn the hearing of the petition and see what happened next.

The court cannot order the petitioning creditor to accept the offer, or the debtor to make one. However, where the debtor makes an offer and the court dismisses the bankruptcy petition on that account, the court will expect the offer still to be open after the petition is dismissed. There are no formal repercussions for the debtor of withdrawing the offer, or even not fulfilling the offer after it has been accepted. However, the creditor would inevitably then restart the bankruptcy process.

There are relatively few other examples where a petition has been dismissed on this ground. One recent case is *Boulton v Queen Margaret's School* [2018] EWHC 3729 (Ch). A private school successfully applied for a bankruptcy order against a parent at that school. The parent disputed part of the debt, but had made an offer to settle the undisputed part of £38,279. The offer was that a third party was going to pay the school in monthly instalments of £10,000. The first instalment had already been paid. Furthermore, the debtor offered security over a property worth substantially more than the undisputed debt. It was held that the school acted unreasonably in rejecting this offer, and so the bankruptcy order was successfully appealed.

5.13.7 The petition is an abuse of process

This is another ground which is commonly argued, but (to set expectations) is rarely successful. An 'abuse of process' occurs when a court process is used for an improper purpose. The purpose of bankruptcy is to provide for the creditors as a whole, and it is abused when the petitioning creditor's real purpose is different. Where a debtor can show that a petitioner is pursuing the petition for an improper purpose, the petitioner will then be expected to show that an order is in the interest in the class of creditors as a whole. This means that an argument about abuse of process is only likely to succeed when other creditors oppose the making of the bankruptcy order, if there are any. If other creditors support the petition, then the court may not let the wrong intentions of the petitioning creditor taint the decision, which will be taken for the creditors as a whole. Whether it does or not will depend on how abusive the petition is, i.e. how far removed it is from the proper purposes of bankruptcy. However, where the other creditors oppose the making of a bankruptcy order, or where there is only one main creditor, the court will dismiss a petition made for an improper purpose.

Common illegitimate purposes are:

- An attempt to stop enforcement of a debt owed to the debtor. Paragraph 2.6 above addressed the question of what happens when the debtor is themselves owed money. An unscrupulous creditor of the debtor may try to take advantage of the debtor's situation by deliberately petitioning for their bankruptcy. This might happen where, for example, a company owes the debtor money, but the debtor owes the sole director/shareholder of the company money personally, and so there is no valid defence of a cross-claim. In these circumstances, the court will be very suspicious of an abuse of process, since it appears as if the petitioner is using the tool of bankruptcy to stop the debtor from collecting the funds from the company. This may also occur when the debtor is conducting litigation against the petitioning creditor.

- A related case is where a petitioner knows that the making of a bankruptcy order has a positive effect on a third party. For example, the debtor might have a contract (perhaps a lease) which expires if a bankruptcy order is made. The petitioning creditor may want this contract to expire, and so petitions accordingly.

- Where the petition is made as part of some wider threat to the debtor, to encourage them to do something unrelated to the payment of the debt. For example, if the debtor is having a personal relationship with the ex-partner of the petitioning creditor, it would be an abuse of process for the creditor to start bankruptcy proceedings hoping to cause the debtor and the ex-partner to break up.

It is nearly always the case that, by the time it gets to the bankruptcy order, there is ill-feeling between the petitioning creditor and the debtor, and so it cannot be enough to dismiss the petition on this basis alone. A distinction is sometimes made between the 'purpose' and the 'motive' of the petitioning creditor.

The motive may be malicious, but the purpose will be related to the effect the bankruptcy order will have. It has been said that someone's 'purpose' refers to some future aim and their 'motive' refers to something which has happened in the past: this is sometimes a helpful framework, but not always. In practice, it is difficult to try to categorise the petitioning creditor's motives and purposes, and easier to show that (regardless of whether it is called a purpose or a motive) the creditor is not interested in the usual legal outcome of bankruptcy.

Although bankruptcy is not intended to be a form of debt collection, a legitimate purpose is to obtain a payment (a 'dividend') from the distribution the Trustee in Bankruptcy will make. Where a creditor has multiple purposes, the petition will only be an abuse of process if there are no proper purposes. This is a problem when using this ground for dismissing the petition: a creditor can nearly always say that they merely seek their rightful dividend. The court has said, in a corporate insolvency case, that it does not even matter if the petitioner's principal purpose was illegitimate, provided that one of their purposes was to receive a dividend: *Ebbvale Ltd v Hosking* [2013] UKPC 1.

Evidence of an improper purpose can also be useful to establish that the creditor has unreasonably refused an offer of settlement as in Paragraph 5.13.6 above.

It is an abuse of process to bring a petition against an individual who is already an undischarged bankrupt. However, it is not necessarily abusive to present a second bankruptcy petition in parallel with the first bankruptcy petition. A creditor might choose to do so and face the cost risk of their petition being dismissed if the debtor is made bankrupt on the other petition. It would be abusive if the second petition is presented for some collateral purpose. A second bankruptcy petition is good for the debtor only inasmuch as it can help the debtor argue for an adjournment (for example, to hear the petitions together, or so that they can be heard separately). Having a second petition is not going to help the debtor dismiss the first petition, which will be assessed on its own merits.

An example of an argument about abuse of process succeeding is *Re Leigh Estates (UK) Ltd* [1994] B.C.C. 292. It concerned a winding up petition rather than a bankruptcy petition, but the principles are similar. The local council presented a petition for unpaid business rates, but the remaining creditors who represented the majority of the debt owed opposed the petition. If the petition had been successful, a third party would have to pay the business rates. The court held that the council's reason for petitioning the court was not for the benefit of the unsecured creditors, but to gain a preference over the secured and unsecured creditors; and the opposing creditors' views were to be accepted.

5.13.8 The creditors are guilty of improper behaviour towards the debtor

The court has general discretion about whether or not to make a bankruptcy order, and it will consider the circumstances as a whole. If a creditor has, for example, threatened physical violence, or illegitimately sought to embarrass the debtor or their family, then the court may dismiss the petition on this basis. If a debtor feels they have been treated unfairly, they should present the information to the court as clearly and as dispassionately as possible. This is related to the 'abuse of process' ground.

The court may dismiss a petition if it considers that the petition is merely extortion of money, i.e. the creditor is seeking more than they deserve. An example of extortion would be if a creditor is owed £10,000 but writes a letter saying they will withdraw the petition if a third party pays them £20,000. However, there is no extortion simply because a creditor has high interest rates or late payment penalties. The creditor would say that these sums are compensation for any delay in payment. The court will probably decide whether a creditor is extorting the debtor based on their history of dealings, and by comparing the amount owed to the amount claimed.

The mere fact that the creditor goes straight to bankruptcy proceedings rather than consider other measures to enforce the debt does not constitute improper behaviour (although see Paragraph 5.13.3 for public bodies). The court is more likely to view this as grounds for adjourning the bankruptcy hearing for allowing time for settlement between the parties.

5.13.9 Bankruptcy would have a serious psychological impact on the debtor; or the debtor is very elderly or unwell

This ground primarily relates to petitions from HMRC and other public bodies. As part of HMRC's Debt Management and Banking Manual (to be found at https://www.gov.uk/hmrc-internal-manuals/debt-management-and-banking/dmbm585185 and https://www.gov.uk/hmrc-internal-manuals/debt-management-and-banking/dmbm585180). HMRC notes that the Equality Act 2010 creates obligations to make reasonable adjustment for taxpayers with mental health issues; or who are unwell or elderly. This does not automatically mean that they have no power to present a bankruptcy petition, but it does mean that HMRC should consider the effect of such a position. This relates to the 'proportionality' ground, because these considerations must feed into the public body's assessment of the harm of proceeding with the bankruptcy. The court can decide that it is unreasonable for HMRC to present a petition without considering the consequences on the debtor.

5.13.10 The petitioner does not attend the hearing of the petition

Under r10.26, a petitioning creditor who does not appear at the hearing may not present either that petition, or any other petition in respect of the same debt, without permission of the court to which the first petition was presented. This means that if the petitioner does not attend – either themselves, or through their legal representatives – the petition will not only be dismissed, but it is likely that the petitioner will not be able to bring another petition for the same debt. This rule is not often called upon. However, even if there are no other grounds for opposing the petition, if the petitioning creditor does not attend the hearing of the petition, the debtor can ask for it to be dismissed.

If the creditor can present a good reason why they did not attend the hearing, the court is likely to give permission for a further petition to be presented. The purpose of the power to dismiss is to prevent a petitioner from behaving improperly or in a cavalier fashion. If the petition is being heard remotely, and the petitioner can show that they (or the court) had an IT error and attempts were made to attend the hearing of the petition, this is likely to be sufficient for permission to be granted.

5.13.11 An Individual Voluntary Arrangement has been approved

For details of an IVA, see Paragraph 1.1 above. Once an IVA is approved by 75% of creditors, all creditors who were entitled to vote are bound by it (s260(2) of the Act). The Act does not specify that a bankruptcy petition must be dismissed, but once an IVA is approved it is a ground for annulling a bankruptcy under s261(2) of the Act, and so there is no point making an order.

5.13.12 The court has no jurisdiction to make the bankruptcy order

See Paragraph 5.2 above for a discussion of 'jurisdiction', which means whether there is a sufficient connection between the debtor and the English court. If the court has no jurisdiction, it must dismiss the petition.

5.13.13 Debtor lacks capacity

'Lack of capacity' in general refers to the mental ability of an individual to understand and make decisions in a legal process. It depends on the decision in question. In *Haworth v Cartmel* [2011] EWHC 36 (Ch) a bankruptcy order was annulled because the bankrupt lacked the mental capacity to engage in the bankruptcy process and so the order should not have been made. HMRC was criticised for being aware of this, but failing to inform the court.

Someone is presumed to have capacity under s1(2) of the Mental Capacity Act 2005 unless it is established otherwise. Someone is not treated as unable to make a decision merely because they make an unwise decision, but only when they are unable to a) understand the relevant information, b) retain that information, c) use the information or d) communicate a decision. Someone who can read this book is likely to have sufficient mental capacity to make decisions. However, this ground may be relevant when advising someone else.

BOX 20: OTHER GROUNDS FOR DISMISSING PETITIONS

There are other grounds for dismissing petitions, which rarely apply but are worth mentioning briefly:

- **Bankruptcy would destroy an important asset**. If so, bankruptcy would be counter-productive for the purposes of providing a return for the creditors. An example would be if the bankrupt was a member of a partnership and likely to receive a dividend, but the bankruptcy order would lead to the debtor being expelled from the partnership.

- The court can strike out a petition on the ground of **undue delay**. If a creditor delays, for example in filing evidence to prove that there are no grounds to dispute the debt, then the court can strike out the petition. The delay would need to be for several months – missing a deadline by a few days is insufficient.

To set expectations, it is worth noting what are not grounds to dispute the bankruptcy petition:

- The petitioner has a **personal grudge** against the debtor. This does not meet the criteria for an abuse of process, for which see Paragraph 5.13.7. This would be characterised as the 'motive' behind the petition, which is irrelevant.

- The **impact of bankruptcy** on the debtor and their family. A debtor will naturally be worried about the Trustee in Bankruptcy selling their house, leaving them and their family homeless or without enough resources to live on. This is not a consideration at the stage of making a bankruptcy order, and so it will not be grounds for dismissal. However, these arguments will affect a possession hearing (see Chapter 6) and may be grounds for challenging the decision of a Trustee in Bankruptcy (see Chapter 8). A court may also view these factors as part of its discretion to adjourn the bankruptcy if there is the possibility of settlement or an IVA: see Paragraph 5.12 above.

> ► **The debtor needs more time to pay.** This is never a ground for dismissal of the petition, but only adjournment: see Paragraph 5.12 above. Even then, the court does not need to adjourn the hearing for this reason, and even at the first hearing the court may decide to make a bankruptcy order.
>
> ► **Other creditors oppose the petition.** Bankruptcy is a class remedy and so one might have thought that if the majority of the creditors oppose the petition, it would be dismissed. This is not the case. If 75% of the creditors by value oppose the petition, it would be possible to approve an IVA. If, however, 25.1% or more of creditors by value are in favour of a bankruptcy petition, the court will not dismiss it on the views of the majority without some further cause. If the remaining creditors believe that the debtor requires more time to pay, this would be grounds to adjourn the petition: see Paragraph 5.12 above.

5.14 Substitution

Since bankruptcy is a class remedy, other creditors can apply to present the petition instead of the petitioning creditor. A creditor can apply to be substituted for the petitioning creditor when the petitioning creditor a) is not entitled to present the petition; b) consents to an adjournment, to withdraw the petition or to allow it to be dismissed; c) fails to appear; or d) appears but fails to apply for the bankruptcy order (r10.27(1)). This rule is partly aimed at stopping the debtor from paying off the one petitioning creditor in full at the expense of the other creditors, thinking that they would need to restart the whole process.

Where this happens, the court can substitute another creditor as the petitioner if they a) have delivered a notice of intention to appear at the hearing, b) are willing to present the petition, and c) at the date the petition was presented, they would have been in a position to present a petition themselves (r10.27(2)). The third of these tests means that, at the time when the petition was presented, the debt was for a liquidated sum equal to or above £5,000, there was a statutory demand served in respect of these debts (or execution of judgment had returned unsatisfied), three weeks had elapsed without payment, and there was no application to set the demand aside. As with the petitioning creditor, the new petitioner may petition in respect of a future debt. However, unless the debt has fallen due by the time of the petition, the court is likely to adjourn or dismiss the petition on the grounds that the debtor might be able to pay it.

Under these circumstances the petition will need to be amended and re-served, and the hearing will be adjourned (r10.28).

5.15 Change of carriage

A hypothetical option for a debtor would be to get a friendly creditor to file a bankruptcy petition, and then agree with the creditor to adjourn the petition indefinitely.

This option is not available. Under r10.29, the court can make a 'change of carriage order'. This would allow any creditor, who has formally given notice that they intend to appear at the hearing, control of the petition instead of the original petitioning creditor. It will do so if the original petitioner intends "by any means" to secure the postponement, adjournment, dismissal or withdrawal of the petition, or simply does not intend to continue proceedings diligently or at all. In practice this rule is only relied on where the court considers that the bankruptcy process is being abused: the mere fact that the petitioning creditor is more tolerant than a supporting creditor will not lead to a change of carriage order. A formal amendment of the petition is not required in these circumstances. The court can make a change of carriage order and hear the petition as presented by the new creditor on the same day, although if the new petitioned debt is disputed it is unlikely to do so.

5.16 Bankruptcy order

If the debtor's arguments for an adjournment or for dismissal are unsuccessful, the court will make a bankruptcy order. This will be dated to the minute rather than just the day.

5.17 Appeals

Appeals to bankruptcy orders as well as other decisions will be discussed in Chapter 15.

5.18 Other forms of bankruptcy

Criminal bankruptcy orders: There are several references in the Insolvency Act 1986 to a criminal bankruptcy order. This no longer exists due to s101 of the Criminal Justice Act 1988. It is unfortunate that the Insolvency Act and the Insolvency Rules have not been amended to show this.

Petitions following a failed IVA: It is possible for a creditor bound by an IVA or the supervisor of an IVA to bring a bankruptcy petition if the terms of an IVA are breached. Under s276 of the Act, the court shall not make an order upon this petition unless it is satisfied that:

> (a) the debtor has failed to comply with his obligations under the voluntary arrangement, or

(b) information which was false or misleading in any material particular or which contained material omissions –

(i) was contained in any statement of affairs or other document supplied by the debtor under Part VIII to any person, or

(ii) was otherwise made available by the debtor to his creditors in connection with a creditors' decision procedure instigated under that Part, or

(c) the debtor has failed to do all such things as may for the purposes of the voluntary arrangement have been reasonably required of him by the supervisor of the arrangement.

This section means that a petition brought by the creditor or supervisor does not need to establish insolvency. The supervisor only needs to show that the debtor has breached the agreement, or supplied false or misleading information. The court has discretion whether to make a bankruptcy order on this ground, as with a creditor's petition. If the terms of the agreement are ambiguous, the court is likely to interpret it in favour of the debtor, given the severity of making a bankruptcy order.

Chapter 6   Possession hearings

A bankruptcy order has been made. The bankrupt's possessions (their 'estate') now belong to ('vest in') the Trustee in Bankruptcy. The Trustee in Bankruptcy will now try to sell ('realise') the estate. The most valuable asset is typically the bankrupt's house. This house may be owned jointly by the bankrupt and their spouse: if so, the Trustee will try to sell the bankrupt's share of the property.

6.1   Overview

The Trustee's first step is likely to be to try to sell the house to another member of the bankrupt's family, if there is one who can afford to pay. This would allow the bankrupt and family to continue to live in their own house, but more importantly (from the perspective of the Trustee) it avoids the costs of further court proceedings, and estate agents' fees if the property needs to be sold on the open market. If a member of the bankrupt's family offers to purchase the house at a fair price and the Trustee does not properly consider the offer, see Chapter 8 on challenging the decisions of the Trustee. The family-purchaser is likely therefore to be given time to gather the funds to buy the property, including time to obtain a mortgage if necessary. The Trustee will not provide a discount to the family member, but instead will focus on getting the best deal for the creditors. However, a potential family member purchaser should be aware that the Trustee will face costs of a public sale and so it is likely to be in the creditors' interests to make the sale quickly. For both reasons, it may be possible to negotiate a discount with a private sale.

However, there may be no family purchaser able or willing to buy the property. This commonly happens when they cannot find a mortgage lender prepared to lend them the money. The family member might also already be in financial difficulty, particularly if they tried to support the bankrupt in the past.

In this circumstance, the Trustee in Bankruptcy will try to find an alternative purchaser. Unless the family living in the property can reach an agreement with a potential purchaser, the Trustee will be likely to try to sell the property 'with vacant possession', i.e. without the bankrupt and their family living in it.

It is often in the bankrupt's interests to leave voluntarily: see Box 23 on page 108. In particular, if the house is partly owned by the bankrupt's spouse, then it is sensible to aim to get the best possible price for the property because some of that money will be returned to the spouse. However, if the house is wholly owned by the bankrupt, then the longer spent in the property the less the bankrupt will need to spend on rent elsewhere.

This chapter describes what rights a Trustee in Bankruptcy has in respect of the family home if an agreement is not reached. A textbook which explains possession proceedings in general is 'Defending Possession Proceedings' by Jan Luba QC. Defending Possession Proceedings also sets out the procedural requirements of a possession claim, which this chapter will not cover.

This chapter only considers the relationship between the bankrupt and their family and the Trustee in Bankruptcy. A third party may also have the right to apply for a possession order, for example a lender who has a mortgage over the property is likely to have the right to sell the property if the debtor stops making mortgage payments. Depending on the mortgage document, the mere making of the bankruptcy order might allow the mortgagee to appoint a receiver to sell the property. If the power to sell is not contained (or excluded) in the mortgage agreement, it is granted by r10.122 of the Rules. It is common for the Trustee to ignore the bankrupt's house if the sale will be dealt with by the mortgage provider and there will be no surplus remaining for unsecured creditors. A Trustee might decide to continue paying the mortgage in order to avoid the mortgagee selling the property prematurely, knowing that these repayments partly go towards the equity in the property and so might be a good investment.

It is unfortunately beyond the scope of this book to describe how to get help rehousing. As soon as it seems possible that they will be evicted, a bankrupt should contact a local homelessness charity, local authority or Citizens Advice (or all three). It is a mistake to wait until after eviction, because it can take time to make the proper arrangements.

This chapter also only considers houses which are the main residence of the bankrupt or their family: it does not apply to second homes, or to property which the bankrupt owns and lets out to third parties. This falls into the estate and will be sold in the usual way. The Trustee does not have any special powers or restrictions against the tenants of a property whose landlord has gone bankrupt.

BOX 21:   WHAT IF THE BANKRUPT WAS RENTING?

The terms of the bankrupt's lease might contain provisions which determine what will apply if the tenant goes bankrupt. This is typically that the lease is forfeited. The landlord will then be able to apply for possession themselves. The general rule is that a creditor cannot take their own steps to enforce a provable debt, after the bankruptcy order is made (s285 of the Act). However, this does not include a claim for possession due to unpaid rent.

If the lease continues, the Trustee will have the power to end ('disclaim') the lease under s315 of the Act. A Trustee in Bankruptcy may permit a bankrupt to continue paying rent in the property the bankrupt previously lived in if they consider the rent to be reasonable expenditure. Rather than disclaim the property, the Trustee may simply decline to pay rent and allow the landlord to forfeit the lease.

Some types of tenancy do not fall automatically into the estate of the debtor, in particular, an assured tenancy, a protected tenancy and a secured tenancy (see s283(3A) of the Act). However, a Trustee can acquire these tenancies by serving notice in writing (s308A) if they do so within 42 days of learning about the tenancy. This may not apply if the tenancies contain prohibitions on assignment. Other types of tenancy, such as a statutory tenancy, are personal to the tenant and can never be disclaimed by a Trustee. A statutory tenancy is created if a person who previously held a protected tenancy remains in possession of property following the termination of the protected tenancy.

A Trustee cannot disclaim a lease jointly held between two tenants. There is also a process for an interested party to apply for a 'vesting order' which would allow another occupant of the property to take over the lease, to allow it to continue (s320 of the Act). In practice, a Trustee considering disclaiming a lease may consider simply giving ('assigning') it to the bankrupt's spouse without a court application, if the spouse agrees to take on all the liabilities under the lease.

BOX 22:   CORONAVIRUS AND EVICTIONS

There have been changes to the procedure for a landlord taking possession of property as a result of the pandemic. These broadly have the effect of making it more difficult for landlords to evict tenants for the non-payment of rent. This is an area of law which might be reviewed if the number of bankruptcies increases and so there is greater pressure placed on local authorities to provide housing support.

This area of the law is regrettably complicated. There are many different forms of tenancy and ways of taking an interest in land. The complexity of the law can lead to injustice, if only by accident. The bankrupt is unlikely to be able to pay for legal advice and is to some degree at the mercy of the Trustee in Bankruptcy.

> ## BOX 23:   CAUTION
>
> This book assumes that the debtor/bankrupt wishes to contest proceedings, and Chapter 3 discusses when this would be sensible.
>
> Possession proceedings can be taken more personally even than bankruptcy proceedings, and so contesting them can cause a great deal of pain and suffering. Even if a debtor makes a sensible and reasonable decision to contest bankruptcy, it is worth reviewing the situation after the bankruptcy order is made to decide whether it remains worth the stress of contesting the possession proceeding. There is unlikely to be significant cost risk involved for the bankrupt, but a third party (such as a wife or husband) could be put at risk of an order to pay the costs of the Trustee in Bankruptcy. That third party might be better off not contesting, because if/when the property is sold, they might receive some proceeds from the sale. The Trustee in Bankruptcy will deduct any cost award the court has made from the proceeds of sale.
>
> It follows that, if the family decide after reading this chapter that they have no right to occupy the house or contest its sale, it may be better to leave the house voluntarily. Family members should try to minimise their involvement in proceedings to avoid the likely costs order. For example, where it is possible to choose, it would be preferable for the bankrupt to make an application and the family member to support it, rather than the other way around.

6.2   Role of Trustee

The Trustee in Bankruptcy controls what was previously the property of the bankrupt. However, this does not automatically mean that they have the right to sell the property if a third party has an interest or is living there with the bankrupt.

> ## BOX 24:   SUMMARY OF THE BANKRUPT'S RIGHTS
>
> Unless the bankrupt can reach an arrangement with a potential purchaser, they will probably have to move out of the property eventually.

If the bankrupt is the sole occupier of the property, then the Trustee can apply for a possession order promptly. If they live with children or a spouse, the bankrupt and their family are likely to be given a year to live in the property from the time when the Trustee in Bankruptcy is appointed. Afterwards, the Trustee may apply for the sale of the property, unless there are exceptional circumstances. An example of exceptional circumstance is when a child is extremely ill and moving would harm them.

The first question the Trustee must establish is how much of the property is owned by the bankrupt, and how much (if any) is owned by their spouse. Even if the property is jointly owned by the bankrupt and their spouse, the property might not be shared 50:50 between the two. The amount of the property owned by the bankrupt is known as their "interest". In the first instance, the Trustee is likely to check the Land Registry and to ask the bankrupt and their family (potentially in the context of a formal investigation – see Chapter 2) how the value of the property is split between them. If a sensible answer is given (for example, 50:50) then the Trustee is unlikely to do any more research. If the answer given is that the bankrupt had no interest in the property at all, but only their spouse did, then the Trustee is unlikely to take this at face value without any further explanation.

Once the Trustee has established that the bankrupt has a certain interest in the property, they must take at least one of five steps under s283A of the Act within three years of the bankruptcy order. Either they can sell the bankrupt's interest; or apply for an order for possession; or for an order for sale, or for a charging order for the value of the bankrupt's interest; or find an agreement with the bankrupt regarding their interest. Failure to take any of these steps within three years of the bankruptcy order leads to the interest in the property returning to the bankrupt. This is known as 'use it or lose it'. The three year time limit begins on the date on which the Trustee becomes aware of the property if the bankrupt does not inform them of its existence within three months of the bankruptcy order. Trustees rarely 'lose it'.

Selling the interest: It will not be necessary to obtain an order for sale if the bankrupt owns a 100% interest in the property because the Trustee would already have the right to sell. However, such a sale will be with tenants in possession, which is less appealing for the purchaser. The **order for possession** will be to remove the bankrupt and their family. Initially this will be an order that the family leave the property. It can be followed by an application for a warrant of possession which allows the family to be evicted by force and the locks to be changed.

Charging order: A charging order puts a 'charge' over the property. It is like a mortgage, which is a charge held by the lending bank. A 'charge' means that when the house is sold the Trustee will receive their money back from the proceeds of sale. The charge will be registered at the Land Registry and so the prospective purchaser should be aware of it and so will not make a payment directly to the bankrupt for the property. A Trustee might obtain a charging order as a first step, and obtain an order for sale afterwards.

Until the **order to sell**, the bankrupt and their family can live in the house unaffected by the fact the Trustee holds a charge over the property. A Trustee may prefer not to apply for a charging order, because until the house is sold the creditors are unpaid, and the house may not be sold for many years. However, a Trustee in Bankruptcy may decide that a charging order is their best outcome, particularly in the event that the bankrupt is taking steps to sell the property themselves. A Trustee may also apply for a charging order if there are exceptional circumstances which prevent them selling the property.

Agreement: This would include an agreement for some future property which is likely to fall into the estate of the bankrupt (such as a future inheritance), in exchange for the bankrupt keeping the property. These are less commonly made.

6.3   Orders for possession

If the bankrupt owns the property outright and is the only occupier, the Trustee can apply for an order for possession immediately. The Trustee cannot remove the bankrupt without an order permitting them to do so. However, these orders are easy to obtain because the bankrupt has no right of occupation.

However, there are rights of occupation in three particular circumstances:

1.   When the bankrupt lives with children;

2.   When the bankrupt lives with a spouse or civil partner;

3.   When the property is co-owned.

6.3.1   Rights of occupation when the bankrupt lives with children

Under s337 of the Act, where a person is entitled to live in a property and they live there with anyone under the age of 18 (i.e. they have children at home) at the time of the presentation of the petition and the making of the bankruptcy order, they have the right not to be evicted by the Trustee, except with the leave of the court. By virtue of s337(2)(a) even if the bankrupt was not in occupation, they have the right to enter into and occupy the house with the leave of the court. The children do not need to belong to the bankrupt (either biologically or in law), but only live there with them. For example, it is enough if the bankrupt was living with a partner and with their children. It is not enough if the children move in after the presentation of the petition.

This application to evict or deny occupation must be made to the court where the bankruptcy order was made under s337(4) of the Act. The court will make the order that it thinks just and reasonable having regard to the interests of a) the creditors, b) the bankrupt's financial resources, c) the needs of the children and d) all the circumstances of the case other than the needs of the bankrupt. In practice, the court will be likely to refuse or adjourn the application in the first year of bankruptcy unless the family have somewhere to move to.

However, under s337(6) after a year has lapsed the court will assume, unless the circumstances are exceptional, that the interests of the creditors will outweigh all others. 'Exceptional circumstances' typically mean that the family have suffered or are suffering from a serious illness. Mere hardship to spouses and young children is not an exceptional circumstance: it is (unfortunately) routine.

6.3.2 Rights of occupation when the bankrupt lives with a spouse or civil partner

A spouse or civil partner obtains an interest in the property under the Family Law Act 1996 even if they have no rights of ownership. Under s30 of the Family Law Act, if one partner is entitled to live in certain property, the other partner has the right not to be evicted or excluded from that property, except with the leave of the court.

Under s336(2) of the Insolvency Act 1986, this right not be evicted continues against the Trustee in Bankruptcy. The Trustee will have to apply for an eviction order under s33 of the Family Law Act 1996 as if it were one partner trying to evict another. If the application is within a year of the property vesting in the Trustee, the court will make the eviction order as it thinks just and reasonable having regard to:

a) the interests of the bankrupt's creditors. The interests of a small business creditor may be given more weight than a large financial institution, if it is more important to the former to be repaid promptly;

b) the conduct of the spouse or former spouse, so far as contributing to the bankruptcy;

c) the needs and financial resources of the spouse;

d) the needs of any children; and

e)   all the circumstances of the case other than the needs of the bankrupt.

After the first year after the bankruptcy order, s336(5) of the Act provides that the court will assume that the interests of the bankrupt's creditors outweigh the other considerations, unless the circumstances are exceptional.

BOX 25:   'COMMON LAW WIVES'

There is no concept in English law of a 'common law wife', i.e. that by living with a partner for a long period of time, someone can acquire legal status akin to that of a husband, civil partner or wife. The law does not recognise the development of stable long term relationships outside of the formal marriage/civil partnership process.

It may be sensible for the partner of someone with serious debt problems to get married in advance of any bankruptcy proceedings. Note that s336(1) of the Act provides that nothing occurring between the presentation of the bankruptcy petition and the making of a bankruptcy order can give rise to any home rights under the Family Law Act 1996. This means that it is too late to get married after the bankruptcy petition is presented (at least for the purposes of remaining in the property).

For a couple facing eviction this is very serious. There is a notice period required before couples can get married, either religiously or civilly. The precise waiting period depends upon the type of marriage. For a civil ceremony, it is a minimum of 28 days of notice (see s31(1) of the Marriage Act 1949). This means that waiting for the statutory demand to come may be too late, since a petition can be presented 21 days later. This period is unlikely to be waived by applying to the Registrar General: rules concerning waiver of the notice period apply to matters like mortal illness. A foreign wedding would be recognised under English law if it was legal in the place it was celebrated, which might be an alternative for some couples.

There are criminal offences which can be committed in relation to marriage, for example by making a false declaration relating to a marriage (see s3 of the Perjury Act 1911). These are not committed by a couple who decide to formalise their pre-existing relationship, even if it is done primarily for the positive legal consequences that marriage brings.

6.3.3 Rights of occupation when the bankrupt co-owns the property with a third party

Where a third party (for simplicity, consider an unmarried partner) of the bankrupt partly owns the property with the bankrupt, the Trustee will apply for an order for sale under s14 of the Trusts of Land and Appointment of Trustees Act 1996. An unmarried partner can co-own the property with the bankrupt even if their name does not appear on the Land Registry. In particular, an unmarried partner may be able to argue that by helping the bankrupt with mortgage payments over a period of time or by contributing to improvements to the house, they have acquired an interest in the property themselves. Their interest would be proportionate to their contribution, but it is not simple to determine what this is: see Box 5 on page 17. In practice, a partner may need to negotiate this share with the Trustee in Bankruptcy.

Under s335A of the Act, if less than a year has passed the court will consider a range of factors, including the financial needs of the partner, the needs of any children, and the conduct of the partner insofar as it contributed to the bankruptcy. After a year, the interests of the creditors will outweigh the other considerations, unless the circumstances of the case are exceptional.

A spouse who co-owns the property and a spouse who does not are in a similar position. This is because s335A imposes more or less the same restrictions on the Trustee as s336 of the Act. However, s335A works to extend this protection to an any third party co-owner, even if they are not married to the bankrupt.

6.4 Low value homes

The court will dismiss an application to sell a property if the house was the main residence of the bankrupt, their spouse or their former spouse and the value of the bankrupt's interest is less than £1,000 (see s313A of the Act and the Insolvency Proceedings (Monetary Limits) (Amendment) Order 2004). A lender with a mortgage might still seek to sell the property.

6.5 Mortgage payments

Frequently when an individual makes mortgage payments, part of the payment goes towards interest on the loan and part of it goes towards paying off the principal amount. Little by little, the houseowner acquires the whole house. A Trustee in Bankruptcy may decide that mortgage payments should continue, perhaps because there are circumstances that mean that the family cannot be evicted and so no purchaser is likely to buy the house, or perhaps because they would rather arrange the sale of the property instead of the bank.

Where the bankrupt occupies the property on the condition that they make mortgage payments, the bankrupt does not automatically acquire any part of the house as a consequence (s338 of the Act). The Trustee is still able to, for example, place a charge over the part of the house which the mortgage lender can no longer claim.

6.6   Objecting to sale

It follows from the above discussion that there is a difference in the test the court will consider depending on whether the objection is made within a year from the bankruptcy order or afterwards. Either way, the sale will only be made with the leave of the court and at the application of the Trustee in Bankruptcy themselves. Unless the Trustee is breaking the rules (and see Chapter 8 if so) there is no need for the bankrupt or their family to make an application to the court – it will be sufficient for them to turn up and oppose the Trustee's application.

The Trustee is likely to name every occupant of the property as respondents to the application. However, it is best for the bankrupt to object to the sale, and not the other residents if possible. In particular, the bankrupt has standing to occupy the house when there are children living there in his own name: there is no need to act in the name of the children. This is to avoid a costs order being made against the other resident. Assuming the bankrupt has fewer assets than liabilities, they are 'judgment proof'. A costs order against an undischarged bankrupt does not fall into their estate and so it is not removed upon the discharge of their bankruptcy (see the definition of a bankruptcy debt in s382 of the Act). However, it is difficult to enforce a debt against someone recently made bankrupt, since they probably have no assets. In practice the Trustee might prefer for the costs to fall as part of their expenses, and if so they will be paid in preference to other bankruptcy debts. If, however, a objection was made by a third party (like a spouse) then they would be liable for the costs of the Trustee if they are unsuccessful; and the Trustee would have a duty to pursue them for costs rather than deplete the assets of the bankrupt's estate by paying the costs themselves. For more details, see Chapter 16 on costs.

If the possession hearing takes place before a year has expired, the bankrupt should submit a witness statement setting out the impact which eviction would have on him and his family members. Points which are likely to be relevant are:

- Any reason why the house is well-located: for example, if it is near the school which the bankrupt's children attend; or proximity to grandparents who provide childcare support.

- The impact on moving: whether this would cause great disruption to the family.

- The financial cost of finding a new place to live on the partner: for example, evidence as to how much this would cost, and information on the partner's ability to pay this sum. It is worth commenting on whether the partner's interest in the property would be sufficient to pay for replacement housing, (but only if it would not be).

- The amount of equity in the house. If the bankrupt has more assets than liabilities, then creditors can be compensated for the delay by receiving a greater sum once the property is finally sold if their debts bare interest. However, if the bankrupt is in this position they would be advised to sell the property themselves: see Paragraph 3.1 above.

The only material which is irrelevant is the needs of the bankrupt themselves. However, judges will consider the bankrupt's needs when this is reflected in the needs of their family. There are circumstances where one member of the family needs to care for another.

The likely outcome of an opposed application made before a year is that the court will make an order for possession to be suspended until the year lapses rather than the dismissal of the application. Failure to oppose an application is likely to lead to the order being effective sooner.

After a year, the bankrupt should submit a witness statement which will need to support the argument that 'the circumstances of the case are exceptional'. This could include:

- If a member of the family is ill, medical information which sets out the detrimental effect a move would have on the family, and how long it might take until the family member recovers (if at all).

- If appropriate, how long that family member has left to live. In *Re Bremner* [1999] 1 FLR 912 the bankrupt was 79 years old and terminally ill. The judge considered the needs of the bankrupt's wife in looking after her husband in their home. The wife offered to allow sale three months after his death, and this was allowed by the judge.

Although it is unlikely that an application for an order for sale will be dismissed if a year passes, it is possible that the court will postpone the order until after a certain event, for example until after a member of the family receives medical attention, or until a child reaches a certain age.

6.7   Dismissal of Trustee's application for possession

Under s283A(4) of the Act, if the Trustee in Bankruptcy makes a failed application for an order of sale, order of possession, or charging order, then the property returns automatically to the bankrupt, unless the court orders otherwise. This is an unusual provision, since it can lead to a windfall gain for the bankrupt for a minor failure by the Trustee. However, as a consequence of s283A, the court is likely to adjourn an otherwise unsuccessful application for a sale rather than dismiss it, in order to avoid this consequence. This might happen if, for example, the application for sale was made before the year long grace period had expired, but it considered that once it lapsed an order for sale would be likely.

Chapter 7　　Bankruptcy offences

There are a large number of criminal offences which a bankrupt may commit. They all ultimately relate to the bankrupt gaining some improper advantage at the expense of their creditors. It is impossible for creditors to seek financial compensation for this improper behaviour, since by definition the bankrupt is unlikely to have the assets to repay the creditors for their debts in the first place. The law steps in and imposes criminal sanctions to punish the bankrupt instead. Under s350(5) of the Act, all prosecutions must be instigated either by the Secretary of State for Business, Energy and Industrial Strategy via the Insolvency Service, or by or with the consent of the Director of Public Prosecutions.

This chapter is about what the bankruptcy offences are, to allow the reader to understand how not to break the law and what a Trustee in Bankruptcy will be concerned about. It does not describe how the offences are prosecuted. A bankrupt accused of a criminal offence should have access to legal aid and so to a lawyer who can explain what the process will be.

Statistics from the Insolvency Service from February 2020 show that there are roughly 100 individuals charged with an insolvency related offence every year. This would include charges for offences relating to companies going insolvent. Approximately 10 individuals are acquitted each year; the remainder are convicted. In its 2018/2019 annual report, the Insolvency Service's target time to instigate a criminal prosecution was fewer than 24 months, and its planning assumption was for approximately 140 to 160 criminal investigations resulting in a decision to prosecute within a year.

The law about bankruptcy offences is mostly set out in Chapter 6 of the Act, in sections 350 to 360, but there are offences elsewhere in the Act and in other legislation.

7.1　Bankruptcy offences in the Act

The main bankruptcy offences in the Act are:

- **Failure to disclose full details of property comprised in the bankrupt's estate to the Trustee.** The bankrupt has a positive obligation to give full information to the Trustee to the best of their knowledge and belief. This includes disclosing details of significant transactions where property would have fallen into the estate.

- **Concealing property or failing to deliver it to the Trustee.** The bankrupt has a positive obligation to hand over all property, although in order to be an offence the minimum amount concealed or kept must be £1,000.

- **Concealing, destroying or falsifying documents relating to the estate.** This includes computer records.

- **Making a false representation** (i.e. lying) to the Trustee, including failing to tell the Trustee of a false claim by a purported creditor.

- **Fraudulently disposing of property** within five years of the commencement of bankruptcy.

- **Removing property** with a total value of over £1,000 from the estate.

- **Failure to account for the loss of a substantial part of property** within the year before the bankruptcy.

- **Leaving England and Wales with property** valued at more than £1,000, or preparing to leave.

- **Obtaining credit without disclosing relevant information** about the bankrupt's status, i.e. that they are an undischarged bankrupt.

- **Trading under a different name to the one in which the bankruptcy order was made.** It is legal for a bankrupt to change their name, but they must engage in business under their previous name until the bankruptcy is discharged.

There is significant cross-over between some of these offences. For example, it is unlikely that a bankrupt who conceals property will make a full disclosure of the property they hold. The Insolvency Service or the Crown Prosecution Service (CPS) will decide which are the appropriate charges to bring. In the event that two charges are proven a judge would not simply sum up the two likely sentences for each charge individually. Instead, the judge will consider the misconduct 'in the round' and treat the additional offences as an aggravating factor.

These offences apply regardless of whether the bankrupt applies for their own bankruptcy or whether the petition is brought by a creditor or IVA supervisor. In practice, the offences are most likely to be prosecuted in higher value cases.

Bankruptcy offences are in addition to other crimes which anyone, bankrupt or not, may commit. In particular, it is still possible for an individual (whether or not they are an undischarged bankrupt) to commit fraud: i.e. dishonestly make a false representation with the intention of making a gain or to cause another to suffer a loss. An act of fraud might be both a bankruptcy offence and an offence in its own right.

However, these bankruptcy offences can only be committed by someone made bankrupt. For example, it is not a bankruptcy offence for the spouse of a bankrupt to remove property with a value of over £1,000: this is simply an act of theft, and so an offence under the usual Theft Act 1968. It is an offence for the bankrupt to lie to their Trustee in Bankruptcy under s356 of the Act; for a spouse it would likely be contempt of court or fraud instead.

Note that it is not an offence to have a transaction at an undervalue, or to grant a preference (see Chapter 2). However, it would be an offence not to disclose to the Trustee that these payments were made.

7.2   Defence of innocent intention

There is a general defence under s352 of the Act if the bankrupt can prove that at the time of committing the offence, they had no intention to defraud or conceal the state of their affairs.

The wording of s352 makes it seem as if the bankrupt has to prove that they are innocent, rather than the normal rule which is that the accused is presumed to be innocent until the prosecutor proves that they are guilty. However, the court interprets it as showing that the bankrupt needs to raise a plausible case that they acted innocently, and having done so the prosecution needs to prove that this was not the case.

The defence does not apply to all the criminal offences, although where it does not there is sometimes a related defence of 'reasonable excuse'. For example, there is no defence of innocent intention for a failure to account for any substantial loss of property in the 12 months before the petition was presented. This failure is an offence under s354(3). However, there is a defence of reasonable excuse for failing to provide this account. It might be, for example, that the bankrupt failed to keep proper records and now cannot remember where the property has gone. Whether this excuse is a reasonable one will be a question ultimately for a magistrate or jury to decide.

There is no defence for engaging in business or obtaining credit without disclosing relevant information about the bankruptcy under s360: the onus is wholly on the bankrupt to take proper steps. The Trustee in Bankruptcy is likely to explain this obligation (as well as all the other obligations) to the bankrupt.

However, if the Trustee fails to do so, or if the bankrupt forgets or does not understand the explanation, this would not stop the act of engaging in business without disclosure from being an offence. Instead, it would be a mitigating factor when it comes to the punishment, or a reason for the Insolvency Service or CPS not to prosecute.

7.3   Punishment

Schedule 10 of the Act sets out the range of sentences for many of these offences. This shows that the maximum sentence is typically seven years. However, in practice it is very rare for the court to be so harsh on an offender. Statistics from the Insolvency Service in February 2020 show that of those convicted of an insolvency offence, approximately half received a community order and half were imprisoned. Of those imprisoned, most were given sentences of under 12 months. Individuals typically were given disqualification orders and costs orders also. This would also include offences in relation to a corporate bankruptcy.

Having a criminal record of any form makes it (even) harder for a bankrupt to get their life back into order following the bankruptcy order.

7.4   Effect of annulment and discharge

The fact that a bankruptcy is later annulled is no defence to the proceedings. However, no proceedings can be commenced after the bankruptcy has been annulled (s350(2) of the Act). In contrast, there can be criminal proceedings for a bankruptcy offence against an individual after their bankruptcy has been discharged, but it has to relate to behaviour before the date of discharge (s350(3)). The difference between an annulment of a bankruptcy and the discharge of a bankruptcy is discussed in Chapter 9.

7.5   Prosecution

The Trustee in Bankruptcy will not be the prosecutor for these bankruptcy offences. Instead, if the Trustee suspects an offence has been committed, they will report it to the Insolvency Service who will make a decision on prosecution. If the Trustee is the Official Receiver, the Official Receiver will refer the case to a different department within the Insolvency Service. If the bankrupt is charged with an offence and pleads not guilty, there will be a criminal trial to determine what happened. Advice on how to conduct a criminal trial goes beyond the scope of this book: a defendant would hopefully have access to legal aid.

7.6   Application for an arrest warrant

The Trustee does have a power to apply to the court for a warrant for the bankrupt's arrest under s364 of the Act, as well as for the seizure of any records or goods in their possession when arrested. This can be done at any time after the presentation of the bankruptcy petition, and is to prevent the bankrupt absconding, removing goods, concealing or destroying records, or failing to attend examination. This is technically distinct from the prosecution of a bankruptcy offence: it is a power the Trustee has to carry out their duties and not punishment for an offence. The application is used in extreme circumstances, for example where the Trustee has credible evidence that the bankrupt is lying to them or falsifying documents. The Trustee cannot arrest the bankrupt or seize any of their records without a warrant from the court. The Trustee themselves will not conduct the arrest, but instead it will be done by 'tipstaff': court employees who act as policemen or bailiffs.

7.7 Contempt of court

There is a category of misconduct which the Trustee in Bankruptcy can, in effect, prosecute. It is 'contempt of court' to make a false statement of truth, or to disobey or disrupt the court process. This is not always formally categorised as a crime, but once proven it still leads to the offender being punished, including potentially being sent to prison.

It is contempt of court to refuse to answer a question while under a public examination (s290(5) of the Act) (see Chapter 2 on examination). This is in contrast to normal civil proceedings, where an individual can always refuse to answer a question if it would lead to exposing themselves or their partner to criminal proceedings (s4 Civil Evidence Act 1968).

Finally, ss312, 333 and 363 of the Act create obligations on the bankrupt to deliver up property and records, to assist the Trustee on request, and to comply with a direction of the court.

Depending on the behaviour, a frustrated Trustee may prefer to bring 'committal proceedings', i.e. a claim for contempt of court, instead of referring potentially criminal activity to the CPS. Committal proceedings, despite their name, do not need to lead to a custodial sentence even if the claim succeeds. They must be made to the High Court to a High Court judge, by virtue of PDIP para 3.2.

Committal proceedings are highly technical. The standard of proof is the criminal standard, i.e. the judge has to be 'sure' that the defendant has interfered with the administration of justice. The procedure is set out in CPR Part 81. As an officer of the court, the Trustee does not require permission to make the application.

It is unclear how often committal applications are made for bankruptcy cases: probably few, given the other options available to a Trustee in Bankruptcy. Figures from the Civil Justice Statistics bulletin for 2019 show approximately

400 committal warrants issued each year, but that figure includes contempt for non-bankruptcy work which will be the majority of cases.

7.8   Bankruptcy offences outside of the Act

It would be helpful if the Act gave a complete list of the possible offences a bankrupt could commit through acting whilst bankrupt. It does not. A bankrupt should also be aware that it is an offence under s11 of the Company Directors Disqualification Act 1986 for an undischarged bankrupt to act as a director, or to take part in the promotion, formation or management of a company without leave of the court. This includes acting as a director of a company incorporated outside of Great Britain if it has a place of establishment inside Great Britain (s11(4)). There is no defence that the accused honestly believes that the bankruptcy has been discharged. Under s13, the maximum sentence is two years' imprisonment and a fine. In order to seek leave, the application should be served on the Official Receiver, who has the right to oppose the application. The principles are similar to a disqualified director applying for permission (see Chapter 14).

Chapter 8　　Challenges to the Trustee in Bankruptcy

This book has described many rules and principles which the Trustee must follow. A bankrupt is in a difficult position if they think that the Trustee is breaking the rules, or acting unfairly. A bankrupt has a general duty to cooperate with their Trustee under s333 of the Act. If the bankrupt fails to comply with any obligation which the Trustee reasonably requires of them, this could be contempt of court and the bankrupt may be punished accordingly (s333(4)).

This chapter sets out how a bankrupt or a friendly creditor can challenge a decision of the Trustee.

In summary, there are two sections a bankrupt can rely on: s303 and s304 of the Act. The difference between the two is that s303 of the Act is for a general application to challenge the Trustee and s304 is for specific wrongdoing where the Trustee has caused loss to the bankrupt's estate or has taken its assets for themselves. A s303 application is to seek a direction that the Trustee does or does not do something: a s304 application typically seeks compensation.

The court also has power under s298 to remove the Trustee from office. This would usually be used only in a situation where there could be a challenge under s303 or s304. This chapter will also discuss the possibility of making a complaint to the Trustee's regulator.

The court's general approach is that it will not interfere with the Trustee's administration of the estate lightly, and so bankrupts should approach this chapter with caution. This is because it would be impossible to work as a Trustee if the court continually scrutinises every decision made. A bankrupt should be selective about what they make a court application over, not just due to the cost risk but also because if the court considers that the application is 'totally without merit' it may make a civil restraint order prohibiting the bankrupt from making any further application without leave of the court. This makes it more difficult to complain even if a meritorious application could be made.

Unfortunately the bankrupt starts on the back foot when making their application. This is for two reasons.

- Firstly, the Trustee in Bankruptcy is an independent professional person, and unless their independence can be shown to be compromised, the court will be inclined to trust their account. This does not mean that the court will automatically disregard the testimony of a bankrupt, but the bankrupt does have more to gain or lose personally, so perhaps more incentive to stretch the truth than a Trustee. However, the court may also have experience of Insolvency Practitioners misbehaving and so a judge will try to approach the case with an open mind.

- Secondly, the court's primary concern will not be the welfare of the bankrupt, but the interests of the creditors as a whole. This does not mean it will bend the rules to suit the creditors. However, it does mean that the court will not let its sympathy for the difficult position of a bankrupt override the need to sell the bankrupt's possessions in order to repay the creditors.

Bankrupts do sometimes succeed in challenging the decisions of their Trustees in Bankruptcy – and (more commonly) Trustees back down before a formal application needs to be made, when they know their actions could be criticised by a judge. Knowledge of the rules of when a challenge is likely to be successful is the best way to ensure that a Trustee follows the law.

8.1   General control of the Trustee by the court

The main section of the Act which permits a bankrupt to challenge the decision of the Trustee is s303:

303 General control of Trustee by the court

(1) If a bankrupt or any of his creditors or any other person is dissatisfied by any act, omission or decision of a Trustee of the bankrupt's estate, he may apply to the court; and on such an application the court may confirm, reverse or modify any act or decision of the Trustee, may give him directions or may make such other order as it thinks fit.

There is no limit on what a bankrupt might wish to complain about. Common complaints are:

1.   **The Trustee wrongly values property**. A bankrupt might feel that they have enough assets to pay off all their creditors, if the assets were sold for their proper amounts. By selling them at an undervalue, the Trustee deprives the bankrupt of the appropriate surplus of the estate.

2.   **The Trustee wrongly admits contested debts**. A bankrupt might object to paying certain creditors because they deny the debt is owed. This might be out of principle, or because the higher amount of proved debt guarantees

that there will be no surplus left for the bankrupt.

3. **The Trustee tries to sell property which does not fall into the bankrupt's estate**. This might be property which did not belong to the bankrupt because (for example) it was owned by the bankrupt's partner, or because it was personal property like a wedding ring (see Chapter 2).

Although the court has the power to control the Trustee in any manner, in general a s303 application has to be related to the obligation of the Trustee: the application must be that the Trustee is in some way not meeting their duties. Note that the Trustee has no duty to be friendly or polite. However, Trustees are subject to 'the rule in *ex parte* James' (pronounced ex-part-ay). This is an obligation to act with integrity. If a Trustee promises to do something, they should do it even if they had no statutory obligation to make the promise in the first place. A Trustee also cannot take advantage of a technical position in law where it would be dishonourable. For example, if a family member of the bankrupt accidentally gave them money without realising that the bankruptcy order has been made, the Trustee should not take advantage of this mistake and distribute the property to the creditors: they should return it to the family member. Trustees are held to high standards, and they must distance themselves from any moral wrongdoing. However, this standard is that a Trustee must not act in a manner 'obviously unjust by all right-minded men', and not that they cannot act in a manner which is merely unfair.

The test for making a s303 application is that the Trustee must have acted 'perversely'. It was described in *Bramston v Haut* [2012] EWCA Civ 1637 at paragraph 69 as:

> *"It follows that it can only be right for the court to interfere with the decision the Official Receiver has taken if it can be shown that he has acted in bad faith or so perversely that no Trustee properly advised or properly instructing himself could so have acted, alternatively, if he has acted fraudulently or in a manner so unreasonable and absurd that no reasonable person could have acted in that way."*

If the Trustee's actions were straightforwardly illegal, like selling property not belonging to the bankrupt, this will be met. However, for the other two examples above, a Trustee has a degree of discretion. There is no objective answer for the proper price to sell property at, or how to value an uncertain debt owed by a creditor, and there is a range of different valuation techniques which a Trustee might legitimately use. This means that the test is difficult to meet. In practice judges themselves have a margin of appreciation for what they consider unreasonable. Where the judge feels that an injustice has occurred, they will find that it meets the test.

The test from *Bramston v Haut* also allows the court to interfere if the Trustee acts in 'bad faith'. This is not a well-defined phrase, but it refers to the Trustee acting maliciously or dishonestly. This standard is likely to be even harder to achieve than 'perversity'. Judges are often reluctant to find that someone has acted in bad faith, and particularly an independent, regulated professional like an Insolvency Practitioner. They will give individuals the benefit of the doubt, unless there is objective evidence to support the application.

The primary relevance of a s303 application is as a check on the Trustee. A Trustee is not going to want to lose a s303 application, because in losing the court is finding that they acted perversely, or in a manner which no reasonable Trustee should have acted. If there are potential grounds for a s303 challenge, a bankrupt should write to the Trustee and set out the grounds of complaint. By threatening to start proceedings, Trustees are forced to take the bankrupt's complaint seriously. See Paragraph 18.1.1 on settlement for more information.

As an illustration, Trustees have been found to have acted perversely when:

- The Trustee did not allow the bankrupt to make a claim against a third party, even though the Trustee did not intend to claim himself: *Heath v Tang* [1993] 1 WLR 1421.

- The Trustee presented their costs bill without a breakdown: *Woodbridge v Smith* [2004] BPIR 247.

Trustees had not acted perversely when:

- Nearly all the money in the estate was used on their fees: *Freeburn v Hunt* [2010] C.L.Y. 1903.

- The bankrupt was not allowed to occupy property even pending sale to his wife: *Supperstone v Hurst* [2006] EWHC 2147 (Ch).

- They settled a personal injury claim for £5,000, when the bankrupt wanted to refuse the offer and continue to trial: *Aslam v Finn* [2013] EWHC 3405 (Ch).

- They refused to investigate or pursue a speculative claim against a third party: *Shepherd v Official Receiver* [2006] EWHC 2902 (Ch).

8.2   Compensation for breach of duty

Under s304 of the Act:

Liability of Trustee

(1) Where on an application under this section the court is satisfied –

(a) that the Trustee of a bankrupt's estate has misapplied or retained, or become accountable for, any money or other property comprised in the bankrupt's estate, or

(b) that a bankrupt's estate has suffered any loss in consequence of any misfeasance or breach of fiduciary or other duty by a Trustee of the estate in the carrying out of his functions,

the court may order the Trustee, for the benefit of the estate, to repay, restore or account for money or other property (together with interest at such rate as the court thinks just) or, as the case may require, to pay such sum by way of compensation in respect of the misfeasance or breach of fiduciary or other duty as the court thinks just.

This is without prejudice to any liability arising apart from this section.

(2) An application under this section may be made by the Official Receiver, the Secretary of State, a creditor of the bankrupt or (whether or not there is, or is likely to be, a surplus for the purposes of section 330(5) (final distribution)) the bankrupt himself.

But the leave of the court is required for the making of an application if it is to be made by the bankrupt or if it is to be made after the Trustee has had his release under section 299.

(3) Where –

(a) the Trustee seizes or disposes of any property which is not comprised in the bankrupts estate, and

(b) at the time of the seizure or disposal the Trustee believes, and has reasonable grounds for believing, that he is entitled (whether in pursuance of an order of the court or otherwise) to seize or dispose of that property,

the Trustee is not liable to any person (whether under this section or otherwise) in respect of any loss or damage resulting from the seizure or disposal except in so far as that loss or damage is caused by the negligence of the Trustee; and he has a lien on the property, or the proceeds of its sale, for such of the expenses of the bankruptcy as were incurred in connection with the seizure or disposal.

In short, the Trustee has to pay compensation if their breach of duty has caused harm to the estate.

The first point for the bankrupt to notice is that the bankrupt can only make a s304 application with the permission of the court. This is not required for a s303 application. It can be avoided if the bankrupt is friends with a creditor who is prepared to put in the application themselves, although the effect of doing so is that the friendly creditor will be at risk of a costs order if the application is unsuccessful.

The second point to note is that the effect of compensation is typically to compensate the estate of the bankrupt and not the bankrupt themselves. This may mean that, from the bankrupt's perspective, a s304 application can be pointless. To give an extreme example: consider a situation where the Trustee in Bankruptcy decided to take the bankrupt's car for themselves and the bankrupt notices one day that their Trustee has turned up to the property driving their old car. This is a case where the Trustee has retained property that comprised (contained in) the bankrupt's estate (s304(1)(a)) and a breach of duty (s304(1) (b)). What the Trustee should have done is sell the car and distribute the assets. However, if the bankrupt makes a s304 application, all the court will do is require the Trustee to sell the car, and perhaps provide compensation to the creditors for any delay or loss in value. This does little for the bankrupt: prior to the s304 application their Trustee had the car; afterwards, their creditors have the car. There is no question of returning property to the bankrupt just because the Trustee has misapplied it.

It follows that a s304 application is only worth making if either a) the bankrupt expects their assets in their estate will be greater than their debts (including expenses) and so the compensation will eventually return to the bankrupt, or b) the bankrupt wants the court to remove the Trustee in Bankruptcy and this is an objective ground for the court to do so. However, type a) bankruptcies are not common, because a prudent debtor will sell their assets before the bankruptcy order gets made (see the discussion at Paragraph 3.1 above). Type b) situations are common, but the bankrupt should be aware that the delay caused by the application could lead to the replacement Trustee in Bankruptcy continuing to review the estate even after the bankruptcy has been discharged. The result of removing a Trustee is that the court will appoint another, this one (hopefully) with more integrity and professionalism. The bankrupt should consider whether the next Trustee will make the same decisions which they found objectionable as the first Trustee. Even if the wrongdoer is rude and unpleasant, it may be better to keep them in the knowledge that the bankruptcy should be over within a year.

Notwithstanding that advice, it is worth briefly reviewing how s304 can be used. The important point of the application is to identify the wrongdoing. This can be money or property the Trustee kept for themselves. Alternatively, it might be a breach of duty by the Trustee. Trustees have a duty to act in the best interests of the creditors. The duty might be breached if (for example) the Trustee had a conflict of interest such as if they personally bought something from the bankrupt's estate, or if the Trustee was negligent in an action, such as they sold a car worth £50,000 for just £1,000.

Under s304(3) if a Trustee disposes of property which was <u>not</u> in the bankrupt's estate, but the Trustee had reasonable grounds for believing that they were entitled to sell it, the Trustee is not liable for the sale. This means that if the Trustee sells a house which was jointly owned on the basis that only the bankrupt owned it, and distributes the entire sales money to the creditors, the co-owner of the house cannot sue the Trustee. The two exceptions are where a) the Trustee had no reasonable grounds for believing they were entitled to sell it, and b) where the Trustee acted negligently. There is a degree of crossover between those two exceptions. Joint ownership of a house is commonly stated on the Land Registry – if it is, it would probably be unreasonable for the Trustee to believe it fell entirely into the estate.

This is a powerful rule for the Trustee to rely on, and bankrupts and others need to be cautious about it. A bankrupt should be aware of what the Trustee is selling, and should be proactive in claiming that property does not fall into the estate. Chapter 2 sets out what falls into the bankrupt's estate. An example of this section being applied is the recent case of *Birdi v Price* [2018] EWHC 2943 (Ch). The claimant was a car mechanic for Italian 'supercars' such as Ferraris, and so he had valuable equipment. Items necessary for the bankrupt's work do not fall into the estate under s283(2)(a) of the Act. The Trustee sold them, and the bankrupt tried to sue him for the loss. As part of the dispute the judge held that the Trustee had reasonable grounds to think he was entitled to sell the equipment and so had a defence under s304(3).

8.3   Complaints to the regulator

The Trustee in Bankruptcy will either be the Official Receiver or an independent Insolvency Practitioner. Either way, they will be closely regulated. Complaints about private practice Insolvency Practitioners can be made online through the Insolvency Service gateway. This is fully set out online at https://www.gov.uk/guidance/make-a-complaint-to-the-insolvency-service. Complaints about the Official Receiver can be made online at https://www.gov.uk/government/organisations/insolvency-service/about/complaints-procedure.

In the year 2018/2019 the Insolvency Service received 378 complaints, of which 38% were upheld or partially upheld.

Neither the Insolvency Service nor the body which regulates the Insolvency Practitioner has the power to direct the Trustee to take a certain action, or to provide compensation for their mistakes. This can only be done by the court through s303 and s304 of the Act. It follows that complaining to the Insolvency Service is unlikely to achieve the objective the complainant desires. It is often used as a threat, but Trustees in Bankruptcy are used to being threatened with complaints. The Insolvency Service may treat complaints with a degree of scepticism because it is likely to receive many meritless complaints, unless objective evidence is provided in support.

The substance of the complaint will need to be that the Trustee is not following the rules of the regulator. This includes the Insolvency Rules and bankruptcy law, but it is likely to be broader: for example, the regulator is a little more open to the general complaint that a Trustee is acting unfairly than the court will be. The regulator may also apply a lower test than the court which, as discussed in Paragraph 8.1 above, will only interfere with a decision of a Trustee if the decision is wholly unreasonable.

In general, it is my opinion that the court route is typically more effective than an online complaint. This is because:

1. It is more public.

2. The court has the power to control the Trustee but its regulator does not.

3. The regulator will take a court finding extremely seriously and is unlikely to second-guess a legal finding. In contrast, the court is not bound to follow the decision of a regulator.

4. Applications to the court contain a statement of truth. As will be discussed in Chapter 18, this means that there can be serious consequences of knowingly providing a false or misleading statement. Conversely, this means that more weight can be placed on what is said.

Complaints are easier to make, because they can all be done online and there is no court fee to pay. However, the ease of making a complaint goes both ways: it often means that complainants do not properly explain why the regulator should intervene. Going to court is expensive for the Trustee, at least in the short term. The Trustee will risk being ordered to pay costs personally if the court decides that neither the bankrupt nor the creditors of the estate should have to pay. The court will expect the Trustee and the bankrupt to try to resolve their problems informally, but making a court application (or threatening to) can be a necessary step for the Trustee to take the bankrupt's complaints seriously. A bankrupt is relatively protected from the cost risk of making an unsuccessful application, since they are unlikely to be able to pay the cost award at least in the short term. This creates an additional incentive for the Trustee to settle.

Chapter 9   The conclusion of bankruptcy: discharge and annulment

A bankruptcy begins on the day when the bankruptcy order is made (s278 of the Act). The default rule is that a bankrupt is discharged a year later (s279(1) of the Act). This chapter describes the effects of discharge, the ways a bankruptcy can be extended and the possible long term effects of the bankruptcy order.

The court can also annul a bankruptcy order under s282 on the grounds that it should not have been made, or because the bankruptcy debts and expenses have been paid. The effect of annulment is as if the bankruptcy order was never made.

9.1 Discharge

The default rule is that bankruptcy lasts a year. It can be lengthened if the Trustee applies to the court if the bankrupt has failed to comply with an Insolvency Act obligation (s279 of the Act). This is known as a 'suspension of discharge'. The court can then make an order which either gives a fixed term extension of the bankruptcy, or gives an extension until after the fulfilment of a certain condition. The bankrupt's activity prior to the bankruptcy proceedings is irrelevant – an extension cannot be given as a form of punishment due to, say, the sheer amount of debt which accrued or any lies told to creditors before the presentation of the petition. The mere fact that the affairs of the bankrupt are complicated is not sufficient to apply for an extension: under s279(4) the court can only make the order if the bankrupt themselves are at fault. This is because a Trustee can continue to investigate the affairs of the bankrupt's estate after the bankruptcy has been discharged. The most common examples of a bankrupt being at fault are when the bankrupt refuses to share information with the Trustee upon their request, including failure to give notice of an asset received during the course of the bankruptcy, and failure to give the Trustee access to their home for valuation purposes.

Under r10.142(2), the Trustee must file evidence in support of their application. Under r10.143, the bankrupt has the power to apply for the court to discharge an order suspending the time period. This is a fast track route to overturning the court's decision.

A significant reason for the bankrupt to cooperate with the Trustee in Bankruptcy is the threat of a s279(2) extension of the bankruptcy period. When deciding how to react to a request from the Trustee, bankrupts should always be aware that even if it is unlikely that they will be fined or imprisoned as a result of their actions, the Trustee can easily apply for an extension.

If desired, it is possible to apply to the court for a certificate of discharge to prove that their bankruptcy is over. This is set out in r10.144. It costs £70 to apply, and £10 per copy of the certificate. It is possible to request the discharge to be put in the London Gazette and locally advertised under r10.144(4), similar to the public advertisement of the original bankruptcy order.

9.1.1 Effect of discharge

The effect of discharge is prospective, not retrospective. The restrictions on an undischarged bankrupt cease (see Chapter 2) and an individual can start to re-build their life. For example, a year and a day after the bankruptcy order is made, absent any suspension, the individual can become a director of a company.

However, even if the Trustee has not finished selling the assets of the former bankrupt, they remain property of the Trustee and theirs to sell in due course. The bankrupt must still cooperate with their Trustee in respect of this property even after discharge. This will particularly apply to the bankrupt's property, if they are entitled to live in it for a year (see Chapter 6).

After a bankruptcy is discharged most debts which the bankrupt previously faced will be forgiven. The creditors will either receive a distribution in the bankruptcy or end up with nothing. In particular, the effect of the bankruptcy being discharged is that, under English law, the bankrupt will not need to repay even a debt owed under foreign law which was incurred before the bankruptcy order. This is the position under English law: a foreign court might not agree.

Due to s281 of the Act, discharge also does not affect:

a) Any security held by creditors.

b) Any debt which was incurred due to fraud. This is interpreted broadly to include all debts which result from the bankrupt's dishonesty.

c) Any criminal fines.

d) Any orders under the Proceeds of Crime Act.

e) Any potential damages claim for personal injury unless the court directs otherwise.

f) Any order made in family proceedings or for child maintenance unless the court directs otherwise.

g) Any other debts which did not fall into the bankruptcy, which includes student loans

Unscrupulous creditors may pretend not to know about the effects of discharge from bankruptcy. If a creditor from before the bankruptcy order asks for payment, it is important not to pay them. Instead, the better strategy is to inform them of the bankruptcy order, and explain that this means that the debt has been forgiven. If they disagree, the bankrupt can invite them to formally sue if they wish to recover their money. The creditor will then be likely to write off the debt instead of spending money litigating when there is no prospect of success.

9.1.2 Bankruptcy restriction orders

There is a catch to the one year automatic release of bankruptcy, which is that upon the application by the Official Receiver or the Secretary of State, the court can make a bankruptcy restriction order against an individual. A bankruptcy restriction order has the effect of continuing certain bankruptcy restrictions, even though the bankruptcy itself might have been discharged. This is set out in Sch 4A of the Act. A bankruptcy restriction order will be made 'where the court considers it appropriate, having regard to the bankrupt's conduct either before or during their bankruptcy': paragraph 2(1) of Sch 4A. The purpose of a bankruptcy restriction order is both to protect the public and to have a deterrent effect. The application must be made within one year from the making of the bankruptcy order, unless the court gives permission for it to be later.

The court will consider whether the bankrupt:

- failed to keep proper records;

- failed to produce these records on demand;

- acted to prejudice their creditors by making a transaction at an undervalue;

- traded when insolvent;

- incurred a debt when they did not expect to repay it;

- undertook 'rash and hazardous speculation' or unreasonable extravagance.

The court will also consider whether the individual had already gone bankrupt within the previous six years.

The court will review the conduct of the bankrupt, but due to the onerous conditions created by the order, it will resolve doubts to the benefit of the bankrupt. It will not do so if their account is obviously untrue: see *Official Receiver v Doganci* [2007] B.P.I.R. 87.

A bankruptcy restriction order must last at least two years and at most 15 years. It creates similar restrictions as if the individual was still bankrupt, such as:

- They cannot obtain credit of more than £500 without disclosing the bankruptcy relief order.

- They cannot act as a director of a company.

- They must disclose their real name when they trade, so the other side can discover that they were once made bankrupt.

- They cannot be a trustee of a charity.

Breaching a bankruptcy restriction order is a criminal offence.

The Official Receiver is likely to tell the bankrupt that they intend to apply for a bankruptcy restriction order before they apply for one. The bankrupt will then have the opportunity to offer bankruptcy restriction 'undertakings' in lieu of a formal order. An 'undertaking' is a promise to the court. Bankruptcy restriction undertakings are a way of the bankrupt voluntarily accepting a bankruptcy restrictions order. The bankrupt is likely to make an undertaking which is less onerous than a full order, similar to a discount an offender would expect for pleading guilty.

The Secretary of State (in effect, another civil servant) will consider the same factors as the court and decide whether or not to accept these undertakings. In practice, the Secretary of State will be anxious to avoid going to court because it is a waste of resources. Instead, the Secretary of State will usually accept any sensible length and scope of undertakings appropriate for the wrongdoing. There can be some negotiation to be done between the former bankrupt and the Secretary of State. Making an undertaking will likely involve the bankrupt admitting at least some of the underlying wrongdoing. On the other hand, it is better for the bankrupt to provide an undertaking and admit some mistakes than to contest the finding in court and lose.

It is possible to mark negotiations around bankruptcy restriction undertakings 'without prejudice' (see Chapter 18).

In general, the order will be less than five years if the bankrupt incurred debts knowing they could not repay them; five to ten years if their behaviour was reckless; and ten to 15 years if their behaviour was dishonest.

Both bankruptcy restriction orders and undertakings are public knowledge: see https://www.insolvencydirect.bis.gov.uk/IESdatabase/viewbrobrusummary-new.asp. The public will be able to see the details of the misconduct on the website for the first three months, and subsequently upon request.

For two examples from 2020: an individual who operated a fish and chip shop and failed to disclose to HMRC that he was self-employed or register for VAT received an order lasting for three years. Based on the length of the order, it seems likely that the Secretary of State accepted that this was an honest if negligent mistake. In contrast, a solicitor who improperly transferred client account money to himself and failed to return it was given a bankruptcy restrictions order lasting 11 years. This reflects the high standard expected of solicitors and other regulated professionals.

Statistics from the Insolvency Service show that there are approximately 450 restrictions made each year. This figure includes both bankruptcy and debt relief restrictions, which are similar but made following a debt relief order (see Chapter 1). Of these, only 30 were restriction orders and the remainder were bankruptcy undertakings. The average length of a restriction order was six to seven years, compared to five years for an undertaking. The five most common allegations made were that the bankrupt neglected their business affairs which contributed to the bankruptcy (132 allegations), the bankrupt incurred debt without reasonable expectation of payment (88 allegations), dissipation of assets (67 allegations), gambling, rash and hazardous speculation (54 allegations) and fraud (42 allegations).

BOX 26: CONTESTING A BANKRUPTCY RESTRICTION ORDER

As the statistics on the average length of a restriction indicate, it is generally in a bankrupt's interest to reach a compromise with the Secretary of State and accept bankruptcy restriction undertakings. Undertakings are likely to be more generous than the order the Secretary of State will seek. However, it is possible that the Secretary of State (via the Official Receiver) makes a mistake about the behaviour of the bankrupt, and wrongly accuses them of improper conduct. If so, it would be a mistake to accept undertakings. Bankruptcy undertakings are (also) a matter of public record and would be strong evidence for a third party to rely on in any subsequent claim.

It may also be a good idea to contest a bankruptcy restriction order if the bankruptcy might be annulled because the debts may be paid or because an IVA may be approved (see Paragraph 9.2.3). This is because the order will not be made post-annulment. In contrast, if undertakings are agreed they will survive the annulment. Delaying the making of the bankruptcy order may give the debtor enough time to escape the restrictions altogether. However, it is unusual for an IVA to be approved so late into a bankruptcy. If the IVA was possible, it probably would have passed before the stage where the Secretary of State is considering a bankruptcy restriction order.

The bankruptcy restriction regime is similar to a director's disqualification order (see Chapter 14 for more details).

9.1.3 Insolvency register

All IVAs, DROs, bankruptcies, bankruptcy restriction orders and undertakings are publicly recorded at https://www.insolvencydirect.bis.gov.uk/eiir/. They will remain on this register until three months after they lapse.

Up until six years after the bankruptcy order is made and discharged, credit rating agencies are likely to have a record of the insolvency, and so there is likely to be a long term effect on the individual's ability to receive credit from institutions like banks, payday lenders, and large shops with formal arrangements to provide consumer credit. A bankruptcy restrictions order may remain on the credit reference file for longer. The six year period arises out of data protection law but there are no restrictions on a creditor treating a former bankrupt differently for an indefinite period of time.

9.1.4 Income payments order or income payments agreement

As discussed in Chapter 2, the income of a bankrupt does not 'fall into their estate'. This means that, in the first instance, the bankrupt can keep their income rather than it pass to the Trustee to distribute it to creditors. An income payments order or income payment agreement is necessary for the income to be claimed by the Trustee. The order or agreement typically lasts more than a year, and so can continue to bind the debtor after their discharge from bankruptcy, as well as any employers or banks involved.

9.1.5 Long term impact

Charitable organisations like the Money Advice Service, StepChange and Citizens Advice will continue to offer help even after the bankruptcy order is discharged. Bankruptcy can be seen as a positive opportunity to rebuild life without debt. The principles of good financial management are outside the scope of this book, but there is plenty of free advice online.

9.2 Annulment

The second route to ending bankruptcy is for the bankruptcy order to be annulled. Annulment can happen even if the bankruptcy has already been discharged (s282(3) of the Act).

An application for the annulment costs £155 for the court fee and uses the standard 'IAA' application form (see Annex 1). There are three general grounds for annulment:

1. The bankruptcy order should not have been made.

2. The bankruptcy debts and expenses have all been paid or secured to the satisfaction of the court.

3. The bankrupt has signed an IVA with their creditors.

The court has discretion over the first two grounds. Since bankruptcy is a class remedy, the court will wish to review the full facts in order to make the right decision for the creditors as a whole. The third ground gives an automatic right to annulment, since all creditors are automatically bound by the terms of the IVA. Taking these in turn:

9.2.1   The order should not have been made

For full details, see Chapter 15 which covers appeals. This ground can be made in parallel with the second ground. An application made under this ground should be sent to the petitioning creditor, as well as the Official Receiver and Trustee. A contentious question is who should pay for the costs of the bankruptcy, given that it should not have been made. The usual options are a) the bankrupt, b) the petitioning creditor, or c) the Trustee in Bankruptcy should bear their own costs. This is discussed in Chapter 16.

9.2.2   The debts and expenses have been paid

Creditors have to 'prove' in the bankruptcy, i.e. demonstrate to the Trustee that the bankrupt owed them money (see Chapter 2). Once all the admitted debts have been paid, the primary purpose of bankruptcy has been achieved. Annulment is more appropriate than discharge, because (in hindsight) the individual was able to pay their debts. The Trustee still has to file a report relating to the circumstances leading to the bankruptcy, a summary of the bankrupt's assets and liabilities at the date of the bankruptcy order and annulment application, any details of creditors who have not proven their debts but are known to have claims, and any other matters that the Trustee sees fit (r10.133(2)). If the Trustee reports that they know of creditors who have not yet proven the debt, the court may direct the Trustee to advertise the application to annul the bankruptcy, or adjourn the application for not less than 35 days in order to give the creditors more time (rule 10.136).

A more difficult issue is that the expenses of the bankruptcy have to be paid. The Trustee will present their bill for their work. This is typically larger than the bankrupt was expecting, partly because Trustees in Bankruptcy do not receive their full fees where an estate has no money to pay them and so they charge high amounts to compensate.

Under r10.134 a bankrupt can challenge the remuneration or expenses of a Trustee if they are also applying for an annulment if the cost is 'in all the circumstances excessive'. They should only do so when their case is strong, because in the event the Trustee's fees are deemed reasonable, the court is likely to add on the additional costs of the application to the Trustee's bill. The court has the power to dismiss this application without an oral hearing ('dismiss it on the papers') if, on its face, it is clear that the application has no merit. The alternative is a laborious review of each challenged item of the Trustee's bill, which is likely to be a time intensive and costly exercise.

The principles of the review are set out in the Insolvency Proceedings Practice Direction part 6, para 21. These are:

1. **'Justification'**. It is for the office-holder who seeks to be remunerated at a particular level and/or in a particular manner to justify their claim. They are responsible for preparing and providing full particulars of the basis for, and the nature of, their claim for remuneration.

2. **'The benefit of the doubt'**. If, after having regard to the evidence and guiding principles, there remains any doubt as to the appropriateness, fairness or reasonableness of the remuneration sought or to be fixed, such element of doubt should be resolved by the court <u>against</u> the office-holder (emphasis added).

3. **'Professional integrity'**. The court should give weight to the fact that the office-holder is a member of a regulated profession and as such is subject to rules and guidance as to professional conduct and the fact that the office-holder is an officer of the court.

4. **'The value of the service rendered'**. The remuneration of an office-holder should reflect the value of the service rendered by the office-holder,

not simply reimburse the office-holder in respect of time expended and cost incurred.

5. **'Fair and reasonable'**. The amount and basis of the office-holder's remuneration should represent fair and reasonable remuneration for the work properly undertaken or to be undertaken.

6. **'Proportionality of information'**. The office-holder should provide a proportionate amount of information considering the amount of remuneration and the value and nature of the assets and liabilities of the estate.

7. **'Proportionality of remuneration'**. The amount and basis of remuneration to be fixed by the court should be proportionate to the nature, complexity and extent of the work that has been completed by the office-holder and the value and nature of the assets with which the office-holder has had to deal, the nature and degree of the responsibility to which the office-holder has been subject in any given case, the nature and extent of the risk (if any) assumed by the office-holder and the efficiency (in respect of both time and cost) with which the office-holder has completed the work undertaken.

8. **'Professional guidance'**. In respect of an application for the fixing and approval of the amount and/or basis of the remuneration, the office-holder may have regard to the relevant and current statements of practice promulgated by any relevant regulatory and professional bodies in relation to the fixing of the remuneration of an office-holder. In considering a remuneration application, the court may also have regard to such statements of practice and the extent of compliance with such statements of practice by the office-holder.

9. **'Timing of application'**. The court will take into account whether any application should have been made earlier and if so the reasons for any delay.

In practice, it is sensible for the bankrupt to send the Trustee an email setting out criticisms of the expenses. The email should highlight individual items in the Trustee's bill, and then link the complaint with the list of nine principles. The court is likely to find a middle ground between the bankrupt's reasonable complaints and the Trustee, who will undoubtedly argue that every penny was properly spent. If the Trustee is unable to give any details of why they charged the amount they did, the bankrupt can say that the Trustee is unable to properly justify their expenditure (principle 1).

The bankrupt will be in a stronger position to criticise the Trustee's fees if they were fully cooperative and did not lead to additional costs. Conversely, the court will be less likely to reduce the Trustee's fees if the Trustee can show that additional fees were incurred due to the bankrupt, such as the bankrupt's failure to fully explain transactions, or failure to keep a proper record, or because they had entered into transactions at an undervalue. It follows that if a bankrupt believes they will be in a position where all their bankruptcy debts can be paid, they should be as helpful as possible to the Trustee and minimise their workload wherever they can.

It is easier for both parties to settle rather than litigate over costs. Unless the Trustee is prepared to take at least 10% off their bill, the bankrupt loses nothing by sending them a draft application on a without prejudice basis and threatening to apply to the court. See Chapter 18 for a full discussion. If the matter does proceed to a formal application, the court can require the bankrupt to pre-pay the full amount of the remuneration as security, and this will be returned as appropriate if the bankrupt is successful. In practice, judges have little patience for arguments over costs. This means that it is important to appear as reasonable as possible in order to proceed with the application.

The Official Receiver has fixed fees where they act as Trustee in Bankruptcy: £6,000 as a general fee, plus 15% of the amount recovered. This will be extremely difficult to challenge as being unreasonably high. However, it provides a useful benchmark for comparison with a private Trustee in Bankruptcy.

> ### BOX 27:   OTHER CHALLENGES TO THE TRUSTEE'S FEES
>
> An alternative procedure for the bankrupt to challenge the Trustee's fees is under r18.35. This route requires the permission of the court. In order to receive permission, the bankrupt must show that there is, or will be (or would be, but for the fees) a surplus to which they are entitled. The difference between this application and one under r10.35 is that it can be made even if not all the creditors are fully paid. It therefore requires the permission of the court, because otherwise bankrupts might complain about their Trustee's expenses even when the creditors are the ones paying. The court has discretion about whether or not to grant permission. If permission is granted, the review process is the same.

BOX 28: ANNULMENT AND DIVORCE PROCEEDINGS

This book is written for debtors undergoing bankruptcy proceedings. However, since bankruptcy is a way to escape paying debts, it can be abused. Sometimes in the course of a contentious divorce, one spouse seeks to use bankruptcy to gain a tactical advantage. They could apply to the adjudicator to be declared bankrupt or invite a friendly creditor to issue a statutory demand and bankruptcy petition, which the spouse decides not to oppose. This way the spouse can appear to have fewer assets than they do, because the family courts will naturally place weight on the existence of insolvency proceedings.

A spouse also has standing to annul a bankruptcy order if they can show they have a legitimate interest in applying. This is most often on the s282(1)(a) ground that the bankruptcy order should never have been made, for example because the bankruptcy proceedings were an abuse of process or because the bankrupt was able to pay their debts at the time. The spouse may want to apply for a transfer of the case outside of the original High Court/County Court to the Family Court, where a judge may be more receptive to their arguments since they will be more familiar with the context of the family dispute.

If the bankrupt is genuinely insolvent, the fact that the bankrupt is motivated by a desire to harm their spouse does not mean the bankruptcy is an abuse of process. In *Whig v Whig* [2007] EWHC 1856 (Fam) a wife sought annulment on the basis that her husband petitioned for his own bankruptcy in order to frustrate her claim for ancillary relief in their divorce proceedings, and that he was able to discharge his debts as they fall due. The judge emphasised that the same rules applied to the Family division of the High Court as to the Chancery division. On the facts, he rejected the wife's allegation that the bankrupt had significant undisclosed assets. Since the bankrupt was unable to pay his debts, he refused to annul the bankruptcy.

If the bankrupt makes an application for annulment, the court may (in advance of making any decision) order for other bankruptcy matters to be stayed (r10.135). This would be relevant if, for example, there was a contested application for an examination or to undo a transaction at an undervalue. The party applying for the stay must let the Official Receiver and Trustee know about the application, so they can make representations if they disagree with the stay.

9.2.3   An IVA has been signed

This is set out in s261 of the Act. Even though a bankruptcy order has been made, it may still be in the creditors' interests to agree an IVA (see Chapter 1). This frequently happens when a third party is prepared to give money to the bankrupt's estate for the sake of their creditors, in order to have the bankruptcy annulled. It can also happen if the creditors can be persuaded that the costs of the bankruptcy are too great, and they would receive a larger return by agreeing to an IVA rather than waiting for a distribution from the Trustee.

Where an IVA has been signed, the court will annul the bankruptcy on an application by the bankrupt, or by the Official Receiver after 42 days from either a) the date when the supervisor files the approval with the court, or b) the date when the supervisor delivered notice of the approval to the creditors (r8.33). The court will not annul the bankruptcy until the 28 day period for the IVA to be challenged has lapsed – see Paragraph 1.1 for brief details of this challenge. In practice, unless the IVA is challenged, the annulment will be uncontroversial.

The terms of the IVA are likely to cover the expenses of the Trustee in Bankruptcy. The Trustee has the standing to apply to challenge the decision of the creditors in passing an IVA under s262(2)(d) of the Act. The Trustee is likely to receive their costs under a bankruptcy due to their high priority in the order of distribution (see Chapter 16). It follows that the Trustee is likely to argue that the IVA was unfairly prejudicial to their interests if they do not receive proper remuneration in the IVA. The supervisor of the IVA is likely to be better placed than the bankrupt to negotiate the matter of the Trustee's expenses.

9.3   Effect of annulment

An annulment (unlike a discharge) acts to undo the bankruptcy process. The aim of annulment is, as much as possible, to reverse the effect of the bankruptcy order as if the bankruptcy order was never made. Under s282(4)(b) of the Act, unless the court appoints otherwise, property automatically re-vests (transfers) from the Trustee back to the debtor.

However, if a Trustee has already sold property, that sale is valid (s282(4)). Similarly, if the Trustee has repaid a valid creditor, the creditor can keep the money. Since the bankruptcy order is undone, all the debts which the debtor owed prior to the bankruptcy order are still due and owing. If the annulment is due to the fact the creditors had been paid in full, then there would be no further debts owing.

If the Trustee has repaid someone who the former bankrupt considered not to be a valid creditor, that payment will not be automatically revoked. Instead, the former bankrupt will either have to claim against the Trustee in Bankruptcy for negligence, or (more easily) against the receiver of money for unjust enrichment.

If a landlord terminated a long term lease upon the bankruptcy of their tenant, there is no automatic provision for the lease to be restored if the bankruptcy order is annulled. The tenant would need to seek 'relief from forfeiture' which requires its own application to the County Court. For details, see a textbook covering land law, like *Residential Possession Proceedings* by Gary Webber and Daniel Dovar. If the lease has been disclaimed, the tenant will need a new lease.

There is, unfortunately, no automatic ability for a debtor who has lost their job as a result of the bankruptcy proceedings to regain it upon annulment. As discussed in Box 9 on page 27, bankruptcy does not automatically terminate employment contracts. Dismissal is a separate decision of the employer. Annulment therefore cannot restore the decision.

The former bankrupt is likely to want to advertise the annulment: they have the right for the Official Receiver to advertise the annulment, just as the bankruptcy order was advertised earlier. This will be a notice in the London Gazette. Advertisement will be the quickest way to notify credit rating agencies and professional lenders like banks that the individual's bankruptcy has been annulled.

BOX 29:   REMOVING ENTRIES AT THE LAND REGISTRY

The former bankrupt will also want the Land Registry to remove the restriction on any property. While the restriction is on the record, potential purchasers will be cautious about buying the property because they may be concerned that the seller is still bankrupt and has no authority to conduct the sale. It will be the former bankrupt's responsibility to apply to the Chief Land Registrar to cancel the restriction. This is done using the AP1 and K11 forms sent to Land Registry Bankruptcy Unit, HM Land Registry Plymouth Office, Seaton Court, 2 William Prance Road, Plymouth PL6 5WS. The forms can be found online, and there is no fee. However, they are not particularly easy to fill in, and it may be worth instructing a professional conveyancer to ensure it is done properly: this should cost a few hundred pounds. The Land Registry will not be proactive in removing the restriction, but it will be removed automatically five years after the date it was made under s8 of the Land Charges Act 1972. The order annulling the bankruptcy must contain an order that the registration of the petition be vacated, identified by the date of registration and the registration number (r8.34(k)).

Annulment under s282(1)(a) automatically cancels bankruptcy restriction orders or undertakings, since the bankruptcy order should never have been made. However, annulment because the debts have been paid or because an IVA has been approved does not have this effect: see paras 10 and 11 of Sch 4A. In any event, a bankruptcy restriction order cannot be made <u>after</u> annulment.

Annulment does not stop proceedings for a bankruptcy offence under Chapter 6 of the Act, but no proceedings can be brought after annulment (s350). This is a compromise position. It may strike the accused as unfair, since it depends on the arbitrary timetables of prosecution proceedings and annulment applications. However, since the Insolvency Service takes so long to institute proceedings (it has a target of 24 months, which it did not meet in 2018/19: see Chapter 7), in practice injustice might not be done. The defence only applies to the Insolvency Act offences and not, for example, to a prosecution under s11 of the Company Directors Disqualification Act 1986 for acting as a director while an undischarged bankrupt. See Chapter 7 for more details on what the bankruptcy offences are.

Chapter 10   Death and Bankruptcy

This chapter is about the rules which apply when an individual dies (1) before the presentation of a bankruptcy petition, (2) after the presentation of the petition but before an order is made, and (3) after an order is made but before the bankruptcy is discharged. It only applies to individuals who are subject to the English jurisdiction (see Chapter 5 for more details).

As a preliminary point, if an individual is seriously ill the court is likely to be sympathetic towards an adjournment or stay of proceedings. However, the court will be reluctant to order a long term adjournment or one which continues for an indefinite length, like an adjournment until the individual dies, unless that is likely within the next few months. See the discussion at Paragraph 5.13.9 above.

This chapter addresses only the bankruptcy aspects of the many problems someone might face. The reader is directed to charities like AgeUK, Marie Curie and Citizens Advice who can help individuals with other problems, ranging from coping with grief to getting help obtaining probate. The Government website https://www.gov.uk/when-someone-dies also has useful resources.

> ## BOX 30:   KEY TERMINOLOGY
>
> An '**estate**' is given a particular definition in bankruptcy law. For example, it excludes clothing required for the bankrupt's basic domestic needs: see Chapter 2 and s283 of the Act. However, 'estate' is also used in inheritance law to mean absolutely all of the property of the deceased.
>
> A '**Personal Representative**' is someone who controls ('administers') the deceased person's estate. This is either the executor named in the will, or if there is no will, or the will did not appoint an executor, or the executor is unable to or unwilling to act, then it will be the 'administrator' of the estate. There is an order of priority for the administrators, beginning with the surviving spouse, then children, then parents, etc. An executor or an administrator can then appoint a solicitor to act on their behalf.

A **'beneficiary'** of an estate is someone who may receive an inheritance from the deceased.

10.1 Death before the presentation of a bankruptcy petition

If the petitioning creditor learns that the debtor has died before they can present a bankruptcy petition, they are likely to reassess their options. Their likely next route would be to inform the person in charge of the estate of the deceased, the 'Personal Representative' (PR), that the deceased had an outstanding debt to them. That individual will be obliged to pay the creditor before making any distribution to the beneficiaries. In the event that they refuse to do so, the creditor can use all the usual enforcement mechanisms if they have a judgment in their favour: third party debt orders (orders that a third party, like a bank, pays the creditor); bailiffs; charging orders, etc. If the PR disputes the debt, the creditor will need to go to court to prove they are owed a debt just as they would against a debtor had they been alive.

> ### BOX 31: WHAT HAPPENS IF THE PR REFUSES TO PAY AN ADMITTED DEBT?
>
> A PR has a duty owed to the beneficiaries of the estate as well as the creditors to pay the deceased's debts. This duty is set out in the Administration of Estates Act 1925, s25. Failure to pay the deceased's valid debts is a breach of duty, and it can lead to the PR themselves being sued for losses caused, as well as a claim against the estate for the original debt.
>
> A PR can apply under s61 of the Trustee Act 1925 to be relieved of personal liability, but only if they can satisfy the court that they have acted honesty and reasonably. It is difficult to see how a PR could act honestly and reasonably if they refuse to pay a debt which they admit is owing, unless the estate is insolvent.

However, if the deceased person is insolvent, their estate cannot meet all of the claims by the creditors. This is not the same as the estate not having enough assets to pay all of the legacies in the will. Whether an estate is insolvent is a question of fact, and it is the duty of the PR to determine whether the estate is insolvent.

Under s44 of the Administration of Estates Act 1925 a PR is not bound to make a distribution before the expiration of one year from the death, including to creditors. A PR should therefore not feel rushed into making a distribution which they are uncertain about.

If the estate is insolvent, or is likely to be insolvent, it must only be administered for the benefit of the creditors and not the beneficiaries under the will. In effect, the PR becomes the Trustee in Bankruptcy whose role it would be to pay the creditors. If the PR is unsure, they should assume the estate is insolvent, and so follow the statutory order for the priority of payment of debts. The beneficiaries under a will are not equivalent to creditors. Instead, all creditors will take priority and the beneficiaries will only be paid if there is a surplus after the statutory regime.

The statutory order is similar to the order of a living person's priority of payments, set out in full at Paragraph 2.14. The main change is that the reasonable funeral expenses of the deceased take priority over preferential debts and so ordinary unsecured debts too. Only secured creditors have higher priority. This is because the PR has a duty to dispose of the body of the deceased. If the deceased dies insolvent, then the funeral costs should be kept as low as reasonably possible.

There are three ways in which the insolvent estate can be administered. It could be done out of court by the deceased's PR, or the PR can apply for the court's direction under CPR part 64, or the court can make an insolvency administration order under the Administration of Estates of Insolvent Deceased Persons Order 1986 ('the Insolvent Estates Order').

BOX 32:   SOURCES FOR THE LAW

The Insolvency Act 1986 still applies to the estate of the deceased, but it is modified by the Insolvent Estates Order. However, these modifications are not shown on legislation.gov.uk. It is confusing to refer simply to the Insolvency Act, and too wordy to refer to the Act 'as amended by the Insolvent Estates Order'. For convenience, this chapter will simply give references to the paragraphs of the Insolvent Estates Order instead of to the sections of the Act which it modifies. The Insolvency Rules 2016 also apply to these cases relying on the Insolvent Estates Order.

10.1.1   Out of court

The PR can take on the role of Trustee in Bankruptcy informally, and pay off the debts in accordance to the statutory scheme themselves. However, unless all the creditors agree with this approach, this can lead to disputes and a PR incurring personal liability. For example, if Creditor 1 holds that another creditor, Creditor 2, was wrongly paid out, then Creditor 1 could argue that the PR was in breach of their duty by paying Creditor 2 and so sue the PR for the damage they caused the estate.

10.1.2 CPR Part 64 application

An application under CPR part 64 allows the PR to delegate decision making to the court: a judge (a Chancery Master) will issue directions as to how an estate should be administered. However, this is a complicated task. It is best relied on where there is uncertainty or disagreement about what decisions the PR should make. The disagreement can then be referred to the court under part 64.

If the court is satisfied that the estate is insolvent, it may transfer the case to the Insolvency Court and use the Insolvency Administration Order route instead: see para 5 of Part II of Sch 1 of the Insolvent Estates Order.

10.1.3 Insolvency Administration Orders

A PR or a creditor of the deceased can make an application for an 'Insolvency Administration Order' (IAO) to the court for an order that the estate of the deceased be administered as bankrupt. This is similar to an ordinary bankruptcy petition. It should be presented to the court where the debtor resided, or carried on business for the greater part of the six months before death. The application should be served on the PR, although the court can dispense with service. It cannot be presented after CPR Part 64 proceedings have been commenced under Part II paragraph 5 of the Insolvent Estates Order, although the court may transfer the case to the local bankruptcy court, and then make an IAO.

The court may make an IAO from a creditor's petition if it is satisfied that the creditor is owed a liquidated debt and there is a reasonable probability that the estate is insolvent. For a PR's petition, the PR must establish that the estate is in fact insolvent: 'reasonable probability' is not good enough. Neither petitioner will need to use the statutory demand procedure.

If the court makes an Insolvency Administration Order, the Official Receiver is appointed the Trustee in Bankruptcy. The estate vests in the Trustee automatically as per s306 and similar to a normal bankruptcy petition. The OR may require a statement of the deceased affairs from the PR, and failure to comply can be a contempt of court. Afterwards, only the OR can make a payment from the deceased's estate. All payments made by the PR are void, and if the PR becomes aware of the petition they must make no further payments or risk personal liability.

As with normal bankruptcy proceedings, any potential claim which a third party has against the estate is paused ('stayed') after an IAO is made. The creditor can then negotiate how much their claim is worth with the Trustee in Bankruptcy as part of the process of 'proving' their debt.

BOX 33: 'SURVIVORSHIP' AND JOINTLY OWNED PROPERTY

This is a complicated area which commonly applies to houses and flats. Consider the situation where two people, A and B jointly own a house. The joint ownership might be that A owns 50% and B owns 50%, or any other percentages. Upon the death of A, A's percentage of the house will fall into their estate and if A dies insolvent, it will be sold to pay creditors. However, it can also be that A and B both own 100% of the property as an undivided share. This is known as a 'joint tenancy'. If A dies, then B would automatically become the sole owner. This is the meaning of the legal concept of 'survivorship'. If the property passes to its joint owner through survivorship, then B owns the property, and A's creditors will lose out. Whether A and B own a property as joint tenants or separately ('tenants-in-common') should be recorded on the Land Registry.

If an IAO is made within five years of the death of the deceased, the court can make an order under s421A(2) of the Act which provides that the survivor compensates the Trustee for the value lost to the estate. From the creditor perspective, this is a reason to apply for an IAO rather than use the CPR part 64 procedure.

One minor difference between IAOs and bankruptcy orders is that the definition of a bankruptcy debt applies with the date of the death of the deceased under para 24 of Part II of Sch 1 of the Insolvency Estates Order, rather than the usual rule which is when the bankruptcy petition is presented under s382 of the Act. There is usually little difference except for the calculation of interest, because the deceased is unlikely to incur further liabilities. The leading case on this deals with the effect of a debt in a foreign currency when there were large fluctuations in the exchange rate: *Lockston Group Inc v Wood* [2015] EWHC 2962 (Ch).

Another difference is that there is no automatic discharge from an IAO: see para 10 of Part II of Sch 1 of the Insolvent Estates Order.

It is possible that the estate was solvent prior to making distributions under the will, the PR made distributions, and a creditor subsequently notifies the PR of the debt. If so, the estate would be insolvent. It is possible that the PR will be liable for the debt personally if they acted negligently in some way: this would be a breach of their duty to administer the estate. However, it could be that the creditor was simply slow to identify their claim against the deceased, and the PR could not reasonably have identified it themselves. It is possible to avoid dispositions made by a personal representative under s284 of the Act (see Box 7 on page 24). This may allow the Trustee to recover a payment made to a beneficiary, although the court may retroactively approve ('ratify') a disposition. Similarly, the provisions for a transaction at an undervalue and a preference apply from the date of death, which gives a long period for making recoveries to the estate.

10.2 How to choose between the three options – from the perspective of the PR

From the perspective of the PR, if there is likely to be a dispute, the out of court process can expose the PR to personal liability and it is the most risky. By applying for an IAO, the PR will devolve all decisions to the Trustee in Bankruptcy. This has the advantage of avoiding the difficulty of corresponding with creditors and contentious court hearings, but it has the disadvantage of potentially being more expensive, and it allows the Trustee in Bankruptcy to review the transactions made by the bankrupt and potentially reverse them. A PR who is also a beneficiary may anticipate receiving money from the estate, and so may rather apply for a Part 64 direction. However, if the estate looks likely to be insolvent, then there is little prospect of an inheritance.

Note that a creditor can present a petition for an IAO and take the decision out of the PR's hands.

BOX 34:   WHAT IF THE PETITIONING CREDITOR
DOES NOT KNOW THE DEBTOR HAS DIED?

If the petitioning creditor does not know that the debtor has died, they will incorrectly present the petition on the basis that the debtor is alive. One would assume that this petition would be void, because the subject of the petition is not a legal person. There is no authority on this point. The court's instinct might be to treat the petition as a defective but correctable petition for an insolvency administration order against the estate of the debtor. However, since there is a specific form for an IAO, this might not be possible. This would at most add a further procedural step for the creditor.

10.3 Death after presentation of the bankruptcy petition

If the debtor dies after the presentation of a bankruptcy petition, the proceedings continue as if the debtor were alive. The bankruptcy petition will be served on the PR, unless the court permits otherwise (para 2 of Part II of Sch 1 of the Insolvent Estates Order). If there is no next of kin and no PR, the court may dispense with service altogether.

10.4 Death after bankruptcy order is made

If the debtor dies after the bankruptcy order is made, a Trustee in Bankruptcy will already have been appointed. They will continue with their primary function which is to sell the assets of the bankruptcy to repay creditors. One practical difference is that the Trustee is unlikely to want to investigate the affairs of the deceased with a view to advising on a bankruptcy restrictions order. However, they will investigate the previous transactions of the deceased if it is likely to lead to increasing the size of the estate, such as identifying any transactions at an undervalue, void dispositions or preferences. In the event that there is a surplus in the estate, the remaining funds will be given to the bankrupt's PR for onward distribution to the beneficiaries.

Chapter 11 Guarantees

A common reason why individuals go bankrupt is because they have personally guaranteed a debt of a company. If a company owes a creditor money, that creditor cannot pursue the directors or shareholders of a company for the debt. The only debtor would be the company. If the company cannot pay then the creditor may be able to have it wound up (see Chapter 12).

However, it is possible for one individual to guarantee the debts of someone else. A guarantee is an agreement between the creditor and the guarantor where the guarantor allows the creditor to enforce the debt against themselves as well as (and sometimes instead of) the original debtor. The rules are the same for a guarantee of another person or another company. In order to be more confident of a return on a loan, lenders frequently seek guarantees from company directors when lending to the company. If the company defaults on the loan, the lenders then seek repayment from the director.

This chapter is about what a guarantee is and how to challenge a guarantee. From a bankruptcy perspective a court will dismiss a bankruptcy petition if the underlying debt is genuinely disputed. It is enough to show that the debtor has an arguable case that the money is not owing (see Chapter 5). If the debt is disputed, the court will dismiss the petition or statutory demand with indemnity costs (see Chapter 16). It is easier to show that a guarantee is disputed than that the guarantee should be overturned. This chapter is important both for the further hearing, and also for settlement purposes. If a creditor will need to take further expensive court proceedings in order to prove that money is owed under the guarantee, and also pay the costs of a failed bankruptcy petition, then it is possible that they would be prepared to settle the debt for a lower amount.

This is a technical area of law. If a guarantee is not written by a lawyer, or if a non-lawyer adapts a legal template and makes substantial changes, it is possible that the guarantee will be invalid on a technical ground and so cannot be enforced against the guarantor. This means that, if possible, it is worth spending money on legal advice on this point. Conversely, if the guarantee is written by a lawyer it is unlikely that there will be a mistake in the contract and so it is less worthwhile to take a risk and spend money getting legal advice on it.

This chapter focuses on the most common reasons why a guarantee is unenforceable. It does not try to give a complete overview of the law of guarantees.

11.1 What is a guarantee?

A guarantee is a promise to pay the debts of another, if that other person fails to do so. It is also possible to promise to be responsible for any loss by the creditor: this is technically known as an 'indemnity'. Many guarantee agreements are also indemnities.

Due to s4 of the Statute of Frauds 1677 a guarantee must be in writing, and signed by the guarantor. This means that a spoken promise to pay someone else's debt is not binding and not enforceable. A digital version with an e-'signature' is sufficient. So may be an email with the name of the guarantor on the bottom where the guarantor intended to use the email to sign the guarantee. From a bankruptcy perspective, there is likely to be an argument over the threshold for dismissing a bankruptcy petition if there is not a clear-cut signature of some form on the guarantee.

There are two common types of guarantee: either the guarantee can cover a specific debt which may exist or may be anticipated, or it can cover a range of debts without one specific debt in mind. The first type is typically used when the lender only intends to make one or two loans to the borrower. The second type is used when the lender may make a range of additional loans – for example, it is possible to use the second type to guarantee an overdraft, where the size of the overdraft may change.

11.2 Why guarantees might be unenforceable

There are three common ways in which a guarantee might not be enforceable:

1.   It might be a valid guarantee, but it does not cover the debt in question.

2.   There has not been a proper demand under the guarantee.

3.   It is void due to duress, misrepresentation or undue influence.

If the guarantee is unenforceable that does not mean the original debt is unenforceable, just that the creditor can only claim against the original debtor and not the guarantor.

11.2.1 Does the guarantee apply to the debt?

A guarantee has to be clear about what debts it covers. A debtor may have several debts with a creditor, and the guarantee might not necessarily cover all of them. It is common for a guarantee to have a clause or a definition which covers 'Guaranteed Obligations', which will set out what precisely the guarantee covers. If the statutory demand or bankruptcy petition is for a debt which might fall outside of the scope of the guarantee, then there are grounds to dispute the demand or petition and it must be dismissed.

11.2.2 Has there been a proper demand under that guarantee

Guarantees typically have requirements about how a demand under that guarantee be made. For example, the guarantee document usually has a section which gives notice requirements. An example is:

> *Any notice or other communication given to a party under or in connection with this guarantee shall be:*
>
> *(a) in writing;*
>
> *(b) delivered by hand by pre-paid first-class post; and*
>
> *(c) sent to the Guarantor at [their address].*

This wording requires notice to be served by post. It follows that notice by telephone call, or by email, would not be enough. Most guarantees provide that until the notice is given, the guarantor does not have any obligations to pay under the guarantee. The usual wording is "*the Guarantor shall immediately on demand pay that amount as if he were the principal obligor*" and a demand must satisfy the notice requirements.

The notification requirements do not provide a long-term escape from liability. As soon as the lender knows about them, it will be simple for the lender to serve the correct notice. The reason this matters in a bankruptcy setting is because a statutory demand has to refer to a pre-existing liability, because it refers to a sum 'payable immediately' (s268(1) of the Act). Until the notice is served, there is no liability. If the statutory demand is served before the notice under the guarantee, it is void and no bankruptcy petition can be brought on that basis.

It might be thought that a statutory demand, which is necessarily in writing and typically personally served, would qualify as a demand under the guarantee. However, it does not. The starting point for the court is that the demand is defective as a matter of substance (and not just a formality) and so it should set aside the statutory demand, and dismiss the petition if it has already been presented. This is not commonly appreciated, and so a debtor relying on this argument should refer the judge to the case of *Martin v McLaren Construction Ltd* [2019] EWHC 2059 (Ch).

11.2.3   Is the guarantee valid?

A guarantee can be invalid for three reasons.

Duress occurs when someone is forced to sign a document under illegitimate pressure. If someone threatened physical violence, either to a person or to property, if the guarantor refused to sign the guarantee, then it is likely that the guarantor can later avoid the guarantee. However, duress requires <u>illegitimate</u> pressure: threatening to call in a debt, or to refuse extra credit, or even to begin bankruptcy proceedings is not likely to be illegitimate pressure. It is also important to show that the pressure caused the person to sign the document: it is not enough if the guarantor was going to sign the document anyway.

Undue influence occurs most often in family situations. The usual example is where someone elderly is pressured into guaranteeing the debts of their children, or where one spouse guarantees the debts of the other or their company. The spouse might say they were pressured into signing a document they did not understand or agree with. There is a presumption of undue influence if one spouse can show that they placed trust and confidence in the other, and the transaction calls for some explanation like the guarantor received no personal benefit through the loan. This presumption can be rebutted by the spouse receiving independent legal advice (see below). It is difficult to show undue influence outside of a family situation, since the law will assume that there is not the trust and confidence between two people doing business as there might be between husband and wife, or between brothers, etc.

BOX 35:   INDEPENDENT LEGAL ADVICE

Due to the risk of a guarantee being set aside for misrepresentation or undue influence, it is common for the lender to insist that the guarantor receives independent legal advice before agreeing to the guarantee. This is in order to prove that the guarantor properly understands their obligations, and that they properly agree to take these on. The process of obtaining independent legal advice is now so common that the court will expect it every time someone guarantees a debt where there is no obvious benefit to themselves. It will not be necessary for a company director guaranteeing company debt but it will be necessary if a non-director or non-shareholder (like an unconnected family member) wants to enter into a guarantee. It is very difficult to set aside a guarantee for undue influence if the guarantor has received independent legal advice, even if it was bad advice.

Misrepresentation occurs when the creditor says something about the guarantee which turns out to be false, and the guarantor only signed the document in reliance on the statement. For example, a guarantee may be void for misrepresentation if a creditor says to a guarantor that the guarantee only covers one debt, but in fact it covers more, and the guarantor is more exposed to liability than they would have wanted to be.

The statement has to be a statement of fact. However, a statement of fact can be inferred from a statement of belief or a future statement. For example, a guarantee could in theory be set aside for misrepresentation if the creditor said that the debtor would not default. The court will infer an implied representation of fact: that the creditor had no reasonable grounds to believe that the debtor would default. This representation would be false if the creditor knew that the debtor had defaulted many times in the past, and as a consequence believed that they would do so again. The representation does not have to be a deliberate lie (although it would be a misrepresentation if it was a lie), but only turn out not to be true.

In order to set aside a guarantee for misrepresentation, a debtor will need to show that they would not have entered into the guarantee but for the representation. This means that (at the very least) the representation has to be made before they sign the guarantee document. In practice, it is not difficult to show that the misrepresentation led to entry into the guarantee for the purposes of challenging a statutory demand or petition, because it is difficult to establish these questions of causation without a thorough look at the evidence, which is not the purpose of a disputed debt hearing. If the debtor does say that the misrepresentation was deliberate, there is a presumption that the lie would have had sufficient influence on the decision to enter into the guarantee. However, this presumption can be rebutted if the facts point otherwise.

There is no duty for the creditor to explain every part of the guarantee; or to answer every question the guarantor has. However, an incomplete representation can be a misrepresentation. If (for example) the guarantor asked what the total amount of debt guaranteed was, and the creditor said the guarantee would cover the principal amount of the loan without explaining the guarantee also covered the interest, that is likely to be a misrepresentation, since it implies that there was no interest or that the interest was not included in the guarantee. The misrepresentation has to be made by the creditor – creditors cannot be held responsible if, for example, the original debtor misrepresented their own financial situation. It is unlikely to be enough if the creditor was silent on something because the law considers that silence does not usually amounted to a positive misrepresentation.

> ## BOX 36:   OTHER REASONS TO CHALLENGE A GUARANTEE
>
> This brief description covers the most common ways guarantees are challenged. Three other ways are to set aside the guarantee for (1) common mistake, (2) for unilateral mistake and (3) to argue that there was a breach of the creditor's duty of disclosure. These are both limited exceptions and rarely succeed. In a sentence: (1) If both parties made a mistake about some fundamental point of a guarantee, such as guaranteeing a company which did not exist, that mistake can render the guarantee void. (2) If one party made a mistake, and the other party realised it was a mistake but still continued, the guarantee can also be void. Finally, (3) if there exists some unusual circumstances which the creditor knew about but the guarantor did not, the guarantee can sometimes be set aside for the non-disclosure. These three circumstances rarely apply: they are an example of a defence which is sufficiently arguable to proceed to directions and a full hearing, but are unlikely to be effective to set aside the demand or petition.

11.3 Evidence to present to the bankruptcy court

This summary of the law is presented so that debtors will be able to present enough evidence that the guarantee is disputed so that a statutory demand or a bankruptcy petition based on that guarantee will be set aside or dismissed.

In order to demonstrate that the guarantee is dismissed, the debtor should put in a witness statement which sets out:

1. When the guarantee was made, and if it was a written guarantee, include a copy as an attachment. If it was not a written guarantee, say so. An oral guarantee would be invalid due to s4 of the Statute of Frauds 1677.

2. If the argument is based on the wording of the guarantee, why the debt itself falls outside of the guarantee.

3. If the argument is based on failure to make a proper demand, set out what demands have been made so far.

4. If the argument is based on duress, what violent acts were threatened or took place which caused the debtor to sign.

5. If the argument is based on misrepresentation, what precisely the creditor said, why it was wrong or misleading, and that the debtor relied on it when

signing the guarantee.

6. If the argument is based on undue influence, what the relationship was between the guarantor and the original debtor, that the guarantor trusted the debtor, and that the guarantor never received independent legal advice.

PART 2   CORPORATE INSOLVENCY

Chapter 12   Companies going insolvent

Chapters 12 and 13 are about companies going insolvent. This chapter sets out the main insolvency processes which a company can go through. The next chapter focusses on a 'compulsory winding up', which is the company equivalent of a bankruptcy order on a creditor's petition.

These chapters will not be as detailed as those for bankruptcy because directors of companies can typically afford to pay for professional advice. They focus on the areas which a director without legal advice needs to know about. For the same reason, they focus on options suitable for small and medium-size companies. A large company with a budget may have more restructuring options open to them.

BOX 37:   TERMINOLOGY

Company law has its own set of specialised terms. A '**director**' is someone in a particular role within the company, although they might have a different job title in practice. The directors of a company are listed on Companies House; although someone who can give instructions that the actual directors to act on ('**shadow directors**') can sometimes be treated as if they were the legal directors.

A '**shareholder**' (sometimes called a '**member**') is someone who owns the company. They do not need to have any degree of influence in the company. For example, owning a share in HSBC is not the same as being a director of the bank.

A company going into '**liquidation**' and a company '**winding up**' are the same thing. This is the process which ultimately ends the life of a company. At the end of the process the company is '**dissolved**' and it is struck off the register of companies. It is possible to restore a dissolved company, but this topic goes beyond the scope of this book.

A '**liquidator**' is equivalent to a Trustee in Bankruptcy: they are an

---

independent professional Insolvency Practitioner who controls the company after it has entered into liquidation. The Official Receiver often acts as liquidator for a company, much like the OR often acts as a Trustee in Bankruptcy over an individual.

'**Bankruptcy**', in English law, is used only for people. The term '**corporate insolvency**' is used for companies. Newspapers sometimes speak of companies going bankrupt: lawyers do not.

In 2019, there were approximately 17,000 company insolvencies. The numbers for 2021 are likely to be higher due to the coronavirus pandemic, but at the time of writing it is unclear how high they will be. 2020 had unusually low numbers of company insolvencies (around 12,500), partly because of emergency measures brought out due to the pandemic.

It is important to say upfront that if a company goes insolvent the people who run the company in general cannot be made bankrupt and they can continue to trade although only by using a new company.

12.1 Corporate insolvency in general

The process of insolvency is different for companies and people. A person must be given the resources to carry on living while the bankruptcy order is in force and the chance to rebuild their lives after the bankruptcy is discharged. A company exists only because the law recognises its existence. When a company goes insolvent all its property can be taken away and the company can be dissolved.

The four most common legal processes that can happen to an insolvent company are:

1. In the short term, a company can go into administration. This protects the company from creditors enforcing their debts (for example, by repossessing property) and allows independent professionals ('administrators') to control the company rather than the directors. The administrators can then decide whether the company or part of it is viable, and if it is not, then the administrators can decide what to do next.

2. The company can enter into a 'company voluntary arrangement' (CVA). This is like an individual voluntary arrangement, but for a company. It occurs when over 75% of its creditors measured by their debt agree to accept a smaller amount, or to postpone the debt. As a result of a CVA, the company is no longer insolvent, since it can presumably meet the new commitments. If it cannot, it is likely to enter into one of the other processes.

3. The company can enter into 'creditors' voluntary liquidation' (CVL). 'Liquidation' refers to the process when the company's assets are sold, and the company can then be dissolved. It is the first stage to the ending of the life of a company. Creditor's voluntary liquidation is when the company decides to put itself into liquidation, but because it is insolvent the liquidation is controlled by the creditors and not the company's shareholders.

4. The company can enter into compulsory winding up. This is the only insolvency process which a company can be placed into involuntarily, although it may agree to give certain creditors the power to apply to the court to put the company into administration. Compulsory winding up can only happen by order of the court, and it is described in more detail in Chapter 13.

These will each be described in more detail below. The two most common processes for SMEs are either voluntary or compulsory liquidation, since administration is expensive and CVAs are unpopular with creditors.

12.2 Limited liability and exceptions to limited liability

Companies are separate legal entities which (nearly always) have 'limited liability'. Limitation of liability means that if a company has a debt, the creditor cannot sue the shareholders for it. This is why nearly every company name ends in 'Ltd'/'Limited' or 'plc' (public limited company).

An exception to the limitation of liability is if the company is 'wrongfully trading', which means that it continues trading when the directors know or ought to know that there is no reasonable prospect that the company will avoid going into insolvent liquidation (i.e. a CVL or a compulsory winding up). If a director continues trading after this point and the company does go into insolvent liquidation, then the liquidator or administrator can apply for a court order for the director of the company to contribute to the assets of the company. The order is typically to compensate the company (and so its creditors) for the loss caused through the additional trading.

A claim can only be made for wrongful trading if the company does, eventually, go into insolvent liquidation or administration (s214 of the Act). It is a defence to this claim that the person took every step with a view to minimising loss to the company's creditors. An example is if the reason the directors continued trading was because they believed they could repay the creditors. The burden is on the directors to prove that this defence applies. The court will expect to see accounting records, a cashflow forecast and a business plan which shows that this was the intention of the directors. A simple example where it may be reasonable to continue trading is if the company sells a time-sensitive product, like fresh milk or Valentine's Day cards, and it is better for the creditors to continue trading to use up the existing supply rather than wait until the assets are worthless.

A director who wrongfully trades is not liable for <u>all</u> of the debts of the company, but only the additional ones accrued through trading. It follows that there can only be a claim for wrongful trading if the company is worse off as a result of the continuation of trading. For example, if a company was losing £10,000 per month and the directors should have known that it would go into insolvent liquidation by 1 January, then the award would be £10,000 for every month the company traded after January.

The directors' liability is to the company and not to any particular creditor: the court will order a payment to the company, which the liquidator will then distribute to the creditors. However, it is possible for the liquidator to sell the claim to a particularly aggressive creditor, who can then pursue the former director on behalf of the company.

> ## BOX 38: CORONAVIRUS CHANGES TO WRONGFUL TRADING
>
> The wrongful trading provisions can encourage a cautious director to stop trading at an earlier position than they otherwise might. This was considered unhelpful during a pandemic when companies' financial situations were unknown. s12 of the Corporate Insolvency and Governance Act 2020 provides that the court should assume that a director is not responsible for the worsening of the financial position of the company between 1 March 2020 and 30 September 2020 and, (through the Corporate Insolvency and Governance Act 2020 (Coronavirus) (Suspension of Liability for Wrongful Trading and Extension of the Relevant Period) Regulations 2020) between 26 November 2020 and 30 June 2021. The net effect is that directors were permitted to wrongfully trade during the pandemic, with a peculiar two month gap when they were not. It is possible that the two month gap will be filled with further legislation once the Government realises its existence.

Seven other exceptions to the principle of limited liability are:

- If someone running the company was <u>fraudulently</u> trading (s213 of the Act). This creates a liability if the business of the company was carried on with the intention of defrauding creditors. The directors will be liable under s213 if, for example, they take out a loan with no intention of repaying it. There is no need to show that the company went insolvent as a result of the trade. Only a director can be liable for *wrongful trading* whereas any manager of the company can be liable for *fraudulent trading*.

- If someone makes a transaction which defrauds a creditor (s423 of the Act). This is typically where a director removes assets from the company, with the intention that the company's creditors will end up claiming against an insolvent company instead. Unlike a claim for fraudulent trading, the company does not need to be insolvent at the time of the fraudulent transaction: a claim can be brought by a victim at any point.

- The directors are in breach of their duties owed to the company. Even here, the directors will not be liable for the entire debts of the company, but only for losses the company incurs or gains the directors make in breach of their duty. More detail is given in Paragraph 12.8 below.

- When someone takes property belonging to the company. This would include, for example, a former director taking a car bought using the company's money and trying to keep it when the company was being wound up.

- The company is being used as a vehicle for a fraud. There are many ways in which to use a company in order to try to avoid an obligation. If someone is under an existing obligation which they try to evade or frustrate by using a company, the court may still impose personal liability.

- Where someone has signed a guarantee, i.e. they agree to take personal responsibility for someone else's debts. See Chapter 11 for more details.

- If a director of another company sets up a new 'phoenix' company which trades under a similar name (s217 of the Act) (see Paragraph 13.2).

For most cases of honest trading, a shareholder or director of the company will not be held liable for the debts of the company. This means that if the company is wound up insolvent, it is not possible to ask the shareholders or former directors to pay for any deficit. The practical point is that it may be positive for a director for their company to be wound up, if that allows them to start again with a clean slate and a new business. Conversely, it is likely to be a poor use of a director/shareholder's personal resources to contest an application to wind up a company, because it may be throwing good money after bad. If the company is wound up, the director/shareholder would keep their own resources, and could put them to better use.

Business mistakes can happen and it is not routine for a director or shareholder to be at personal risk from their company being wound up. In particular, it is not a crime to be unable to pay a company's debts, even if they are unpaid taxes. Personal liability applies only where a director acts particularly recklessly, or dishonestly, and seeks to benefit at the expense of others.

12.3 Before a company goes into liquidation

It follows from the rules on wrongful trading that the director(s) of a company should cease trading as soon as the company seems unlikely to avoid liquidation. Failure to do so is wrongful trading and creates personal liability for the debts of the company. It is possible to trade out of insolvency. Wrongful trading only applies when a reasonable director would realise that insolvent liquidation is inevitable. The standards of a 'reasonable director' are measured objectively: it is not enough that a director subjectively thought that their company would succeed, even if they had some justification and acted in good faith, if the director was being unreasonably optimistic. This is another reason why a director should think carefully before contesting a winding up petition. In this respect, the consequence is more serious if an individual trades through an insolvent company facing a winding up petition than for an individual who continues trading facing a bankruptcy petition.

12.4 Administration

Administration is a half-way position between the normal operation of a company and it being in liquidation. The control of the company is taken out of the hands of its directors and given to an administrator, who must be a qualified IP. The administrator will then decide whether it is possible to rescue the company, or whether there is some solution other than liquidation which is better for the company's creditors. If neither is possible, the administrator will put the company into liquidation and typically act as its liquidator. The administrator is paid from the assets of the company, although an administrator can refuse to act if they do not think it is likely that the company has enough assets to repay them, or they might insist on a personal guarantee.

A company can put itself into administration by a decision of the shareholders of the company, or its directors, without the need to go to court. It is not possible for this process to take place if a winding up petition has already been presented: in those circumstances, the company will need a court order. In practice, once a winding up petition has been presented it is often too late to go into administration successfully and so judges are reluctant to make an administration order. The situation is more complicated if the company has creditors who have a 'floating charge' over the assets of the company. If there is a floating charge holder, they will not have a veto over whether the company can go into administration using the out of court procedure. However, floating charge holders will be able to choose which administrators to appoint, overriding the views of the directors. The floating charge holders can usually put a company into administration themselves without consulting the directors if sums owed to them have not been paid.

BOX 39:   WHAT IS A FLOATING CHARGE?

This book has described security by giving the example of a mortgage over the house. The lender has the right to the sales proceeds of the house to repay its loan. A mortgage is a fixed charge: it is a charge over a specific, fixed asset – the house. The borrower is not able to sell the house without the permission of the mortgage holder, who will typically require full repayment before granting permission.

A company can also create a floating charge, which is a charge over property which the borrower is able to use or sell. The most common example of a floating charge is when lending has been secured against the book debts of the company, but the company is still allowed to trade and accrue/discharge these debts. Another example is a floating charge over the stock of a company, for example a clothes shop may give a floating charge over its clothing. A floating charge provides some security for the lender, but also allows the borrower flexibility to use the underlying asset. An individual cannot create a floating charge.

The floating charge will 'crystallise' if there is a default on the underlying loan, i.e. it converts from a floating charge into a fixed charge against the assets held at that moment in time. From then on, the borrower would be unable to sell those assets.

The floating charge holders have less protection in the event of the company's insolvency because the secured assets might have been disbursed. However, they are compensated by being given more control over how and when a company should be placed into administration.

Some creditors are given the right to appoint administrators under the terms of their loan.

While a company is in administration there is an automatic moratorium which prevents a creditor from bringing or continuing legal proceedings against the company. This is meant to give the administrator time to fulfil their main function without being distracted by the claims of particular creditors.

A common outcome of administration is that the business of the insolvent company is sold as an operational, trading entity (known as a 'going concern') to a different company. If this is arranged in advance of going into administration, this is known as a 'pre-pack'. The creditors of the old company receive the sales money which the administrator will distribute according to the statutory scheme.[7] A 'pre-pack' sale is likely to be a better outcome for creditors than if the old company were liquidated. The business of the company it is likely to be worth more if it is sold as a going concern instead of going into liquidation. This is because most companies are more valuable than the sum of their component assets. For example, a factory may have expensive machines, but if they are specialised and require skilled employees to operate them, then the machines by themselves may be worthless. The most common purchaser of the company is usually the owner of the old company, who is prepared to make a personal investment to keep the business trading.

Stop press: There are new regulations which limit the ability of an administrator to sell a substantial part of the company's assets to someone connected to the company, such as the previous owner, within the first eight weeks of the administration. A pre-pack sale to a connected party now requires either creditor approval, or an independent opinion from an evaluator, to show that the terms of the sale are reasonable.

It is expensive to instruct an administrator to run a company. The administrator is likely to charge per hour, and they would need to work many hours in order to keep the company going. For this reason, administration is rarely used for small companies, except to oversee a a 'pre-pack' sale of the business. For a larger company with more resources, administration is suitable if there is a prospect of making changes to the company to allow it to become a viable business.

12.5 Moratorium outside of administration

A recent development in the law permits the company to enter into a short moratorium without the need for administrators to run the company. This can be for up to 20 business days, but if creditors consent this can be up to a year in total.

This will require the directors to formally state that in their view the company is, or is likely to become, unable to pay its debts, and there must be an IP 'on hand' as a monitor who is willing to certify that in their view it is likely that a moratorium would result in the company being rescued as a going concern. The company cannot have been subject to a CVA or administration in the previous 12 months. It is possible to apply for a moratorium even if there is an outstanding winding up petition, but the directors cannot use the out of court process to do so. The monitor must bring the moratorium to an end if they think that it is no longer likely to result in the rescue of the company, the company has

---

[7] *The order of distribution is similar to that for creditors of a bankruptcy (see Chapter 2).*

been rescued, they cannot carry out their functions due to the directors not providing information, or the company cannot pay moratorium debts which have fallen due.

It is hoped that this process will be cheaper than administration because it requires less support from an external IP, and so it will be a more feasible option for an SME.

12.6 CVA or CVL?

Two unhelpful acronyms often used in corporate insolvency law are 'CVA' and 'CVL'. A CVA is, as mentioned above, a company voluntary arrangement: an agreement to restructure the debt of a company. If 75% of creditors by the value of their debt agree to the terms of the CVA, all creditors will be bound by it. The basic structure of a CVA is that all creditors will be paid a smaller percentage of their debt, and at a later point in time. A creditor with more than 25% of the debt can 'block' the passing of a CVA.

The debts, and hence votes, for a CVA are calculated as of the date the CVA is proposed. Future debts – in particular, debts the tenant company will owe a landlord under their lease – will only be admitted for more than £1 if the CVA supervisor agrees to place a higher value on them (r15.31(3)).

A CVL is a creditors' voluntary liquidation. If the directors of a company believe that, because the company is insolvent, liquidation is inevitable, they should go into liquidation voluntarily. The process of the liquidation is dictated by the creditors, because their interests will override those of the shareholders. The actual liquidation will still be run by an Insolvency Practitioner, but one who will take instructions from the creditors and not the directors/shareholders of the company.

In practice, the directors of a company do not 'choose' between a CVA or a CVL. If a CVA can be passed, this is likely to be the better outcome. However, this requires support from the majority of creditors. If a CVA cannot be passed, then the directors typically choose between putting the company into administration or liquidation.

12.7 Process of an insolvent company going into liquidation

Liquidation is similar to bankruptcy because both processes are focussed on selling the   assets of the company to repay the creditors. However, once the company has no assets remaining, the company will then be dissolved and no longer exist.

As set out in Paragraph 12.1 above, there are two types of liquidation a company can enter: compulsory liquidation and voluntary liquidation. The next chapter discusses compulsory liquidation. Voluntary liquidation can be achieved by a vote of 75% of the shareholders (measured by the number of shares) voting to wind up the company at a company meeting. The directors of the company must send a statement of affairs to all known creditors within seven days. The shareholders will nominate a liquidator, but the creditors get the final say. The resolution to wind up the company must then be sent to Companies House within 15 days of being passed.

If a company is unable to pay its debts, or if it seems inevitable that the company will be unable to pay, then the company must stop trading: see Paragraph 12.2 above for the consequences of continued trading. The directors should contact an Insolvency Practitioner to discuss what happens next. If the company does not have enough money to do even this, the cheapest next stage (from the director's perspective) is to inform the creditors that their debts cannot be paid, and invite them to present a winding up petition to put the company into compulsory liquidation.

12.8 Review of transactions and duties of directors

Directors have a duty to act in the best interests of the company: see s172 of the Companies Act 2006. This duty is owed to the company, and not to any individual shareholder. However, the duty is typically to act in the best interest of the company's shareholders as a whole. This means that, for example, directors should ensure that the company is as profitable as possible, bearing in mind that a director might legitimately consider a broad range of factors which promote the profitability of the company, such as its reputation and need for investment.

The duty to act in the best interests of the company changes when the company is approaching insolvency or when it is insolvent: directors should no longer consider the best interest of the company's shareholders but instead they will owe a duty (still to the company) to act in the best interest of the company's creditors. This means taking steps to ensure that creditors are paid and the company does not incur further debts.

Since these duties are owed to the company, they can only be enforced by the company. In an insolvency situation, this means that the administrators or liquidators of a company are able to sue any director who was in breach of their duty if that caused the company loss.

An administrator and a liquidator will also have the powers to review the transactions of the company similar to that of a Trustee in Bankruptcy: see the description of preferences, transactions at an undervalue, and void dispositions at Paragraph 2.6. In a company setting, Insolvency Practitioners will be particularly concerned that the directors of a company might have used the company's assets or opportunities for their own purposes, rather than for the benefit of the company as a whole.

> ## BOX 40: CORONAVIRUS AND TRANSACTION AVOIDANCE
>
> Usually, like a bankruptcy petition, transactions entered into by the company after the presentation of a winding up petition will be void, unless approved by the court. However, the current rule set out in para 9 of Schedule 10 of the Corporate Insolvency and Governance Act 2020 is that if the winding up petition was presented between 27 April 2020 and 31 March 2021, the transactions will only be avoided from the date when the court made a winding up order. This rule is currently due to expire on 30 June 2021, but it may be modified in the future.

Chapter 13   Compulsory liquidation

The previous chapter discussed the main corporate insolvency processes: administration, creditors' voluntary liquidation, and company voluntary arrangements. These options typically are used with the agreement of creditors and the company and so they do not usually require involvement of the court to resolve a dispute.

The court needs to be involved where the company goes into compulsory liquidation. This is the company law equivalent of a creditor presenting a bankruptcy petition. A creditor who is owed £750 has the right to petition the court for the company to be wound up on the grounds that it is unable to pay its debts (s122(1)(f) of the Act).

13.1 Winding up petitions

It is possible but (unlike bankruptcy) not essential to issue a statutory demand in advance. This step is commonly done because it gives the company formal notice that a winding up petition is on its way, and so increases the pressure to pay the debt. Service of a statutory demand on a company is much easier than on a person: the demand can simply be left at the registered address of the company. There is no procedure for a company to apply to set aside a statutory demand. Instead, a company which receives a statutory demand but disputes the debt should apply to prevent ('restrain') the presentation of a winding up petition. This is done using the usual insolvency application notice (see Annex 1). An injunction will be given if the court considers that the petition will be an abuse of process, i.e. because the debt is disputed, because there is a cross-claim or set-off, or there is some other abuse. The principles are similar to opposing a statutory demand (see Chapter 4). Typically applications to restrain presentation of winding up petitions and applications to set aside statutory demands have similar contents: they both anticipate why the final order should not be made. For example, both applications are likely to contain witness statements about why the debt is disputed.

One important difference between bankruptcy and winding up petitions is that winding up petitions need to be advertised in the London Gazette. This means that other creditors and banks tend to find out more quickly about a winding up petition, and so a company's bank account is likely to be frozen faster than a person's. In practice, it then becomes impossible to trade and so function as a company. If a company has a reason to argue that it should not be wound up, then the company will need to apply for an injunction restraining advertisement of the petition under r7.24. This is usually a similar application to one preventing the presentation of the petition, albeit made a little later in the process. The company will need to show why the petition should not be advertised: typically, that it will suffer irredeemable prejudice, and the petition is in any event an abuse of process.

Both applications to restrain presentation of a petition and to restrain advertisement of a petition should be made to the court in which a petition is pending or would be heard (r7.24).

BOX 41: CORONAVIRUS AND WINDING UP PETITIONS

No petitions for winding up a company can be presented if they rely on a statutory demand served between 1 March 2020 and 30 June 2021. If a demand was served outside of that period, the creditor must not present a petition between 27 April 2020 and 30 June 2021 unless they have reasonable grounds for believing that coronavirus has not had a financial effect on the company, or the company would have gone insolvent in any event. In effect, the process of compulsory liquidation set out in this chapter is put on hold. This deadline has been extended before and it is possible that it will be extended again. In practice, this has meant that very few companies have been wound up against their wishes over the course of the pandemic.

Under r7.10(4), the petition must be advertised not less than seven business days after the company was served with the petition, and not less than seven business days before the winding up hearing. The first requirement is to allow the company the opportunity to apply to the court for an injunction which would stop the advertisement of the petition in order to avoid the public suggestion that the company is insolvent. The second requirement is to give creditors time to decide whether they wish to appear at the hearing in order to support or oppose the petition. It also prevents the use of a winding up petition as a means of enforcing a private debt. As discussed in the Introduction to this book, insolvency is a class process. The court may view failure to advertise a petition as an attempt to abuse the insolvency process by gaining an illegitimate personal advantage.

Most winding up petitions are heard in London. It is the location of choice for HMRC. However, petitions are also heard at the District Registries, i.e. the local branch of the High Court. This has hearing centres in Birmingham, Bristol, Leeds, Liverpool, Manchester, Newcastle, Preston and Cardiff. It is possible to submit a petition online, but there will always be a hearing to determine the outcome.

Bankruptcy petitions are heard one at a time, with the parties walking in and out of the hearing room. In contrast, winding up petitions (at least in London, where most petitions are listed) are heard in one large room with all the companies and creditors represented. It is also, unlike bankruptcy petitions, an occasion where barristers wear their wig and gown.

The winding up list in London is busy. It runs every Wednesday in the Rolls Building near Fetter Lane in Holborn. The list of companies can be found at https://www.justice.gov.uk/courts/court-lists/list-companies-winding-up. Typically there are between 100 and 200 petitions heard beginning at 10.30am, and finishing around 1pm. This means that each petition must be quick: ideally around 30 seconds. If the company does not turn up, the petition will succeed and the hearing will last ten seconds.

Most petitions follow the same format:

1. The usher reads out the name of the next company on the list: "*ABC Services (London) Limited*".

2. The barrister for the creditor stands up and says "*Judge, I appear for the petitioning creditor. The company owes my client £10,000, arising from unpaid invoices. The papers are in order. We seek the usual compulsory order*". The 'usual compulsory order' is an order that the company must be placed into liquidation, and the costs of the petition be paid to the creditor. 'The papers are in order' means that the barrister considers that the proper documents have been filed and at the correct time, and so there are no defects to bring to the judge's attention. The alternative would be to draw attention to the mistake, and ask for it to be waived or an adjournment for it to be corrected.

3. The company (either a director of the company, or a barrister on their behalf) will stand up and say "*Judge, I appear for the company...*", followed by normally:

    a) "*...The petition debt is disputed. We ask that the case be listed for directions*". This is a request that there be a subsequent hearing to determine whether the debt is disputed, and the 'directions' are an order that the company and creditor give evidence about whether or not the petition debt is disputed. This is the equivalent to a disputed debt hearing in bankruptcy (see Chapter 4).

b)   "... *The company is seeking alternative finance options. We ask that the petition be adjourned for xx weeks*". Here the company acknowledges the debt, but is requesting time to pay. At the first hearing, as in bankruptcy, the judge is likely to adjourn the petition for a few weeks to give the company that time. At each subsequent hearing, it becomes less likely that the judge will give a further adjournment, especially if there has been no progress towards obtaining that finance.

c)   "... *The company is negotiating a CVA. We ask that the petition be adjourned for xx weeks*". Here the company is attempting to enter into a CVA, described above at Paragraph 12.1. If it has contacted an Insolvency Practitioner, or if it is the first hearing, the court is likely to adjourn the petition. However, the judge might ask whether it is likely that the petitioning creditor has more than 25% of the debt. If so they can block the CVA and so the judge would refuse the adjournment on this ground.

4.   The creditor will then respond and give a reason why the usual compulsory order should be made that day.

5.   If there is another creditor in the room, they may then voice their support for either a usual compulsory order or an adjournment.

6.   The judge then decides what should happen. The main area for the judge's discretion is how long an adjournment to grant. If it is not the first hearing, the judge may decide that no adjournment is appropriate and will make the usual compulsory order by saying "Usual compulsory order; main proceedings". The judge will make a snap decision because there are many petitions on the list.

7.   The usher will then call the next petition.

It may be possible to agree an adjournment with the petitioning creditor in advance. If so, the creditor will ask for an adjournment outright rather than for the usual compulsory order. The creditor will say "*We do not oppose an adjournment of xx weeks*" and the representative from the company will say "*That is my application*".

If the petition contains a defect, the petitioning creditor will draw this to the judge's attention in their opening remarks – if they do not, then the company will say, indignantly, "*The papers are not in order, because...*". The judge will decide whether to waive the defect, or to order that it be rectified, or to dismiss the petition outright. As with bankruptcy petitions, the latter is only done if the defect is particularly serious such that an adjournment will not remedy the problem, or that it suggests that the petition is an abuse of process. A typo in the company's name in the petition, for example, is likely to be waived. Failure to advertise or to give sufficient time is likely to lead to an adjournment. Failure to serve the petition is likely to lead to dismissal, unless the failure was to file papers demonstrating service in which case the petition is likely to be adjourned. The judge may decide to adjourn or dismiss the petition even if the company does not turn up, although they are more likely to waive the defect if it seems to them that an adjournment will have no practical benefit because the company has ceased trading.

If a petition is complicated, i.e. it cannot be dealt with within a minute, the judge may decide to hear it "second time round". This means it will be sent to the back of the list and heard once all the other petitions are finished.

The barrister at the front with piles of paper and very many cases represents HMRC, who are the petitioning creditor in around 30% of petitions. If the company wants to agree an adjournment with HMRC, it is important to turn up early because they are likely to have many other cases to deal with.

BOX 42: THE COMPANY INSOLVENCY PRO BONO SCHEME

In the Rolls Building in London, there is a scheme run by law students at City University and volunteer barristers who will offer free legal representation for company directors who would otherwise appear in person. Be aware that it does not run during the university summer holiday even though the court is sitting. It opens at around 9.30am on the morning of the court hearing, and it is a good idea to get there early in order to have maximum time with the volunteer barrister. The scheme will allow the barrister to speak on behalf of the company, if a company director asks them to. It is possible to ask the volunteer any legal questions you have about the company's insolvency and obtain some free legal advice. The volunteer may not answer questions if they are too far removed from questions about the winding up petition, or if there are many people who need help and there is not enough time. The scheme uses consultation room 17 on the second floor of the Rolls Building. If the scheme is in operation there will be a large banner outside room 17 and outside the winding up court room so people know.

In the author's opinion, every director without a lawyer would be better off using this scheme rather than trying to speak in court by themselves. The court also benefits, since it allows the busy list of companies to be dealt with more quickly.

Useful tips for the winding up court are:

- If possible, use the City University scheme (see Box 42 on page 181).

- If it is the first or second hearing of the petition, say so. The judge is more likely to grant an adjournment.

- If seeking time to pay, say what steps are likely to be taken in the next few weeks. However, be aware that the court will not agree to a very long adjournment, and will not require the creditor to wait more than a month or two in order to receive the money which they are owed.

- If the debt is disputed, say so upfront, and ask for directions. The judge will not have time for a full explanation and will have little patience to hear the petitioning creditor argue that they dispute that the debt is disputed. Prepare a three sentence explanation of the dispute in case the judge asks.

- Be prepared to wait. If a petition is listed for "not before 11am", it will certainly not be heard before 11am and perhaps not before 11.30am either. However, use the waiting time to watch the barristers and try to mimic their style, which is to be as concise as possible.

- Do not be upset if the company is wound up. As discussed in Paragraph 12.2, this is unlikely to affect the personal assets of the individual directors or shareholders, and they can set up a new company and continue business under a different name.

- Write down what you would like to say, and make sure it can be said within 30 seconds. It is difficult to be concise when standing on your feet. If it cannot be said in 30 seconds, ask for it to be heard the second time around. When it is heard, aim for less than 2 minutes of talking.

13.2 What happens next?

Nothing dramatic happens when the usual compulsory order is made. Instead, the Official Receiver will contact the directors of the company within a few days to begin the process of liquidation. The creditors may choose to instruct a private liquidator rather than rely on the government, but they will not spend money doing so if the company only has minimal assets. The Official Receiver usually requires directors to fill in the 'Preliminary Information Questionnaire' which asks basic questions about the company's affairs, in advance of a formal interview.

Much like the Trustee in Bankruptcy, the liquidator's role involves getting information on the assets and debts of the company, getting access to and selling those assets, and distributing the proceeds to the creditors. The Insolvency Service had an internal target of 27 days to complete the first interview with the directors following a winding up order in 2019/2020. In practice it is likely to take a few days more, but not many. The liquidator will review the accounts for suspicious transactions and speak to the former directors about what went wrong, but if the company was unable to pay its debts simply because its business was unsuccessful, the liquidator is unlikely to take any further steps. The liquidator will send their final account to the creditors, and to Companies House, and the Registrar of Companies will automatically dissolve the company.

The Official Receiver has a duty to investigate the causes of the failure of the company and its affairs generally after a winding up order is made (s132 of the Act). If the Official Receiver considers the directors have demonstrated that they are unfit to be concerned in the management of the company, the OR will consider whether the individuals should be disqualified as directors (see the next chapter).

From the perspective of the directors of the company, two important points to note are that they should be open and honest with the liquidator; and they should be careful to distinguish between what is the company's property (which will need to be sold) and what is their own. For example, if a car was bought using company funds, then the liquidator has the right to sell it. It may be possible to arrange a deal with the liquidator to buy any company property using personal funds. Liquidators are normally happy to accept these deals, because they know that second-hand property is typically not worth much, and it can be costly to arrange their sale. Directors, employees and former directors have a duty to cooperate with the liquidator under s235 of the Act. Former employees only have a duty to cooperate if they were employed within a year of the winding up order (s235(3)(c)).

There is one restriction on what a director can do next, which is a prohibition on 'phoenixing'. A phoenix is a mythical animal which dies and is immediately reborn as if nothing had happened. So too, a director is not allowed to set up a new company with the same or similar name to the old company, under s216 of the Act. It is acceptable for the new company to trade in the same industry, or to service the same customers, but it is potentially a crime to use the same name. Three exceptions are when the court gives permission, the liquidator agrees or if the second company was already known by the prohibited name. The liquidator might agree if the director does a deal with the liquidator to 'buy' the goodwill from the old company. The director also needs to give specific notice of this acquisition to the creditors. The company might already be known by the prohibited name if, for example, there was a group of companies ('ABC Limited', 'ABC (London) Limited', 'ABC plc') and only one of these companies went insolvent.

Chapter 14 Directors' disqualification hearings

The general rule is that being a director of a company which enters into liquidation does not stop that person starting a new company and acting as a director. However, although it does not happen automatically, the court has the power to make an order under the Company Directors Disqualification Act 1986 (CDDA) to disqualify someone from being a director. A director's disqualification order would prevent them from taking any part in the formation or management of a company for a period specified in the order. The restriction applies whether they are formally a director, or have similar levels of control over a company (known as a 'shadow director'). A disqualification order is potentially a serious problem for the individual concerned. For example, if someone is self-employed, it means that they can only work as a sole trader or as a partner in a partnership and they will no longer have the protection of a limited liability company. It would also be a matter on the public record that the court held that someone was unfit to be a director.

There are typically around 1,200 director disqualification orders and undertakings a year across Great Britain.

This chapter is about director's disqualifications, how to try to avoid disqualification, and what to do if it becomes unavoidable. It focuses exclusively on the most common form of disqualification which is under s6 of the CDDA. This section applies when a company goes into liquidation or administration. For simplicity only 'liquidation' will be referred to, but the same rules apply for administration.[8]

14.1 What is director's disqualification?

A liquidator is required to submit a report about a director to the Secretary of State for Business, Energy and Industrial Strategy if it appears to them that the conditions for disqualification are satisfied. The condition is whether the

---

[8] *A third possibility is if the company enters into 'administrative receivership': this is beyond the scope of this book, and is less common.*

director's conduct as a director makes them *"unfit to be concerned in the management of the company"*.

This must be submitted within three months of their appointment. They do this online via the website at https://report-director-conduct.service.gov.uk/. However, if the liquidator discovers some new material after three months, they must send that to the Secretary of State as soon as reasonably practicable (s7A(5) of the CDDA).

The Secretary of State (via civil servants working for the Insolvency Service) can then decide whether to start disqualification proceedings against the director of a company that became insolvent. The civil servants will consider the likelihood of the case succeeding, and whether there are other public interest factors such as the cost effectiveness of proceeding. The Secretary of State has three years from the date of the liquidation of the company to decide to bring proceedings: after then it requires the permission of the court to continue (s7(2) of the CDDA).

Whether an individual is 'unfit' will depend on how they acted as a manager of the company. The court will consider the list of factors set out in Schedule 1 of CDDA. These are paraphrased below:

1. The extent to which the person was responsible for breaking any applicable law.

2. Where applicable, the extent to which the person was responsible for the company becoming insolvent.

3. How often the misconduct in paragraphs 1 or 2 happened.

4. The nature and extent of any harm caused, or any potential harm which could have been caused, by the person's conduct.

5. Any misfeasance or breach of any fiduciary duty by the director.

6. Any material breach of any legislative or other obligation of the director which applies as a result of being a director.

7. The frequency of conduct of the director which falls within paragraph 5 or 6.

In short, the court must consider whether they were in breach of their duties owed to the company, or any material breach of the law, and the frequency of such misconduct. The court can also make a disqualification order if the director is found liable for fraudulent or wrongful trading without the need for the Secretary of State to bring proceedings.

If the court is satisfied that the individual is unfit, they will be disqualified for between two and 15 years, depending on the severity of the offence. The range of two to five years is for cases where the misconduct was not particularly serious; a period of six to ten years is for serious cases, and in excess of ten years is reserved for the particularly serious cases. To give three recent examples which are taken from the public record from 2020:

a)   An individual who ran a security company but failed to comply with its obligations to register for (and pay) approximately £100,000 PAYE with HMRC was disqualified for two years and six months.

b)   Three individuals who ran a restaurant in Poole and failed to submit accurate VAT and corporation tax payments for £650,000 were disqualified for six years.

c)   A solicitor who ran a company which had misleading marketing and financial material and attracted investment from the public and its clients of £1.3m was disqualified for 13 years.

Aggravating factors are the amount of money involved (which relates to the harm caused to creditors); whether the director relied on professional advice or should have done; and the level of sophistication of the individuals and their misconduct.

It is a criminal offence to act as a director in breach of a disqualification order, and that person will also be personally liable for all the relevant debts of the company if they do manage one. Someone disqualified from being a director also cannot be a trustee of a charity without permission; and professionals should report the disqualification to their regulatory body.

A relatively new feature of disqualification proceedings is that the court can now order an individual to pay compensation to a particular creditor or to a group of creditors (via the Secretary of State) or to the company to replenish its assets. The first case was reported in November 2019 and the compensation was equal to the funds which the director had taken from the company. A compensation order can only be made after a disqualification order.

It is possible to avoid formal disqualification proceedings if the Secretary of State accepts formal 'disqualification undertakings'. This has the advantage to both sides of avoiding the costs of going to court. A director is likely to be disqualified for a shorter period of time if they offer disqualification undertakings, similar to a defendant who gets a reduced sentence by pleading guilty to a crime. If a director considers it likely that a disqualification order will be made against them, offering or accepting undertakings is a way to minimise its impact. Disqualification undertakings are still a matter of public record.

> ### BOX 43: DIRECTOR'S DISQUALIFICATION AND BANKRUPTCY
>
> An undischarged bankrupt automatically cannot be a director due to s11 of the CDDA 1986. However, it is also common for bankruptcy restriction orders and bankruptcy restriction undertakings to extend the length of disqualification (see Chapter 9 for full details). In this respect, a bankruptcy restriction order is like a director's disqualification order.

14.2 How to avoid disqualification proceedings

The only guaranteed way to avoid disqualification proceedings is for the company not to go into insolvent liquidation. The court would then have no ability to make a disqualification order.

If the company has gone insolvent, then the next best way to avoid proceedings is to persuade the liquidator of the company not to refer the case to the Secretary of State; or in a bankruptcy case, to persuade the Trustee not to apply for a bankruptcy restrictions order. This can be achieved by not committing any improper acts which warrant further review, or (at least) having a credible, honest explanation for why certain transactions are less suspicious than they appear. A liquidator has a margin of discretion about whether to refer a particular director to the Secretary of State, and in the absence of a referral the Secretary of State might not know that the director had done anything wrong.

Liquidators will primarily be concerned about transactions where the directors, or people connected to the directors like their family members or friends, benefited at the expense of the company. Being able to explain why this was not the case will reassure the liquidator. The liquidator is a qualified Insolvency Practitioner and will be experienced in looking at fraudulent, doctored or incomplete accounts, and it will be counterproductive to try to deceive them. Similarly, if the accounts are inaccurate or incomplete it suggests that the director ran the company badly, and is possibly indicative of misconduct.

The best approach is to be as helpful as possible to the liquidator in the hope that they will finish their job quickly and move onto the next company. It will be worth putting together what accounts the company has; and at the very least putting the receipts and letters in chronological order. In general, the more cooperative the directors are with the liquidator, the less likely the liquidator is to refer the case to the Secretary of State out of caution. Cooperation is not going to turn black into white, but it may help in a marginal case. It may be possible to make a voluntary payment to cover any loss creditors have suffered as a result of what might be considered misconduct - the liquidator might see this as the sign of a responsible director, and so decline to refer the case

The Insolvency Service statistics show that the largest number of allegations in director disqualification statistics relate to unfair treatment of the Crown. In 2019/20 this allegation was made in approximately 60% of cases. In practice 'unfair treatment of the Crown' means more than simply not paying HMRC the correct taxes, because all insolvent companies have unpaid debts. Instead, the allegation is that the directors deliberately favoured private creditors over HMRC and possibly attempted to defraud HMRC in order to pay less tax. Although it is difficult to prove cause and effect, this statistic at least suggests that the Insolvency Service are sensitive to how HMRC is treated as a creditor; and so to avoid disqualification it may be important to show that HMRC was given fair treatment by the directors in the final few months of the company's trading. HMRC can suggest to a liquidator that they consider that disqualification proceedings would be justified.

14.3 What to do if the Secretary of State brings proceedings

Due to s16 of the CDDA, the Secretary of State will give at least ten days' notice before starting proceedings against an individual. In practice, the civil servants aim to give substantially longer. Although there is no requirement for this notice to set out the grounds for seeking a disqualification order, the notice usually does so in practice. If the notice fails to explain what the grounds are, the director should write back and ask for clarification. In practice the Secretary of State tries to contact prospective defendants in advance of any proceedings in order to set out its case and hear any response, before deciding whether to make a formal claim.

This section covers two topics: firstly, how and when to negotiate director's disqualification undertakings; and secondly what to do if agreement cannot be reached and the Secretary of State brings proceedings.

14.3.1 Disqualification undertakings

The basic principles of negotiation for disqualification undertakings are similar to negotiating any settlement, set out in Paragraph 18.1.1. All negotiation which the director does not want the court to see should be entitled 'without prejudice save as to costs' in case agreement is not reached. The other side will be the Secretary of State via in-house government lawyers working for Insolvency Service. They are likely to be conscious of wasting resources and keen to reach a settlement. At the same time, their job is to ensure that individuals who are unfit to be directors are excluded from that role.

The advantages of offering undertakings are that it is likely to lead to a lower disqualification period; and that it can escape a possible costs order which would be made against the director if they were unsuccessful at their hearing. If the court proceedings commence, the court has discretion to award costs as it sees fit, but if this is agreed between the director and the Secretary of State the judge is likely to order as agreed. Undertakings can be offered at any time and even at the entrance to the court it might be sensible to offer undertakings.

One tactic for offering disqualification undertakings is to assess what the likely disqualification period is if all the allegations are proven, and to admit only to the less serious allegations. It is more difficult to prove a serious allegation of misconduct because, although the standard of proof is only whether it is more than 50% likely that the misconduct occurred, the court will consider that it is inherently less likely that someone would commit more serious misconduct and so it is harder to prove in any case. This usually means admitting to being negligent in the conduct in question but not committing it dishonestly.

In general, the earlier in the process undertakings are offered, the more favourable to the director they can be. If the civil servants working for the Secretary of State have not finished their investigation, they will not be too set in their findings and too fixated on a particular length of disqualification. Settlement the day before the court hearing will irritate the civil servants, who will feel that it should have taken place earlier, and there would only be minimal extra costs to proceed to court. Having said that, if offering undertakings at an early stage, it is important not to raise alarm bells. The undertakings should be framed as a frank confession in the hope of putting an end to the investigation, and on the understanding that the Secretary of State would reduce the length of the undertakings in recognition of this honest conduct.

There is a complication with offering undertakings if the allegations are less serious, and the most likely disqualification period sought is two or three years. It is not possible to accept undertakings for less than two years, and so there is effectively no discount available for cooperating. In these circumstances it is better to write to the Secretary of State and suggest they do not bring proceedings at all because they are unlikely to succeed, and make an undertaking to pay compensation. For example, the individual who failed to register for PAYE may have been able to avoid proceedings if they had agreed to make a voluntary payment into their company from their personal assets. It may be worth accepting undertakings to be disqualified for two years even if that is likely to be the order made by the court in order to avoid a subsequent costs or compensation order.

Statistics from the Insolvency Service from 2009 to 2019 shows that around 80% of cases are settled with disqualification undertakings and only 20% result in a court order. The percentage that end with a court order is likely to include convictions following committing a criminal offence relating to a company, where there is no possibility of an undertaking. The true number of cases which settle out of those which are able to end in undertakings is likely to be greater than 80%.

14.3.2 Disqualification hearings

At the centre of a disqualification case is a statement by the Secretary of State of the matters which are relied on to find that the director was unfit to be concerned in the management of a company. This is required by rule 3(3) of the Insolvent Companies (Disqualification of Unfit Directors) Proceedings Rules 1987.

The majority of the hearing will be spent trying to establish whether these allegations are true; and if some or all of the allegations are proven, what the appropriate penalty is.

The Secretary of State has a duty to present the case fairly, similar to that in a criminal case. This includes not omitting significant material in the director's favour and addressing any explanation the director makes.

Even though director's disqualification hearings are similar to criminal prosecutions, there is no right to receive legal aid to allow poor directors to be able to afford legal representation. This means that directors may need to represent themselves at this hearing. Chapter 18 discusses advice for litigants in person in general, but there are particular points which directors should be aware of for disqualification hearings:

1. There are two general arguments. Firstly, the director can argue that the misconduct never took place or that it happened in a manner which was less serious than the Secretary of State suggested. This is a question of fact, and the director will need to bring evidence that the truth supports the defendant's account. The second is to accept that the facts happened as the Secretary of State alleges but that, properly understood, the director had not committed misconduct, or has not shown that they are unfit. This is about emphasising those facts which imply that the director is not a villain, but their behaviour has been misunderstood. Typically a defence to proceedings has elements of both, but if the Secretary of State is able to prove the underlying facts in full, it is unlikely that the second area will prevent a disqualification order. If the court rejects the director's account of the facts and finds that they had given misleading evidence, the judge is likely to impose a more serious order.

2. The court should not apply hindsight when judging the defendant. At the disqualification hearing the court will be aware that the company later went into liquidation but at the time that was not obvious. What is important is whether the director made reasonable and honest decisions at the time,

based only on the knowledge which was (or should have been) available. In practice, it may have been possible for the company to continue trading out of its financial difficulties.

3. Evidence of bad character (e.g. previous misdeeds and crimes) should not be used in order to prove that a director was not fit to hold office. However, it can be relevant to the question of how long a director should be disqualified for, once the main finding is made. Evidence of good character is used in the same way.

4. The court should consider the director's personal responsibility, as opposed to the misconduct of others. A director has to act independently: it is no defence to say that they did what they were told. Having said that, one director cannot be held responsible for the acts of another. Where directors delegate responsibility between them (for example, where there is a designated Finance Director) it would be natural for the other directors to be more focussed on their own area of responsibility.

5. Instead of using a witness statement, evidence should be given by 'affidavit'. This is a form of witness statement where someone (typically a solicitor) administers the same oath which a witness makes when their evidence is used in court, but in advance. If it is not possible, or too expensive, to find a solicitor who will help the director with this oath, then the court is likely to be pragmatic, and to rely on a witness statement given by a litigant in person, provided that they confirm its contents under oath. County Courts are meant to administer the affidavit free of charge if someone turns up with a written statement.

6. Disqualification hearings are robed, i.e. barristers will wear wigs and gowns. This is more intimidating. However, directors should know that, for a judge, a barrister wearing robes is not at all intimidating or authoritative and so they will not be as influenced by the formality as a litigant in person might be. The judge will try to see past what the lawyers are wearing to listen to the arguments. Barristers do not wear robes in most civil (as opposed to criminal) cases. However, disqualification proceedings are similar to criminal trials in that the aim is to protect the public, rather than to provide compensation to a claimant.

14.4 Application for permission to be a director

Even if a director has been disqualified, it is possible for them to apply for permission to act as a director during the disqualification period. The court will not grant permission to act as a director generally, but will consider an application to act as a director for a particular company. Permission may be granted if there are some exceptional extenuating circumstances which means it is unlikely that the director will commit further misconduct. Permission is not often sought. It is difficult for the applicant to show why it is appropriate to grant permission, because the court has already found that the restriction is necessary and appropriate. The court takes a two stage approach to applications: firstly an applicant must show why they 'need' to be a director, and secondly how the public will continue to be adequately protected. The court is generally more interested in the interests of third parties such as the company which needs a director than in the individual needing to continue their livelihood. When considering the protection to the public, the court will also consider the general deterrence effect of an order which is undermined if permission is given. However, the court's main concern is that the director does not commit the same misconduct again. This is easier to show if the original finding was of negligence and not dishonesty: the director can say they intend to rely on professional advice and have learnt not to make decisions without it.

The court often imposes safeguards when granting permission. An example might be an order that the director is not to be paid more than a certain amount, the company is to appoint a particular auditor and an independent director, or the director is personally ordered to ensure the accounts are audited and filed at Companies House within the proper time limits. This may be expressed as a condition of granting permission, or an undertaking to the court. The difference is whether permission is automatically revoked if the condition is broken, or if the director is in contempt of court for breaching their undertaking.

PART 3   APPEALS

Chapter 15   Appeals

This chapter sets out the rules for appealing the decision of a court. There are three ways of reversing a decision in insolvency proceedings. Firstly, the court has the power to 'review' its decision. A court which can make an order in insolvency proceedings has the power to review, rescind or vary that order (s375 of the Act for bankruptcy; and r12.59 for corporate insolvency). Secondly, there can be a (true) appeal. This must be heard by a High Court judge (see Part 4 of the Insolvency Proceedings Practice Direction, para 17.2). Finally, in the case of a bankruptcy order, the debtor can apply under s282 for the order to be annulled.

It will be noted that having three routes is generous. In most other areas of law, litigants only have the ability to appeal a decision. Insolvency law is exceptionally onerous and so the law-makers were concerned that judges should reach the correct decision. This chapter sets out how to apply for a review, an appeal and an annulment. It then discusses the tactical considerations behind these options.

In all three cases, if the other party to a decision agrees that the decision was wrongly made it may be possible to make an application by consent for the court to vary its order.

15.1 Reviews

The ability for the court to review its own decision is unusual. It has been described as a 'safety valve' power for the court. Permission is not required to apply for a review.

The leading case behind a review is *Papanicola v Humphreys* [2005] EWHC 335 (Ch). At paragraph 25, the judge said:

1.   The section gives the court a wide discretion to review, vary or rescind <u>any</u> order made in the exercise of the bankruptcy jurisdiction.

2.   The onus is on the applicant to demonstrate the existence of circumstances which justify exercise of the discretion in his favour.

3.   Those circumstances must be exceptional.

4.   The circumstances relied on must involve a material difference to what was before the court which made the original order. In other words there must be something new to justify the overturning of the original order.

5.   There is no limit to the factors which may be taken into account. They can include, for example, changes which have occurred since the making of the original order and significant facts which, although in existence at the time of the original order, were not brought to the court's attention at that time.

6.   Where the new circumstances relied on consist of or include new evidence which could have been made available at the original hearing, that, and any explanation by the applicant gives for the failure to produce it then or any lack of such explanation, are factors which can be taken into account in the exercise of the discretion.

The purpose of a s375 review is to re-evaluate the court's decision based on some new material. This could include significant new factors which the court did not consider at the first hearing. This could, for example, include the fact that the debtor was not represented at the first hearing, and having instructed a solicitor, the solicitor can bring new points to the court's attention. The onus is on the applicant to say what exceptional circumstances have now arisen. If nothing has changed, the applicant should use the appeal mechanism rather than a review.

The review can be of any decision whatsoever. A debtor who unsuccessfully applied to set aside a statutory demand may, upon receiving new material, apply to the court to review its decision. However, where the review is of the bankruptcy order, the court will be especially anxious that the order was not made in unjust circumstances, and may exercise any discretion in favour of the applicant.

However, the circumstances are rarely sufficiently exceptional for the review to succeed. A rather unusual example of a review being successful is *Haworth v Cartmel* [2011] EWHC 36 (Ch) which was also mentioned in Paragraph 5.13.13above. The applicant had been made bankrupt on the petition of the HMRC. The applicant also had various mental illnesses and received disability benefit. She accepted personal service of a statutory demand, but told the process server she could not open an envelope because she was "under the Mental Health Act". Ms Haworth had a phobia of post. She probably lacked capacity to even accept service, due to her mental state. It turns out that no tax was due, but HMRC did not know this until tax returns were filed after the making of the bankruptcy order. Ms Haworth successfully applied for the order to be rescinded.

In *Yang v Official Receiver* [2013] EWHC 3577 (Ch) the court allowed the review and then rescission of an order when the petition debt was based on unpaid council tax. This was eventually set aside by the valuation tribunal, but only three years after the making of the bankruptcy order. The court felt it could not annul the order under s282(1)(a) because it had been properly made at the time. Instead, it rescinded the order.

The difference between rescission and annulment is that rescission ends the bankruptcy early but treats the order as having been properly made. Unlike annulment, there is no requirement for the Official Receiver to publicise the rescission of a bankruptcy order. The former bankrupt is still able to ask the Official Receiver to publicise the rescission. If the OR does not then it would be sensible for the former bankrupt to take steps to publicise the rescission themselves, for example by putting a notice in the London Gazette. Since third party lenders will be aware of the original bankruptcy order, they will assume the bankruptcy continues unless notified otherwise.

It is also possible to apply for a review of a decision made in a corporate insolvency under r12.59(1). The process for applying to rescind a winding up order is set out in PDIP para 9.10. The application must be made within five business days after the date on which the order was made. The application must be supported by a witness statement which should include details of assets and liabilities and (where appropriate) reasons for any failure to apply within five business days. An application cannot be made by just the company, but instead it must be by either a shareholder or a creditor (by themselves or jointly with the company). The usual costs order if the application is unsuccessful is that the shareholder/creditor pays the costs of the petitioning creditor.

15.2 Appeals

The appeal process for an insolvency order is similar to other civil cases. The main distinguishing feature of an insolvency appeal is that an appeal of a decision of a district judge will be heard by a judge of the High Court. The High Court is busy, and there is likely to be a significant delay before the case is listed, unless it is urgent. If the original decision was made by a circuit judge, the appeal will still be to a High Court judge.

Unlike a review, an appeal can only be on the grounds that the judge was (1) wrong or (2) unjust because of a serious procedural irregularity (CPR 52.21(3)). 'Wrong' means either (1a) an error of law, or (1b) an error of fact, or (1c) an error in the exercise of the court's discretion.

Taking these in turn:

Wrong: Error of law. Of the grounds of appeal, the most common and the most likely to succeed is that the judge properly made an error of law. An error of law means that the judge's decision failed to apply one of the Insolvency Rules or the Insolvency Act, or any other law.

Wrong: Error of fact. This is the least common ground of appeal. The appeal court is unlikely to find that the judge made a critical factual mistake, because the lower judge had all the facts at their disposal and was well placed to make the correct decision. The appeal court is not going to hear additional evidence which demonstrates that a certain witness was mistaken (for example), although this could be relevant to a review. An appeal is not a retrial, and so the court will not be interested in hearing the same evidence again. Provided that the other side agreed with the judge's factual finding, an appeal on this ground is unlikely to succeed. The other consideration is that a judge in a civil case does not decide that something definitely happened, but only that it was the most likely outcome. This is known as the 'standard of proof' being that of the 'balance of probabilities'. An appeal on the ground of an error of fact might succeed, if the judge makes a finding for which there is <u>no</u> evidence to support a finding. An example would be if the judge found that a transaction did not happen when there was a receipt demonstrating that it did, unless the judge also made a finding that the receipt was unreliable.

Wrong: Error in the exercise of discretion. Judges are given a large degree of discretion, and the appeal court will not 'interfere' with that use of discretion simply because it would have adopted a different approach. The appeal court will need to be satisfied that the decision taken went beyond the reasonable exercise of the judge's discretion, which is a high threshold.

Serious procedural irregularity. Although it is easy to criticise the decisions made by judges, in general these decisions are made in a procedurally correct manner. A judge will require a lot of persuasion to hold that the lower court's decision was made with a serious procedural irregularity. The qualification 'serious' means that it is not enough to merely point out some problem with the process, but show that this seriously affected the ability of the applicant to make their case. This could be, for example:

- If the judge made their decision without hearing from the debtor, or if the judge gave no reasons or inadequate reasons for rejecting the debtor's application. However, this rarely happens.

- If the judge is biased or has a conflict of interest. The accusation is frequently made. It is very rarely proven, primarily because English judges tend <u>not</u> to be biased, and they are aware of their own potential conflicts. The fact that a judge has heard a related case before is not a conflict of interest: judges are expected to be able to make independent decisions and assess each case objectively. A professional connection between the judge and the legal team (for example, the barrister and the judge were members of the same set of barristers' chambers) is unlikely to be enough for the judge to be considered conflicted. A personal connection could be.

- The judge made a snap decision after a short period of time, rather than decide to adjourn the case and re-list it for a longer hearing slot. In *Black v Sale Service and Maintenance Ltd* [2018] EWHC 1344 (Ch) the judge dismissed a complicated application to set aside a statutory demand in 15 minutes without reading the witness statement evidence, even though at the outset consensus had been reached that directions would be given. This was held to be a procedural irregularity, the decision was quashed and a hearing listed for 2½ hours. However, less extreme circumstances may be considered a valid decision within the discretion of the judge.

If the judge was unfriendly, curt, or in a bad temper this does <u>not</u> constitute a serious procedural irregularity.

It is possible to appeal a decision on multiple grounds. However, it is sensible to only put forward the strongest grounds of appeal. This is likely to be that the judge has made an error of law. In general, making a weak argument and a strong argument strengthens the weak argument and weakens the strong argument.

Common areas of appeal for a bankruptcy order are:

1. The judge incorrectly held that the debtor was validly served with a document (error of law: see Paragraph 5.8).

2. The judge refused to adjourn a hearing (error of discretion/serious procedural irregularity: see Paragraph 5.12).

3. The judge wrongly held that a debt was not disputed on substantial grounds (error of law: see Paragraph 5.13.5).

4. The judge made a debtor bankrupt when they had no jurisdiction to do so (error of law: see Paragraph 5.2). For example, the debtor did not fall within the English bankruptcy regime, or the hearing was being heard in the wrong court.

5. The judge made a debtor bankrupt but the petition was an abuse of process (error of law: see Paragraph 5.13.7).

Note that merely identifying an error will not be enough. The applicant will need to be able to show why, but for that mistake, their case would have succeeded. If the appeal court agrees that the decision was an error, they are likely to reverse the decision of the previous judge. In the case of a procedural irregularity, the typical remedy is to have a retrial rather than decide the case again on appeal.

In order to appeal, the dissatisfied party requires permission. This can firstly be obtained from the lower court, by asking for permission to appeal the decision made. An application for permission is done immediately after the order being appealed is made. The applicant should politely set out to the judge why they thought their decision was wrong or made as a result of a serious procedural irregularity. It is unusual for the original judge to grant permission to appeal, because having just made their decision, it is unlikely that they consider it to be wrong or unjustly made. The applicant can also ask for a stay of the order, regardless of whether or not the judge grants permission to appeal (see Box 44 below). Unless permission is granted by the original judge, the applicant has 21 days from the date of the order to apply to the High Court for permission to appeal. The written application should set out the grounds of appeal.

BOX 44: STAY OF JUDGMENT

An order is effective immediately from the day it is made (see CPR 40.7). In particular, it is effective before a record of the order is sealed by the court. In order to avoid the effect of an order, a party needs to apply for 'a stay of execution', i.e. an order that the original order be put on hold, pending the appeal. A debtor may need to immediately ask the judge to make a stay of an order, at least on an interim basis if they plan to apply for permission to appeal the decision. The debtor can also apply to the higher court for a stay.

15.3 Annulment of a bankruptcy order

The court has the power to annul a bankruptcy order if at any time it appears to the court that, on any grounds existing at the time the order was made, the order ought not to have been made (s282(1)(a) of the Act).

An application for annulment is broader than an appeal. This is because:

- An application for an annulment can be made at any time, but an appeal must be made within 21 days of the decision, unless an extension of time is given.

- An application for an annulment can be made by any person interested in the application, as opposed to an appeal of a bankruptcy order which is limited to the debtor (or a creditor presenting the petition). A s282(1)(a) application could be made, for example, by a spouse.

- An application for the annulment is not limited to the evidence before the original trial judge, provided it evidences "grounds existing at the time the order was made". For example, if a bankrupt manages to appeal and overturn a judgment which was the basis of the debt in the bankruptcy petition, the bankrupt will be able to apply to annul the bankruptcy order: in hindsight, the debt was not owed. However, there would be no grounds to appeal the order because at the time the order was made, the debt was owed.

- An application for the annulment is not limited to an argument made before the first judge. This means that if a bankrupt did not have legal representation and so failed to properly put their case, there is a good chance that the court will hear an application to annul the bankruptcy, provided that the legal representatives are able to show that an important point was not made by the bankrupt. In contrast, appeal courts are reluctant to hear new arguments in order to encourage parties to make all their points the first time around.

- Like an application for a review, permission is not required to apply to annul.

One way in which it is more difficult to succeed in an application for an annulment than for an appeal is because annulment is a discretionary power. If an appeal court finds that the grounds of appeal succeed, the court cannot choose to let the decision stand. However, the court might decide not to annul a wrongly made bankruptcy order. For example the court may decide not to annul an order if a bankrupt is hopelessly insolvent and so bankruptcy is inevitable and in the best interest of the creditors. Similarly, although there is no time limit for making an application, the court may decide that due to the bankrupt's delay, it would not be appropriate to annul the bankruptcy.

An order for annulment can be made whether or not the bankrupt has been discharged from bankruptcy (s282(3)). This would permit an individual who was wrongly made bankrupt to clear their name. However, it is not always in the interests of an individual to annul a bankruptcy, even if it was wrongly made, because the effect of the bankruptcy being discharged is that the majority of the individual's debts will be forgiven. Annulment would restore these debts.

The court approaches an application for an annulment in three stages: firstly, what were the grounds existing when the order was made; secondly, on those grounds should an order have been be made; and thirdly if the order should not have been made, should the court annul the bankruptcy order? An application should identify each of these three stages and argue for them separately.

If the bankruptcy order ought not to have been made, the general rule is that the petitioning creditor is liable for the bankruptcy costs caused by the petition, and not the former bankrupt. This would include the fees of the Trustee in Bankruptcy. However, this is only the starting point of the costs argument. If the former bankrupt is held responsible for the order being made, then they may be ordered to pay the subsequent costs.

BOX 45:   FAILURE TO ATTEND COURT

The courts adopt a generous interpretation of 'ought not to have been made' for a s282(1)(a) annulment. The court has held that an order ought not have been made, for example, where the bankrupt did not attend court because they had been misled into thinking it would be adjourned. If the bankrupt fails to attend court it is likely that the court would not have heard their argument that the bankruptcy order should not be made, which can be the basis for a s282(1)(a) application.

There is no advantage to a bankrupt of deliberately not attending a hearing but choosing to make a s282(1)(a) application instead. Firstly, the application is harder than simply opposing the hearing. This is because as well as needing to demonstrate that the order should not have been made, the bankrupt will need to show that the court ought to annul it. Secondly, by the time the application is made the bankruptcy order would also have been made and be effective, meaning that the negative effects of bankruptcy would already have started.

There is no equivalent to the annulment process for companies. However, if the company has the assets to pay all of its creditors and the liquidator, the court may order a stay on the enforcement of the winding up order under s147 of the Act. In effect, the liquidation ceases and the directors take control of the company again.

PART 4 COSTS

Chapter 16   Costs

'Costs' in this book, refers to legal expenditure. Litigation is extremely expensive. In general only 60-70% of the costs can be recovered by the winning party. This means that if someone decides to apply to court, or decides to defend court proceedings, they should know that even if they are successful, they are likely to be paying 30-40% of their legal costs themselves. If the claim is against an insolvent person, the estate might not have enough assets to pay even the amount the claimant is entitled to.

Costs are therefore an extremely important tactical consideration. An understanding of the costs which a creditor faces is necessary to decide how to deal with them in correspondence, in particular in order to reach an out of court settlement such as an IVA. It should also be useful when reviewing the other side's costs schedule – see Box 52 on page 219.

After a bankruptcy order is made, all pre-bankruptcy costs orders will be unenforceable and a creditor will need to prove in the insolvency to receive payment. This means that, pre-bankruptcy, a debtor who knows they are insolvent might not care about paying for a costs order: whether they win or lose, the costs will have no marginal effect on their lives.[9] However, all costs orders made after a bankruptcy order are still enforceable, even if the bankrupt is unable to pay them. A bankrupt who makes an unsuccessful application (for example, a s303 application to challenge the Trustee) or a bankrupt who unsuccessfully opposes an application (for example, an application to suspend the discharge of the bankruptcy under s279), and who then receives an adverse costs order may be made bankrupt a second time. Alternatively, the costs order may remain unpaid but the creditor may decide to enforce it several years later if the bankrupt is wealthier in the future. A costs order is enforceable indefinitely, although after six years interest may not accrue and certain enforcement processes require the court's permission.

This chapter has three aims. Firstly, it tries to estimate the likely cost of the stages of litigating a bankruptcy or winding up petition. Secondly, it sets out the

---

[9] The individual might care about the costs order for other reasons, for example in case it is considered as part of the conduct justifying a bankruptcy restrictions order.

principles and specific rules which the court applies when making costs orders. Finally, it discusses the costs of a Trustee in Bankruptcy or liquidator.

16.1 Costs at different stages

> ### BOX 46:   A WORD OF WARNING
>
> This section makes broad estimates. These are presented with no knowledge of the specific facts which the reader is facing. It is foolish to place too much weight on these estimates. However, an estimate is often better than nothing. A debtor who has some money to pay legal fees needs to use this money wisely, which can mean picking battles. Solicitors often give fee estimates for free upon seeing a set of papers. This means that this chapter may be the starting point of the exercise, but it should be possible to get more precise estimates for free.
>
> This section should be read in conjunction with Chapter 17 if the reader is considering which lawyers to instruct.

The costs of litigation can be broken into:

a)   Solicitors' fees

b)   Barristers' fees

c)   Court fees

d)   Process servers' fees

16.1.1 Solicitors' fees

Most solicitors operate on an hourly rate basis: i.e. they charge a fixed amount per hour that they work.[10] The alternative is a 'fixed rate' basis: the rate of work will attract a fixed amount regardless of how long it takes the solicitor to complete it. There are disadvantages of both methods from the client's perspective: the first leads to solicitors working too much; the second too little. A firm working on an hourly rate is likely to estimate how many hours it will be, but unlike a fixed rate fee, they will not be bound by the answer. My advice is not to pay attention to the difference. The Senior Courts Costs Office published figures

---

[10] *This chapter refers to solicitors, but the same observations apply to legal executives. See Paragraph 17.1.1 for further details on the differences between these two types of lawyer.*

in 2010 which offer guideline hourly rates for solicitors in different parts of the country.

Table 1: Official guideline hourly rates from 2010							
Pay band	Fee earner	London grade 1	London grade 2	London grade 3	National grade 1	National grade 2	National grade 3
A	Solicitors and legal executives with over 8 years' experience	£409	£317	£229 to £267	£217	£201	£201
B	Solicitors and legal executives with over 4 years' experience	£296	£242	£172 to £229	£192	£177	£177
C	Other solicitors or legal executives and fee earners of equivalent experience	£226	£196	£165	£161	£146	£146
D	Trainee solicitors, paralegals and other fee earners	£138	£126	£121	£118	£111	£111

Hourly rates excluding VAT

See https://www.gov.uk/guidance/solicitors-guideline-hourly-rates.

'London grade 1/2/3' and 'National grade 1/2/3' are defined on that page, and roughly correspond to how expensive rent is in that part of the country. Oxford is 'National grade 1' and Scarborough is 'National Grade 3', for example.

These figures are notoriously out of date. Solicitors in 2021 charge approximately 50% more than they did in 2010. An adjusted table would be:

Table 2: Author's estimate of hourly rates for solicitors			
	Location		
Experience	London	More expensive part of country	Cheaper part of country
Partner	£550	£350	£300
Experienced associate	£350	£250	£200
Trainee or paralegal	£200	£150	£100

Hourly rates excluding VAT, point estimate

Within 'London', there is a wide range of solicitors' firms. The most prestigious multi-national law firms would charge substantially more than the amounts in Table 2. However, these firms are unlikely to be instructed in a small bankruptcy or winding up petition.

In general, most of the difficult drafting and thinking should be being done by the experienced associate and most of the printing and form filling should be being done by a trainee or paralegal. A partner should have relatively little oversight unless the case is particularly complicated or high value.

At the time of writing, there are discussions about the Senior Courts Cost Office updating its guidance. This would be a controversial decision, since it will inevitably expose some solicitors as over-charging.

Stop press: The Civil Justice Council has published a suggested update to the official guidelines, which broadly agree with the estimates at Table 2 above. It can be found at page 98 at https://www.judiciary.uk/wp-content/uploads/2021/01/20210108-GHR-Report-for-consultation-FINAL.pdf but these have not yet been approved.

Hourly rates tell only half the story. It is also important to know roughly how many hours and how much experience is required for each stage of proceedings. This assumes that the client has roughly got their papers in order and so solicitors do not have to do unnecessary work: see Paragraph 17.2 for more details. The following table gives estimates for both debtors and creditors because it is important for debtors to appreciate the costs their opponents are incurring. The time includes meeting the client, advising on the merits, corresponding with the other side and a barrister, and the hearing itself.

Table 3: Author's time estimate for hearing	
Stage	**Time estimate per category of solicitor**
Initial advice – debtor or creditor	3 hours for an associate
Issue statutory demand	1 hour for an associate; plus 2 hours for a trainee
First bankruptcy hearing or hearing to set aside a statutory demand	10 hours for an associate; plus 5 hours for a trainee
Additional hearing lasting 30 minutes	10 hours for an associate; plus 5 hours for a trainee
Additional hearing lasting 60 minutes	20 hours for an associate; plus 10 hours for a trainee
Possession hearing	10 hours for an associate; plus 5 hours for a trainee
Challenge to the Trustee in Bankruptcy (for the Trustee)	15 hours for an associate; plus 10 hours for a trainee
Appeal	15 hours for an associate; plus 10 hours for a trainee

To give a working example: a common occurrence is for there to be no hearing to set aside the statutory demand, but three bankruptcy hearings: the first in the wrong court, the second setting directions, and a substantive hearing lasting an hour. For a creditor in a more expensive part of the country but outside of London, this is likely to cost approximately £15,000, excluding VAT. If the debtor does not have many assets, the Trustee in Bankruptcy might not be able to pay this costs bill even if it was admitted in full, in which case there would be no money left to repay their actual petition debt and the petitioning creditor would finish the process having lost money. Not all creditors will be able to recover VAT.

This is the situation for a typical bankruptcy case. A debtor may apply to set aside the statutory demand, insist the hearing is listed for two hours to address all the evidence, and in the event the application is unsuccessful, seek multiple adjournments of the bankruptcy petition to seek further time to pay. The reader can see that this can easily cost £40,000 or more in solicitors' fees alone.

See Chapter 17 for tips for how to choose appropriate solicitors. It will be appreciated that where solicitors have an hourly rate, it can be cheaper to use an efficient but more expensive firm over a cheaper, but less efficient firm. A cheaper solicitor may also be less knowledgeable or experienced: specialists typically charge a premium for their expertise.

16.1.2 Barristers' fees

Barristers' fees are complicated by the fact that many barristers do not accept 'direct access' i.e. they will not work with the debtor or creditor directly, but only if the debtor/creditor uses a solicitor.

In general, barristers who specialise in insolvency law are often less likely to be 'direct access' qualified. These are likely to be the barristers located in central London, in chambers that specialise in insolvency law and do not practice in areas of law like family law. Barristers' chambers that cover a wide range of law, including those not located in central London, are more likely to do direct access work.

For a simple case where the matter at stake is under £100,000 there is less benefit using an extremely experienced barrister. Barristers' experience is measured in 'years' call'. this is the time from when they were formally called to the Bar. This is an unhelpful measure, because a barrister may be called to the Bar but not have completed their training ('pupillage'). A barrister who has just completed their training may be in their first year of call if they are late with their paperwork, or they may be in their third year of call if they struggled to find a chambers to train them. Nonetheless, years' call is the measure which is on most barristers' websites.

Table 4: Author's estimated hourly rates for barristers		
Experience	Specialist	Non-specialist
3 years' call or less	£100	£75
Over 3 years' call but less than 7 years	£200	£150
Over 7 years' call	£300	£200

Hourly rates, excluding VAT

Some barristers, typically with over 15 years' call, are given the title of 'Queen's Counsel', abbreviated to 'QC'. This is in recognition of their outstanding skills: similar to a promotion. However, it would be unusual for a QC to appear in an insolvency claim where the matter at stake was less than £1m.

Barristers typically only appear in hearings and give legal advice on the proper strategy. A barrister may be asked for their opinion on the merits of a case: this is typically around ten hours' work. Barristers are not usually asked to draft routine documents like statutory demands or bankruptcy petitions, although they might draft grounds of appeal. They may be asked to review witness evidence.

Barristers often also work on fixed fee bases for routine hearings like bankruptcy petitions. Assuming they are instructed by a solicitor, a specialist barrister of under three years' call would charge roughly the following fees for a simple hearing:

Table 5: Author's estimate for a barrister's fixed fees for a specialist insolvency barrister of under three years' call	
Hearing	Fee
First hearing where the parties expect directions	£400
Additional hearing lasting 20 minutes	£500
Additional hearing lasting 60 minutes	£750
Additional hearing lasting half a day	£1,500
Possession hearing lasting 15 minutes	£300
Challenge to the Trustee in Bankruptcy (for the Trustee)	£1,000
Drafting appeal	£750
Winding up petition hearing (in London)	£100

Figures exclude VAT, additional charges for travelling time and train fares

If the barrister is direct access, they will need to do substantially more work to prepare for the hearings. The time it will take will be comparable to that of a solicitor in Table 2 above.

> ## BOX 47:   WHAT ABOUT WINDING UP PETITIONS?
>
> In general, it is cheaper for a creditor to wind up a company than bankrupt an individual. There is no requirement to serve a statutory demand, and hearings are shorter. A solicitor could prepare the paperwork in 2-4 hours; and barristers typically charge around £100 per winding up hearing. The cost of a disputed debt hearing is comparable to those of a hearing to set aside a statutory demand.

16.1.3   Court fees

Court fees are only payable by the person applying to court. For a debtor/bankrupt, this would only be to appeal or challenge a Trustee. In particular, only the petitioning creditor needs to pay fees for a bankruptcy petition.

Unlike most legal costs, if the court awards costs in favour of one party, this will include 100% of the court fee.

Most court fees are set out in the leaflet EX50 which can be found at https://assets.publishing.service.gov.uk/government/uploads/system/uploads/attachment_data/file/789201/ex50-eng.pdf.

Common court fees are set out below.

Table 6: Common court fees	
Hearing	**Fee**
Serve statutory demand	No fee: not court proceedings
Application to set aside a statutory demand	No fee
Debtor's application to become bankrupt	£680
Bankruptcy petition (paid by petitioning creditor)	£280 court fee, plus £990 as a deposit for the Official Receiver
Any application in existing bankruptcy proceedings	£95
Request for a certificate of discharge from bankruptcy	£70
Appeal to High Court	£240

> ## BOX 48:   HELP WITH COURT FEES
>
> There is a scheme for waiving court fees. The basic rules are that an individual can apply for 'remission' (i.e. not to pay) in the following circumstances:
>
> ► If the debtor or their partner is under 61, they need to have savings of less than £3,000. If they are over 61, they must have savings of under £16,000; and
>
> ► The applicant needs to earn less than £1,085 a month before tax if they are single, or £1,245 if they have a partner, or receive at least one of the following benefits:
>
>   • Income based job seekers allowance
>
>   • Income related Employment and Support Allowance
>
>   • Income support
>
>   • Universal credit, and the debtor earns less than £6000 a year
>
>   • Pension credit
>
> These rules are not generous.

16.1.4 Process server's fees

Statutory demands and bankruptcy petitions must be delivered by hand to the debtor. The process server then needs to give a witness statement confirming that they successfully delivered the documents, or that they went to the appropriate addresses but no one was there. If the documents are not delivered personally, it is usual to attempt a second or third appointment, and to try business addresses as well as personal addresses.

It might be thought that the requirement for personal service would substantially add to the costs of the bankruptcy. However, because it does not matter who serves the documents (it does not need to be done by a qualified lawyer), process servers are typically quite cheap. On average, it costs approximately £100 to instruct a process server, which would include multiple visits. This would be the same for both statutory demands and bankruptcy petitions.

> ## BOX 49: LITIGANTS IN PERSON CAN CLAIM FOR THEIR COSTS
>
> A litigant in person can claim for the costs of their time at £19 per hour: see CPR Practice Direction 46 paragraph 3.4. This means that if someone spends 10 hours preparing and attending their case, and they then succeed and the judge awards them their costs, they can claim £190. A litigant in person can also claim their expenses in the same way as other litigants – for example, their train fare, or any costs of printing. If the litigant in person can prove financial loss as a result of their reasonable preparation for the case, they can claim this loss back as an alternative to the £19/hour figure (CPR 46.5(4)(a)). If, theoretically, the litigant in person was self-employed and had to turn down work in order to focus on the litigation, they can claim for the profitable business they declined. It is difficult to quantify this sum, or to prove that it was incurred, and so the £19/hour figure is more often claimed.

16.2 Principles of costs awards

At the end of every hearing, the judge will decide the question of who will pay the costs of the hearing. The judge has a large degree of discretion in deciding what the fair outcome is. However, the general rule is that "costs follow the event", i.e. if someone 'wins', they should get their costs. To give an example, if an application is made to set aside a statutory demand, and the demand is set aside, then the debtor is likely to be awarded their costs. If the application is dismissed then the creditor is likely to be awarded their costs.

There are many possible costs orders a judge can make, but the most common ones are:

1. Costs for [party]. This means that the named party, whether the creditor/ debtor or applicant/respondent receives their costs. If the court has summarily assessed the costs (see details below), it will order a specific amount to be paid in respect of costs: "[losing party] to pay [winning party]'s costs, summarily assessed as £[amount]". Otherwise, it will order "Costs for [party], to be assessed if not agreed".

2. Costs in the case/costs in the petition. This means that the costs of the hearing will be rolled together with the outcome of the case or petition itself. If the bankruptcy petition succeeds, the creditor will claim the costs of the hearing. Otherwise, the creditor will have to pay the costs of the hearing. This is the default option for a hearing which leads to an adjournment,

because no party has 'won'. It is also the default option for a directions hearing, even if one side 'won' by getting the directions they asked for.

3. No order as to costs. This means that each side will pay their own costs.

4. Costs reserved. This happens when the court does not want to decide what the costs position should be, and so 'reserves' its decision for another time. If no further decision is made, the costs will be costs in the case.

If the judge makes an order which does not say what the costs of the hearing is, the rule is that no party is entitled to claim their costs (CPR r44.10).

Costs orders typically state a time by which the costs must be paid, such as: "*A to pay B's costs, summarily assessed as £10,000, by 4pm on Wednesday 12 May 2021*". If a costs award does not say when it is to be paid, the rule is that it must be paid within 14 days (CPR r44.7). It is possible to ask for additional time: a judge will usually allow 28 days for payment if the paying party asks for it, but rarely allow more than six weeks.

BOX 50: THIRD PARTY COSTS ORDERS

The court has the power to order a third party, i.e. someone who did not appear in the case, to pay the costs of the case. This is unusual. They will be ordered if the non-party controls the litigation, or if they are to benefit from it. Judges sometimes say the third party has to be 'the real party' to the litigation. Two examples will illustrate when this might happen. Firstly, a third party costs order could be awarded if a director caused their company to contest a loan which they had personally guaranteed, but the company was insolvent. The company would not benefit from the litigation, only the director would. Secondly, if a bankrupt contested possession of a property where the court was satisfied that the bankrupt did not live there, but only a spouse did, that would suggest that the spouse was the 'real party' to the litigation. There is a requirement to add the non-party to the litigation and give them the opportunity to attend the hearing where the court will consider the matter further, by virtue of CPR rule 46.2. In practice, this means that for lower value cases it is expensive and so impractical to seek a third party costs order.

Having decided who (if anyone) is going to be awarded their costs, the judge's next decision is how much of the costs will be awarded. In a case where the costs are under £50,000; the costs will nearly always be determined there and then. This is known as summary assessment, i.e. the court will not go through the detailed evidence of the expenditure. The assessment will be done quickly: usually in around five minutes at the end of a hearing. If the paying party is a litigant in person, judges intervene more than they usually do to reduce the bill. A cost assessment can, however, happen at a dedicated separate hearing known as a 'detailed assessment' if the court decides. This usually happens only if one or both parties request a detailed assessment.

An exception to the rule that the court will assess costs summarily after determining a matter substantively is after making a winding up or bankruptcy order. A bankruptcy or winding up order includes, unless otherwise ordered, that the costs will be awarded to the petitioning creditor 'to be assessed if not agreed'.

BOX 51: COSTS OF THE BANKRUPTCY OR WINDING UP PETITION

The court does not usually assess the petitioning creditor's costs after making a bankruptcy or winding up order. Instead, the petitioning creditor will seek to agree costs with the Trustee in Bankruptcy or liquidator. If they do not agree, the question of costs can go to a detailed assessment. The Insolvency Service's guidance at paragraph 39.16 of its Technical Handbook states that petition costs, including court fees, can normally be paid without detailed assessment provided they do not exceed £2,000 for a company and £1,500 for a bankruptcy. This guidance is out of date: a petitioning creditor can expect to recover more than this by agreement. Instead, the Trustee/liquidator is likely to take some rule of thumb adjustment, like making an offer of 70% of the petitioning creditors' costs. If the Trustee/liquidator does not agree what costs are payable, it will proceed to a 'detailed assessment'. The costs of the detailed assessment will be paid for out of the estate of the insolvent person/company. It follows that it is in all parties' interests to agree a suitable figure: any disagreement simply wastes further costs.

The judge will only award costs which were reasonably incurred, reasonable in amount and proportionate. There is inevitably scope for discussion about what 'reasonable' means in this context. As a starting point, the judge will decide whether to assess the costs in one of two ways. These are known as the standard basis and the indemnity basis.

As the name suggests, the standard basis will be the default option. The meaning of the 'standard basis' is that where there is a doubt about how reasonable the cost expenditure is, it will be resolved in favour of the party who is paying the bill. In practice, this means that only 60-75% of the expenditure will be paid. A judge who awards costs on the standard basis will be guided by the paying party to see what expenditure could be said to be unreasonable, in order to reduce the cost award. For example, the judge might decide that the solicitor was too expensive, or that work was done by a partner which should have been done by an associate, or that the solicitor did the work too slowly. These are all reasons to reduce the cost bill.

The second way in which the court can assess the costs is the indemnity basis. This will also not allow a cost which was unreasonably incurred or unreasonable in amount and it will resolve all doubts about reasonableness in favour of the receiving party. There is no need for the expenditure to be proportionate. This means the court will be reluctant to reduce the costs bill. Typically an award on the indemnity basis will cover 75% to 90% of the costs requested, but it is not uncommon for it to be 100%.

An underlying principle of modern litigation is an expectation that parties will try hard to settle the cases out of court without the need to litigate at all. Therefore, in a sense it is a failure on both parties that the problem has not been resolved already. The reason a party who wins is not awarded all their costs is recognition that they could and should have tried harder to settle.

With that principle in mind, an order of indemnity costs is used as a penalty where one party has behaved inappropriately, and the winning party therefore had little choice but to go to court. The court does not punish improper conduct by deciding the entire case against the problematic party: this would not be fair, because the case should be decided on the evidence. Instead, the court shows its disapproval by giving an unfavourable cost award. This would include refusing to award costs even if the party was successful.

Improper conduct would include:

- Failing to abide by the court's orders. For example, if a party did not disclose a document they were ordered to, or was late in submitting an application which caused the other side prejudice, or repeatedly missed deadlines.

- Making arguments which were not just wrong, but obviously wrong or vexatious.

- Abusing the court process. This broadly means using a court process for the wrong purposes, for example, requesting multiple adjournments supposedly in order to gather evidence for a longer trial, and then not turning up for the hearing.

The test for awarding indemnity costs is that the behaviour falls 'outside of the norm'. Minor breaches should not give rise to indemnity costs. The court will view behaviour generously and it will generally require persuasion to hold that a party was abusing the court process, or deserves to be sanctioned in some way.

In an insolvency context, 'abusing the court process' has a particular meaning. It is an abuse of process to present a petition in respect of contested debts. If a debtor can successfully show that a debt is disputed, either when setting aside a statutory demand or when disputing a petition, then the general rule is that since the creditor is abusing the insolvency process, the debtor is entitled to their costs on an indemnity basis. This does not need to be followed, and if the debtor themselves is culpable (for example, because they did not disclose their objections early enough) then the result can be adjusted.

In a detailed assessment, the court applies the same principles, but with more rigour since it is a dedicated separate hearing and so there is more time to scrutinise these costs. Unless there is a significant dispute between the parties on the correct costs, a detailed assessment is usually a waste of resources: it would be cheaper for both parties simply to agree a figure. A party might prefer a detailed assessment if they require time to pay. However, the court usually orders the costs of the costs dispute to be paid by the paying party, unless the paying party made an appropriate offer in advance.

BOX 52:   COSTS SCHEDULES

A litigant in person who seeks their cost on the £19/hour basis should say how many hours they spent working on the case, ideally broken into how many hours on which days and what they were doing at that time.

However, professional lawyers are likely to use a particular 'costs schedule' or 'statement of costs' which sets out their costs in the following form: page from form N260, to be found at https://assets.publishing.service.gov.uk/government/uploads/system/uploads/attachment_data/file/688587/n260-eng.pdf.

The judge will then review the figures and criticise them. It helps for the party paying to have reviewed the figures as well. Common complaints are: a) the hourly rate is too high, b) too many hours were spent on a particular activity, c) the work was done at too senior a level. A statement of costs should be filed at court and served on the other side at least 24 hours in advance of a hearing. It is sensible to review the other side's statement of costs before the hearing. Little time is given to cost assessment and so it is necessary to prepare the arguments in advance as a contingency. People often confuse the number of hours with the number of items on the template form. When correctly filled in, the first column should say the number of hours in the box, in order to multiply it by the hourly rate in the second column to achieve the amount claimed in the third column.

16.3 Fees of the Trustee in Bankruptcy or liquidator

This topic is relevant when a bankruptcy order is later appealed, rescinded, reviewed or annulled (see Chapter 15). This would include when the bankrupt actually has the assets to pay their creditors. As discussed in Chapter 3, it is sensible to pay the bankruptcy debt if at all possible. This is primarily in order to avoid the charges which this section describes. However, sometimes a bankrupt has more assets than they realised, for example because some property sold for a higher amount than expected. If the bankrupt does not have the assets to pay the creditors, then the bankrupt is unlikely to be concerned how much the Trustee in Bankruptcy charges: whether they charge a little or a lot will not affect their return, which is going to be nothing.

In these circumstances, the court has to decide who, if anyone, will be responsible for the fees of the Trustee in Bankruptcy. A former bankrupt has the right under rules 10.134 or 18.35 of The Insolvency (England and Wales) Rules 2016 to challenge the fees of the Trustee as being unfair. This process is described in Paragraph 9.2.2 and Box 27 on page 142.

This topic is also relevant to negotiating settlement with a creditor on the grounds that they would receive less in the bankruptcy or liquidation than they would if they settled. The Trustee or liquidator is likely to take a significant amount of the assets of the estate, which would take priority over a distribution to unsecured creditors.

The Trustee may be either the Official Receiver or a private Insolvency Practitioner. Either way, they will charge fees for their time running the estate of the bankrupt.

The Official Receiver has published their charges online (see https://www.gov. uk/government/news/changes-to-official-receivers-fees).

The key information is:

- There is a fixed single fee of £6,000 regardless of the role of the Official Receiver.

- Where the Official Receiver also sells assets, they will charge 15% of the amount received from the sale as a fee.

- Where the Official Receiver sets up an Income Payments Order (see Chapter 2) they will charge £150.

This applies whether the Official Receiver is a Trustee in Bankruptcy or liquidator of a company. The bottom line consequence is that if someone has assets of £20,000 after accounting for the costs of sale, then there will be at most £12,000 available for distribution to creditors in the bankruptcy, and this sum would be distributed pro rata to the bankrupt's creditors. It would not be worth spending a significant sum of money to present a bankruptcy petition when there are limited prospects of the debt being paid.

When it comes to private Insolvency Practitioners, there are two main methods of charging: either IPs charge per hour for their time or they charge as a percentage of the amount received from sales. The latter is more common, because a creditor is unlikely to be willing to 'throw good money after bad', and so pay for an IP to work when there is doubtful prospect of recovery. IPs are more accustomed to taking the risk of no recovery, particularly since if there is nothing to sell then it will not use up much of their time. The creditors are in charge of setting the fees of the Trustee in Bankruptcy, although in most cases they accept the rates of whichever IP they choose to instruct.

It can safely be assumed that a private Trustee in Bankruptcy will charge more than the Official Receiver does. If an IP is charging as a percentage of receipts, as a rule of thumb this will be around 25% of the estate. Part of the rationale for such a high charge is that a Trustee can be instructed to manage an estate, and then discover that the estate has no assets and so even the Trustee will make no recoveries. Trustees in Bankruptcy charge a higher amount when they can recover money to compensate for the cases when they lose out. Alternatively, if an IP is charging per hour it is common for them to charge between £250 and £450 per hour, depending on their experience and location within the country, with a lower sum for administrative work done by a more junior member of staff.

PART 5   LITIGATION

Chapter 17   Litigation tips for those with legal representation

This chapter gives tips to the reader who is able to afford representation about who to instruct, and how the reader can make the most out of their representation. For those unable to afford representation, see Chapter 18.

BOX 53:   LEGAL AID

Technically legal aid exists for bankruptcy cases when the individual's estate includes their home: see paragraph 33(2) of Schedule 1 to the Legal Aid, Sentencing and Punishment of Offenders Act 2012. This legal aid, in theory, should pay for the debtor to get legal representation at the bankruptcy and subsequent possession hearings. The reader may wonder why a homeowner would receive legal aid, but an individual unable to afford their own home would not.

However, due to stringent eligibility criteria, homeowners are also unlikely to receive legal aid. Where an individual has disposable capital of more than £8,000 or a monthly disposable income of more than £733, they are ineligible to receive legal aid for this debt claim.

In the event that an individual is eligible for legal aid, the following website enables individuals to find a solicitor who will work for legal aid rates for a bankruptcy case: https://find-legal-advice.justice.gov.uk/. Since the amount given for legal aid is approximately £180 as the 'Schedule Authorisation Standard Fee', it might be doubted whether any professional solicitor would be prepared to offer significant help even to an individual who did qualify, although non-profit-making bodies like local law centres might be prepared to do the work at a loss.

It is unclear from the Legal Aid Authority's statistics whether any individuals received legal aid in respect of a bankruptcy hearing in 2019.

The message of this chapter is that since lawyers are expensive and typically charge per hour, it is important to be savvy about the use of their time. After an initial meeting, which is frequently given for free, every minute is likely to be logged and charged for.

This chapter first discusses how and when to instruct a direct access barrister, a solicitor and other legal professionals (including professional McKenzie friends), and how to choose the right lawyer. It then gives advice on how to minimise the use of their time.

This chapter represents the author's personal opinion.

17.1 How to choose a lawyer

A potential client has two important choices to make. Firstly, they need to decide what kind of lawyer they wish to instruct. At present there are several different types, and from the perspective of a non-lawyer there is little difference between them. Secondly, they need to decide which lawyer to pick.

17.1.1 What kind of lawyer?

There is a difference between a barrister, a solicitor, a legal executive, a solicitor's agent and a McKenzie friend:

- Historically, all clients would consult a solicitor as a first step. They can be viewed as 'general practitioners' in the legal world, with a broad range of experience and so often less specialisation. Insolvency is not a topic all high street solicitors encounter, in contrast to 'non-contentious' matters which do not require going to court, like buying and selling property or writing wills. Some solicitors take an additional qualification which permits them to speak in the High Court, and they can describe themselves as 'solicitor-advocates'. All solicitors are technically able to appear in the County Court, although not many choose to do so unless they are qualified solicitor-advocates.

- Barristers typically specialise in litigation. Historically, they could not be instructed by members of the public. This has now changed and certain qualified 'direct access' barristers can be instructed by members of the public. However, many barristers (including the author) still do not take direct access work. This is because they prefer not to work directly with the client and would rather have a solicitor in between. The traditional explanation for this two stage system is that it allows the barrister to be more independent and objective, since they are further removed from the client's case. As a generalisation, direct access barristers can be at the less specialised end of the profession, at least when it comes to insolvency law.

- Legal executives are similar to solicitors, but there are more vocational entry criteria to becoming a legal executive. Legal executives usually specialise in one area of law, whereas solicitors typically have broader specialisms. It is relatively unusual to instruct a legal executive to deal with a bankruptcy case.

- Solicitors' agents (sometimes called 'County Court advocates') are typically individuals who have finished their legal studies, but have not yet qualified as lawyers because they have not completed the practical training. It is unclear precisely when a solicitors' agent is entitled to appear at a hearing.[11] In practice, solicitors' agents are instructed when the matter is routine and likely to be uncontested or uncontestable. It would be rare for a debtor to instruct a solicitor agent (via their solicitor) because they would only attend the hearing of an application or petition when there is a substantive dispute. Similarly, a creditor is unlikely to use a solicitors' agent if they think the matter will be disputed.

- McKenzie friends are not qualified lawyers and so they are not able to offer legal advice or conduct litigation by filing documents on behalf of the client – it may even be a mistake to describe them as 'lawyers'. The description McKenzie friends began as a free service, where a friend may want to assist another in court. They were given some recognition by judges in the family law case of *McKenzie v McKenzie* [1970] 3 WLR 472, which is how they got their name. Unfortunately the practice developed beyond free advice given by a friend. Non-qualified 'lawyers' offer their services as McKenzie friends for a fee. The fee is often low, occasionally as low as £30 an hour. In my opinion this is a problematic situation and I would not recommend anyone spends money on a McKenzie friend. It would be better to use a qualified lawyer's time judiciously and receive limited but high quality advice for a few hours than to spend the same amount and receive more but low quality advice.

In my opinion, the lawyer most parties need is someone who is familiar with bankruptcy law. As this book demonstrates, there are many rules and procedures which need to be followed. It is not a subject which lends itself to 'dabbling'.

17.1.2 How to find an appropriate solicitor

It is a mistake to rely on a solicitors' website because this can exaggerate the scope of work the solicitors do. Instead, clients should find a solicitor by going through one of the insolvency professional organisations. For example, a client should look for a solicitor who is a member of the Insolvency Lawyers

---

[11] *Those who are looking for more information may find the Bar Council's guidance useful: https://www.barcouncilethics.co.uk/wp-content/uploads/2017/10/Solicitors-Agents-Guidance-1-.pdf.*

Association: https://www.ilauk.com/membership/our-members or R3 ('the Association of Business Recovery Professionals') https://www.r3.org.uk/index.cfm?page=get-advice/find-a-practitioner. Note that many members of R3 will be IPs rather than lawyers.

Another technique would be to find a specialist barristers' chambers and call the clerks and ask for a recommended solicitors' firm in an area close to the debtor. The clerks may be able to recommend an appropriate firm, although they may do so on the loose expectation that the solicitors will return work to chambers. A potential supervisor of an IVA is also likely to be able to recommend appropriate solicitors.

17.1.3   How to find an appropriate direct access barrister

If a debtor instructs a solicitor, the solicitor is likely to be better placed to choose a barrister. This section provides guidance for how to find an appropriate direct access barrister.

- Barristers typically work in 'chambers'. This allows the more junior barristers to learn from the more senior barristers, since they interact and can ask each other for advice. Barristers who work in chambers of just one or two lack this interaction.

- It is easy to use the Bar Council's 'direct access portal' to find barristers: see https://www.directaccessportal.co.uk/search/1/barrister. However, avoid barristers who claim to specialise in too many fields: this means it is unlikely they spend much time doing bankruptcy work. For example, it is unusual for a bankruptcy specialist to do criminal law, family law, employment or personal injury law.

- Although the barrister needs to be familiar with the insolvency rules, there is little marginal benefit from having many years experience. For example, unless the case has unusual complexity – which can perhaps be estimated by seeing whether by applying the rules in this book you can predict the answer – a barrister of ten years' call is not necessarily better than one of five years' call. However, as a rule of thumb it may be sensible to instruct a barrister within five years' call of the barrister on the opposing side, if this is known.

Outside of the major cities, it is difficult to find a specialist barrister and particularly one who takes direct access clients. It may be worth paying for a barrister to travel to the hearing, given that a few hours' of travel time is likely to be small compared to the total preparation time the barrister will take for the hearing. Note also that even if a bankruptcy petition is originally listed to be in a County Court near to the debtor, if it is opposed it can only be heard in certain specialist courts (see Chapter 5). These tend to be in areas where there is more legal expertise.

BOX 54:   WORD OF MOUTH

A common way of finding a lawyer is word of mouth. Be aware that a lawyer who dealt brilliantly with a friend's case might have no insolvency experience whatsoever. The best lawyers will not accept a case outside of their specialism. If you prefer to choose a lawyer based on word of mouth, then try to find a contact in a similar position to you, who either had a company go insolvent or themselves were in a bankruptcy situation.

17.2 How to best use a lawyer

A potential client is in a difficult position. A lawyer typically knows more about the law than they do. It is not easy to give the lawyer informed instructions about how they should use their time. Instead, typically lawyers make recommendations to the clients about what they should do, and the clients will be expected to either approve or disapprove of their plan. Lawyers could be said to have a conflict of interest because the more work they recommend, the more hours they will be able to charge for.

If the budget is no problem, then it is better to ask the lawyer to do all of the work. It is obvious to the opposing side and to the judge when a document has been prepared by a professional and when it has been drafted by a layman. The judge will do their best not to hold lack of representation against a party, and particularly a debtor or bankrupt who (by definition) has limited resources. However, generally a professional will be more able to persuade the judge of their client's case than their client themselves. This is partly because this is the full-time role of a lawyer, and so they are experienced. It is also because it is difficult to maintain the objective stance needed to persuade a judge when addressing one's own personal situation. Often a litigant in person will have a good point, but they present it badly because they are overly passionate, or unable to distinguish between the important and unimportant features of their case. This is especially likely to happen when a debtor faces a possible bankruptcy order: this is naturally an emotional area, but an emotional presentation of a case is rarely persuasive. Judges are human, but they also have to apply the law.

For a client with a limited budget, it is helpful to be clear about what work the lawyer is meant to do, and what work the client is willing to do themselves. This allows the client some control over what they spend their resources on. The client should discuss their objectives with the lawyer early in the case – typically the objective is either to dismiss a bankruptcy petition or to delay it as long as possible in the hope of achieving a settlement or for business to pick up. This will determine the next few stages of a bankruptcy case. The lawyer and the client can then discuss how the future work will be divided. A lawyer can fairly say that they are not prepared to work on a piecemeal basis if this means they would be unable to perform their role competently. This is particularly likely if the lawyer's work will be filed in court and so there would be a reputational impact of producing sub-standard work.

Although every case is different, the following list discusses what work is more or less suitable for a lawyer to do:

1. **Advising on whether to go bankrupt**. The main factors are discussed in Chapter 3. It can be very expensive to contest a bankruptcy petition inappropriately. In the event that a debtor is unsure, it is worth paying for robust advice.

2. **Settlement offers**. When a debtor offers to pay a creditor, it is more credible when that offer is relayed via a solicitor. This involves minimal time by the lawyers, since they simply have to rephrase an offer made by their client and type it onto paper with a written letterhead.

3. **Gathering evidence**. This is one important area where a proactive client can save the lawyer's time. Debtors commonly require evidence to prove, for example, that a debt is disputed. Sending a lawyer a disorganised file of papers, or sending documents one by one, will inevitably increase the amount of time it takes for the lawyer to process the information and turn it into a usable format. A non-lawyer can a) organise papers in chronological order; b) write a table with a column for the name of the document, a column that gives a brief description or summary, and a column which gives it the date it was written; c) produce clean machine-readable scans, or give the originals in a chronologically organised file; d) collate all the emails between the relevant people into one place; and e) summarise the key events in a table in chronological order. If in doubt, however, it is better to send the lawyer more information than less, since lawyers are typically quick at distinguishing relevant from irrelevant information.

4. **Producing documents**. Most lawyers will understand if the client prefers to draft their own documents, and then ask the lawyer to spend a certain number of hours improving it. This is unlikely to lead to as good a result as if the lawyer had drafted it from scratch, but often that is not possible given the budget. This also applies for correspondence with the other side: it may be quicker for the debtor to write a first draft and for the lawyer to tidy it up rather than the lawyer to write a draft, send it to their client for comments,

respond to these comments and send on to the other side. Lawyers are, however, more sensitive about what goes on their professional letterhead if it is going to be seen externally and in particular by a judge.

5. **Representation at hearings**. Once the papers are prepared, it is relatively easy to represent oneself at a hearing. However, it is an intimidating situation, and so there is a degree of personal preference involved in the decision of whether or not to instruct a barrister to appear at the hearing. My advice would be not to instruct a barrister if the hearing is likely to be simple, such as an agreed adjournment or an obviously disputed debt. If the hearing is likely to be complicated and winnable (e.g. there is only a weak argument that the debt is not due, or that there had been a serious procedural error), it is worth instructing a barrister. The barrister would hopefully be able to give the argument more credence than the lay client could. If the client is very likely to lose a hearing, it is again better not to instruct a barrister. If the aim of a short hearing is to request a longer hearing (which would inevitably be listed further into the future), a professional barrister is more likely to be able to explain why a case is complex and requires a longer listing time.

BOX 55:   HEARINGS WHERE THE PARTIES HAVE AGREED WHAT THE OUTCOME SHOULD BE

It is common for matters to be agreed in advance of the hearing. This agreement should be recorded in writing so there is no scope of disagreement. Since insolvency petitions are a class remedy, and so in theory other creditors may wish to attend and will be unaware of the agreement, the court is less inclined than in other areas of law to make decisions without a hearing.

Although it is impossible to be sure that the other side will not break a promise to have an agreed adjournment (or an agreed withdrawal of the petition), the consequences of a party agreeing to do something, and breaking that promise before the court are extremely serious. The decision will have been obtained fraudulently and is liable to be overturned. A barrister will probably be in breach of their professional ethical code if they ask the court for a certain outcome knowing that the parties had agreed a different outcome and in reliance on that agreement the other side had not attended. The court will have little hesitation in ordering a stay, or a review or appeal, if it is satisfied that this is what happened. The deceitful party will be liable to face an indemnity costs award, and a petition might be dismissed as an abuse of process. However, before a debtor takes a decision not to attend or send representation, it is important to be sure that the outcome has been clearly and unambiguously agreed.

If someone instructs a solicitor and they appear to be running out of funds, the solicitor should be in a position to help the client get further free ('pro bono') legal advice, although it certainly cannot be guaranteed. This might include a referral of the case to the charity 'Advocate' which can offer free representation by barristers or to the pro bono department of another law firm. If someone can only afford a few hours of a solicitor's time and the case is meritorious – i.e. that based on the principles in this book, the petition should be dismissed – the best use of that money might be to ask them to prepare the papers for onward referral to a pro bono charity. An unmeritorious case is unlikely to receive pro bono advice. However, legal advice charities typically take a generous approach to their cases and prefer not to judge against the potential client if they can avoid it. The charity Advocate sometimes takes on cases in order to give important advice to the client that they have a weak case, and it would be in their interests to stop litigating.

Chapter 18   Representing yourself

If a debtor is content to go bankrupt, there is no need to attend the final hearing. There is no need to even respond to any letters from the petitioning creditor, or notices of the hearing sent by the court (although it is important to respond to the Trustee in Bankruptcy after the bankruptcy order is made).

However, if the debtor does not want to go bankrupt, it will be important for them or their legal representative to attend the hearing unless the outcome of the hearing is agreed. The court will assume that non-attendance is a sign of consent. It may be useful to write to the other side, and it is very likely to be helpful to prepare written materials to give to the court in order to persuade the judge of whatever outcome is desired.

This chapter gives advice to a debtor on writing to a petitioning creditor, written documents for court and how and what to say in court. It is written for debtors facing a bankruptcy petition, but the same principles apply for a company facing a winding up petition.

18.1 Writing to the petitioning creditor

There are four broad purposes of writing to the petitioning creditor:

- In order to reach an agreement without requiring the court to make a decision.

- In order to comply with a court rule, which would include the rule that a debtor needs to send notice of their opposition to a bankruptcy petition (see Chapter 5).

- In order to send ('serve') applications or the evidence which the debtor wants to use in an upcoming hearing.

- As part of the 'pre-action protocol' in advance of making an application to court.

Debtors are expected to be upfront about their position and the evidence they rely on, but in practice the court will be very reluctant not to admit evidence before it. In order to prevent being ambushed at the last minute, the creditor may ask the court to adjourn the hearing, and seek the costs of the failed hearing to be paid by the debtor. Instead of agreeing to an adjournment, the creditor might try to persuade the court not to admit late evidence, or suggest the hearing goes ahead anyway.

It follows that it is sensible to correspond with the other side when:

1. The debtor is looking to settle the case, and so requires the consent of the petitioning creditor. The two most common examples are when the debtor would prefer to sign an IVA to avoid being made bankrupt and when the debtor seeks the agreement of the creditor to adjourn a particular hearing; or

2. The debtor is able to pay the creditor, but there is still a dispute at the hearing. This primarily would happen when the debtor disputes that the debt is owed to the creditor.

18.1.1   Settlement

In order to write effective settlement letters, it is worth considering that:

*   The aim of the letter is to persuade the creditor to agree to something that they otherwise would not have wanted to do. There is nothing to be gained by criticising them for their many faults, because it is unlikely that they will be minded to agree a compromise if they feel challenged. All most creditors want is for their debt to be paid.

*   In order to persuade the creditor, it is best to explain why the debtor's proposal is in the interests of the creditor after all. If an IVA is proposed, this means explaining why the creditor would receive more money through agreeing to the IVA. If a delay is proposed, this means demonstrating that it is likely that, with a further delay, the debtor will have more access to funds and will therefore be able to pay the debt.

*   This may require evidence. There is no reason why a settlement offer cannot contain attachments which show, for example, an Insolvency Practitioner's estimate of a likely distribution upon a bankruptcy order being made.

*   It helps if the debtor can credibly say that they would prefer to spend their money on legal fees contesting the bankruptcy petition than give it to the creditors. This would reduce the likely return a creditor would receive, and so they would be more likely to agree to a settlement.

*   In general, a creditor is likely to lose money through litigation. This is because

i) not all their costs can be recovered, and ii) the best the creditor will receive is a costs award in their favour and (other than petition costs), this will rank them as an unsecured creditor and so they will only receive a fraction of their funds back in the final distribution. The most common strategy for settlement is to show the creditor that it is cost-effective to settle. This can be done by estimating the creditor's costs of their proposed approach, and explaining why those costs will not be recovered.

- There are rules which prevent settlement offers being shown to the court. This is known as 'without prejudice privilege'. It applies to both the creditor and the debtor, and so even if the creditor admits something in the context of a settlement letter, the debtor cannot then show that letter to the court. It can be convenient to show the judge settlement correspondence not for the actual hearing, but to demonstrate that one party acted unreasonably and so the judge should make a particular cost award. In order to present this correspondence, the correspondence must be 'without prejudice save as to costs', i.e. it is privileged for the main part of the hearing, but it is not privileged for a decision on costs which happens at the end. It is routine to include the words "without prejudice save as to costs" on all correspondence which aims at settling a dispute, even if the dispute is a minor one. It may be tempting to break this rule if the creditor makes a concession in 'without prejudice' correspondence which supports the debtor's case. However, judges are used to ignoring evidence which they were not meant to see, and they are likely to view a deliberate breach of the 'without prejudice' rule as the sort of conduct which justifies indemnity costs (see Chapter 16).

- The opposite of a 'without prejudice' offer is an open offer, which is usually marked as 'open' in order to signal that the party making the offer intends to rely on the letter before the judge making the decision. Do not make any admissions in an 'open' letter which you might regret later on. In a 'without prejudice' letter it may be sensible to use conciliatory language like "*Although I recognise this argument may not succeed…*" in order to appear reasonable. However, if it is used in open correspondence the opposing side can read it out to the judge and submit that even the debtor does not believe their own case. Without prejudice privilege applies whenever someone is trying to settle a dispute, unless it is clear that they intend for it to be 'open'. However, it does not necessarily cover an admission of liability or fault, and so it is still worth being cautious in 'without prejudice' letters.

- Even in a 'without prejudice' letter, some lawyers think it is sensible to write strongly worded responses. These letters can exaggerate the strengths of their client's case: they are not written to give a neutral assessment. A debtor should not be shocked by strong wording in a letter from the other side and should try not to be offended by it. They should expect to be told that arguments they think are persuasive are in fact meritless. This argumentative language is even more common in open prejudice where the lawyers think it is possible that the court will see the correspondence. There is nothing to be gained by being rude in correspondence. However, there is also no point complaining about a lawyer defending their own client's case, unless it strays into abuse. Unless the lawyer's response contains explicit insults, racist language or swear words (which is highly unlikely), there is not likely to be any grounds to complain.

- On a related note, just because a lawyer writes to say that a case is very strong and bound to succeed does not mean that their client is not prepared to settle. This could be because it is not worth fighting even a strong case; but it could also be because the case is not as strong as the lawyers say it is, and they know it. There is no penalty for exaggerating the prospects of success to the other side.

There is an example settlement letter in Annex 1.

18.1.2 Disputed debt

The reason it is particularly important to write to the petitioning creditor if the debt is disputed is because the court might find that a debtor acted unreasonably by not sharing that fact and award the costs of a hearing against the debtor even if the debtor subsequently succeeds in dismissing the petition. As set out in Chapter 16, this can be a substantial sum of money. Assuming the debt is genuinely disputed, it is relatively easy for the debtor to ask the court to dismiss the petition: as set out in Chapter 4, the test is only that there is some real prospect that the debtor will be able to show that the money is not owing. It follows that the debtor is no worse off by sharing this evidence early. At best, a creditor might even agree to withdraw the petition.

18.1.3 Sending documents

Unless a person is ordered to send something by post, it is enough to send the other side an email with the document as an attachment. The email should say, at a minimum, what the documents are and why they are sent. An email saying: "*Please find attached documents which I will rely on in the upcoming hearing*" will be enough.

BOX 56:   WHO TO CONTACT

If the other side is represented by a lawyer, there is a rule which says that all letters should be sent to their lawyers rather than to the individual directly. This can be frustrating, because often two individuals who know each other will be able to reach an amicable compromise; but if all the letters are sent via lawyers then this becomes more difficult. One solution is to suggest (via the lawyers) a face-to-face meeting between the debtor and creditor or a telephone conversation. If the debtor has no lawyer it is fair to suggest that the creditor speak on a 'without lawyers' basis as well. However, a creditor may wish to have their lawyer present as a means of protecting themselves (or simply feeling important) and there is little that a debtor can do.

On the other hand, this is a rule which can be broken with relatively little consequence, provided it is only broken once or twice. It may be helpful to let a mutual contact know that the debtor wants to speak, and to ask them to contact the creditor directly. The worst that can happen, at least in the short term, is a cross letter from the creditor's solicitors reminding the debtor of this rule. If, however, after being warned several times about the rule the debtor continues to flout it, it might be a matter relevant to an application for indemnity costs. The court is likely to sympathise with an unrepresented party and see the sense in a meeting without lawyers; and similarly the court is likely to look kindly on all genuine attempts to settle without going to court.

18.1.4 'Pre-action' correspondence

The court will expect all parties to give notice before they start court proceedings as part of the 'pre-action protocol'. The pre-action protocol is set out at http://www.justice.gov.uk/courts/procedure-rules/civil/rules/pd_pre-action_conduct.

This is an opportunity for the other side to change their position before the court gets involved. If the debtor has a strong case it is usually sensible to be as upfront as possible about why. A debtor's failure to follow the pre-action protocol will provide the creditor with an argument when it comes to costs: they should not be liable for the debtor's costs due to their breach of the protocol, causing excess costs to be incurred. The pre-action protocol is of less importance for applications to set aside a statutory demand, where the debtor is under time pressure to make the application within 18 days. However, for applications against the Trustee in Bankruptcy, following the pre-action protocol is an indication that the bankrupt has a credible and respectable case.

> **BOX 57:   USING THE CREDITOR'S RESOURCES WISELY**
>
> A savvy debtor with limited legal representation can ask the other side's lawyers to perform certain administrative or agreed tasks.
>
> If the debtor is having difficulty finding a particular legal case, for example because it is not available on a website like Bailii (https://www.bailii.org/), then it is possible to ask the other side to send a copy. The creditor might refuse, but the debtor will then be able to say to the court that they would have liked to refer to a particular case, but for the creditor's refusal. Since it will cost the creditor almost nothing to share the authority, and benefit both the debtor and the court, the court is likely to disapprove of the creditor being unhelpful. This will not affect the merits of the case, but it is a point which goes to costs and potentially also to an adjournment.

18.2 Written documents for the court

At different stages, a debtor may need to produce the following documents:

1. An application to set aside a statutory demand.

2. An application to un-freeze a bank account (an application for a 'validation order').

3. A notice of opposition.

4. A witness statement and evidence to oppose the bankruptcy petition.

5. A summary of the points they intend to make at a hearing (a 'skeleton argument').

6. A notice of appeal, including grounds of appeal.

Examples of all these documents are in Annex 1.

General writing tips for the court are as follows:

1. Use short numbered paragraphs. This is a good way of structuring what the document is trying to say. Try to keep to at most one argument per paragraph, or use sub-paragraphs if there are lots of points. A common mistake by non-lawyers is to write one very long paragraph rather than many short ones. This makes it difficult to understand what the person's point is. A

paragraph should usually have between two and eight sentences.

2.   Make sure the document has a beginning, a middle and an end. The beginning will usually set out the facts as briefly as possible, say what the debtor is seeking, and summarise the rest of the case. The middle will normally set out a) any relevant legal test; b) the facts as applied by this test. The ending can be brief, and simply repeat what the debtor wants the judge to do.

3.   If it is possible, type up the document. Use 'justified' text – on Microsoft Word this is achieved by clicking on the icon which normally makes the text begin on the left hand side, middle or right hand side of the page; but use the right-most box which has four lines of the same size. Use 1.5 line spacing – on Microsoft Word, this is achieved by highlighting all the text (ctrl A) and then pressing ctrl and the number 5 at the same time. Use the Arial or Times New Roman font, size 11 or 12. These minor formatting points make the document look more credible.

4.   Describe the events chronologically. A case is likely to have many facts, and in order to persuade a judge it is important that they understand the full picture. This can only be achieved if the facts are presented in a logical manner. The easiest way to do this is chronological, because the judge will be able to see how the events unfolded.

5.   Focus on the facts of the case. The court will be familiar with the law, and so it will be able to piece together the legally correct conclusion once it understands what the facts are. It is important for the author to understand the law in order to know what facts need to be presented, but it is a waste of space to quote long sections of familiar law.

6.   Make sure that there are no bare denials or assertions of fact or law: instead, give reasons why something is the case. Rather than say "X is wrong", say "X is wrong because...".

7.   Use neutral language. The judge will decide whether something is 'outrageous', 'back-stabbing', 'unfair' or any other adjective. For example, it is more persuasive to say that "X promised that he would do A, but he then did B" than to say "X lied". This is because the judge will be able to put two and two together, and by presenting the facts in anything but a neutral manner, the debtor will look biased, aggressive and unreliable. It is very hard to be neutral about one's own case: if it is possible, ask someone unconnected to the facts to review the document from the perspective of a judge. This rule can be relaxed slightly when speaking before the judge.

8.   It is also a mistake to over-state how strong a case is. A judge will not believe that a case should succeed simply on the say-so of the person presenting

it. However, if a particular point is difficult, it is better to acknowledge this orally rather than in writing, because the other side will be better able to exploit the acknowledgment.

9. In an application document, say as little as possible. A few sentences can set out what the application is about. Keep the main material about the facts and why the application should succeed to an accompanying witness statement.

10. Assume the judge knows the law, but nothing else. It will be necessary to explain technical language. If, for example, the dispute relates to the supply of some service, it will be necessary to use simple everyday language to explain what each person actually did.

It is important that a document contains no mistakes, and tells the truth without being misleading or exaggerating. Once it has been sent to the other side, they may refer to it as the dispute progresses. Written documents are opportunities to tell the court the debtor's version of events, but they are also ways in which the debtor can trip up due to admitting something inadvertently or exposing the weakness in a case.

BOX 58:   MAKING APPLICATIONS

This book often refers to making an application, for example, to set aside a statutory demand, to challenge a decision of a Trustee or to restrain presentation of a winding up petition. This usually means completing the insolvency application notice form IAA (see Annex 1 for an example), signing it and sending a copy to the appropriate court by email. The applicant usually includes a witness statement which provides evidence in support of the application. The court office will then require a fee to be paid, unless the applicant has 'help with fees' (see Box 48 on page 214). Most fees cannot be paid online by litigants in person, and instead are usually paid by cheque. The court will stamp ('seal') the application, and either send ('serve') it to the respondent themselves or send it back to the applicant to serve.

18.3 Skeleton arguments

A skeleton argument is a summary of the arguments a party intends to make before the judge. They are expected for every substantial hearing, which is in practice every hearing which lasts more than 15 minutes. Good advice on how to prepare a skeleton argument can be found at https://www.biicl.org/files/2223_ skeleton_arguments_guide.pdf.

There is a difference between a witness statement and a skeleton argument. A witness statement is where someone gives evidence about what they saw, did or heard. It will include documents relevant to what happened at the time as an exhibit, i.e. in an annex at the back. The witness statement tells the story of what happened which gave rise to the dispute. A skeleton argument puts this into the legal framework and explains to the judge why they should make a certain decision as a consequence.

BOX 59:   COURT BUNDLE

The default rule is that the party who is making an application to the court has to prepare the 'court bundle', i.e. a paginated file with the application, witness statements and supporting evidence. However, if one side is represented and the other is not, the court is likely to expect the represented side to prepare the bundle even if they are the defendant/respondent. This is particularly true if the hearing will be remote, and so it will be more likely to use a digital hearing bundle.

It is best to agree a time with the other side to email one another ('exchange') the skeleton arguments. Email the skeleton argument and evidence to the court at least three days in advance, but bring along several additional copies since you should be prepared for the papers to be lost in transmission. The email address can be found online at https://courttribunalfinder.service.gov.uk/ courts/. Find the correct court, and the email address is likely to begin with either 'Applications' or 'Enquiries'. The safest thing to do is to email both. If the court replies using a particular email address, or recommends you use one, then follow that advice.

BOX 60:   SENDING DOCUMENTS TO COURT

The County Court email may have an automatic reply, but there is no guarantee that anything sent to court will actually be received by the judge in time for the hearing. Always bring (at least) two spare copies of whatever you would like the judge to see – one for the judge, and one for the other side. Unfortunately the court administration staff are overwhelmed with work and under-resourced. Hand any material to the ushers who are at the registration desk at the front of the court building. Alternatively, give the material to the court clerk inside the court room at the start of the hearing. If the judge has time, they will send the parties away in order to read it in advance.

18.4 Appearing in court

If a person has never been in a court room before, it can be daunting to walk in for the first time. It is sensible to go to a court in advance, to watch someone else's hearing and to see what actually happens. Unsurprisingly, it is not like the scenes on television.

Most court hearings are open to the public. Nonetheless it is sensible to ask an usher (a member of the court staff) before walking in. It is also sensible to ask the usher what kind of case the hearing is. There is some value in watching a hearing which is not bankruptcy-related, because the key features are all the same. However, family cases and criminal cases are very distinct and are more likely to mislead than to be useful.

Upon entering a court building for your own hearing, the first thing someone should do is to notify the usher that they have arrived. The usher will mark this down and ensure that the hearing does not start without the person present. The usher is likely to be the first member of the court staff someone would see immediately after security, but in the case of doubt ask the security guard where the ushers are. Give the usher a copy of your skeleton argument, even if it has been sent to the court already. The second thing to do is to find the list of cases for that day, which will be a series of A4 pieces of paper attached to the wall or on the ushers' desk. Bankruptcy cases are typically listed by reference to the surname of the debtor and corporate insolvency cases are listed by the name of the company.

The set up of a court room is always the same: at the front will sit the judge on a slightly raised platform. The judge will enter from their own door at the back of the room, but they may be sitting down before or after the debtor's own case is called. In front of the judge will be a desk for the judge's usher. To one side is likely to be a desk where a witness will sit, probably with a Bible for taking oaths. In front of that will be two desks, and the usher is likely to say which one is for the debtor and which for the creditor. If they do not, typically the applicant/petitioner sits on the left facing the judge and the respondent/debtor on the right, but in general there is no wrong desk to choose. These desks are for the creditor and debtor, with a barrister or solicitor if they have instructed one. At the very back of the court room there will be some additional chairs for members of the public.

18.4.1 Cross-examination

Cross-examination is where a witness is asked questions about their evidence by the other side of a dispute. It is not very common to have live witness evidence in a bankruptcy hearing and so there is not often cross-examination of witnesses. This is because, in practice, most evidence will be written down on paper. If the judge needs to decide between two alternative cases based on witnesses, it is likely that the debt is disputed and so the bankruptcy petition will be dismissed. It is theoretically possible to have an argument between witnesses about some aspect of the bankruptcy process, for example, whether an individual was personally served. In practice this is rare. This means that the cross-examination which is likely to be a large part of most non-bankruptcy cases does not often happen. Most of the time the parties simply show the judge pieces of paper, and explain why the paper means the petition should/should not be dismissed.

BOX 61: REMOTE HEARINGS

At the time of writing this book, most court hearings have taken place either online or by telephone since the beginning of the coronavirus pandemic in March 2020. This includes bankruptcy hearings: para 4 of the pandemic-related Temporary Insolvency PD (October 2020) says that all bankruptcy petitions (from 1 October 2020) must be listed as remote hearings if they are in the Insolvency and Companies Court list in the High Court in London.

It is the decision of the judge whether to have the hearing in-person or remotely. If the judge prefers a remote hearing, the judge will decide whether it be by a video-conferencing platform like Skype or Microsoft Teams, or whether by telephone. This situation looks likely to continue until the end of the pandemic, and possibly beyond. A party cannot insist that the hearing takes place in person, even if they are a litigant in person. The court will say what format the hearing will be in the 'notice of hearing' which is sent to all parties.

A remote hearing offers disadvantages to both sides: for example, the lack of face-to-face contact makes it difficult to read the judge's expression; there is no easy way of handing up pieces of paper to the judge; and there are no conversations between the parties before the hearing to try to agree matters by consent. However, litigants in person are likely to be particularly disadvantaged by having a remote hearing because it adds another obstacle to someone unfamiliar with the court process.

Resolution, a family law organisation, has guidance for litigants in person on the technical details of remote hearings which applies to insolvency law hearings as well: https://resolution.org.uk/looking-for-help/splitting-up/your-process-options-for-divorce-and-dissolution/representing-yourself-in-court-as-a-litigant-in-person/guidance-for-litigants-in-person-on-remote-hearings-in-the-family-court/.

18.4.2 Addressing the court

It is useful to remember when speaking to the judge:

- District Judges are called 'Sir' or 'Madam', Circuit Judges are called 'Your Honour', Insolvency and Companies Court Judges are called 'Judge' and High Court Judges are 'My Lord' or 'My Lady'. It may be simpler to politely say 'you'.

- Never speak when the judge is speaking. Try not to interrupt your opponent: this will only annoy the judge. If there is something important they got wrong, save it for a reply. This is true for all hearings, but particularly so for remote hearings where it is impossible to hear two people talk at once.

- If the hearing will not be long enough to properly explain your case, say so in advance and explain why. A judge will expect to be able to hear the full case in the time slot provided, but they will understand if that is unlikely.

- Make it clear what you want from the judge: an adjournment, dismissal of the petition, or whatever. Say this at the beginning and at the end of your time.

- Ask the judge if they have read your skeleton argument. If they have, there is no point in reading it out word for word. However, it would be sensible to summarise the key points: the judge cannot be expected to remember all of it.

- It is very difficult to respond to the other side there and then. This is not strictly necessary, and so it may be better to use the time to present your own case rather than respond to the other side.

- The judge may ask a question. Try to answer it immediately, rather than putting it off until later. If you do not know the answer, say so.

- Stay calm and neutral. Nothing is gained by shouting, or getting upset. If you find this difficult, then try to write down everything you think the judge should know in advance, and then ask the judge to read the submissions. Explain that you are not confident speaking but that you would be happy to answer any questions the judge has.

- The judge should be experienced in dealing with people who are not lawyers. If you do not understand something, ask what it means and the judge should be able to explain.

- Time in the court room moves quickly. Use it wisely. This can only be done if you prepare what you are going to say in advance. It is perfectly acceptable to read out a prepared speech, although it is more engaging to speak naturally rather than read.

- It is acceptable to ask the judge whether they have any questions. This is not usually done by professional lawyers, but it can be helpful when the judge is hearing from a litigant in person who might not have explained their case very well.

BOX 62:   WHAT SHOULD I WEAR?

Wear something respectful but comfortable. Lawyers wear suits most days, but judges are aware that many people do not wear suits in their everyday lives. There is no point spending money buying a new outfit for court. Wear the smartest outfit in your wardrobe. There is no requirement for men to wear ties, but it is common. Women will often wear something neutral and formal. Unlike on television, barristers will be wearing suits rather than wigs and gowns, unless it is a winding up hearing for a company (see Chapter 13) or a director's disqualification hearing (see Chapter 14). The judge may be wearing a black robe, but may also be in a suit, depending on their preference.

18.4.3 Order of proceedings

The first thing the judge is likely to do is to confirm who the parties are, and who represents them. After that, the order of speaking is as follows:

- First the applicant begins. If this is a hearing of a bankruptcy petition, it will be the creditor presenting the petition. If it is an application to set aside a statutory demand, it will be the debtor presenting their application.

- Afterwards, the other side will respond; and the first side will have the right of reply.

- The judge will make their decision, which is typically read out as an 'oral' or 'ex tempore'[12] judgment.

- Next, the winning side will ask for their costs and the judge will make a decision on this request.

- Finally, if the losing party feels the decision was wrong for some appealable reason (see Chapter 15), they will ask for permission to appeal.

---

[12] *This Latin phrase means 'read out' and is pronounced 'ex temp-or-ree'. Most legal Latin has been phased out but unfortunately this term remains common.*

PART 6   ANNEXES

Annex 1   Model Documents

This section contains examples of:

a)   A letter of settlement.

b)   An application to set aside a statutory demand.

c)   Notice of opposition to a bankruptcy petition.

d)   An application for a validation order to unfreeze a bank account.

e)   Statement of costs.

f)   A skeleton argument opposing the making of a bankruptcy order.

g)   Grounds of appeal.

> ## BOX 63:   HOW TO USE THESE DOCUMENTS
>
> These are examples of what a sensible document might look like. The information is fictional, and illustrates the rules set out in the main text of this book. However, the documents are properly formatted and have an appropriate structure and tone. There is no one correct way to write a document for the court, but there are more ways of writing documents badly than correctly. See Chapter 18 for general advice on drafting.

Letter of settlement

[Address of the creditor's solicitors]

Without prejudice save as to costs

18 October 2021

Dear Sir or Madam,

OFFER OF SETTLEMENT

I am writing in response to the bankruptcy petition which I received on 2 September 2021. I will contest the petition for reasons I will set out in the Notice of Opposition in due course.

However, you should know that even if the petition was not opposed, I am not able to pay your client the demanded sum of £14,000. I currently have £400 in my bank account. I have a large mortgage remaining over my house and my car is eight years old. I estimate that at most my total assets are worth £40,000. I attach a recent statement from my mortgage provider and my bank account to confirm this. If I were to be made bankrupt, this would be divided between all my creditors, which total £60,000. After deducting the costs of the bankruptcy (which will be strongly contested), there will be less than £20,000 in my estate. The Official Receiver would then charge a £6,000 fee for the administration of the estate not to mention a further 15% of all the assets recovered. Assuming the full amount can be realised, then the total amount which will be distributed will be roughly £10,000. Of this, your client would be likely to receive less than £4,000 and is likely to have spent more than that on unrecoverable legal fees. If your client continues to present the bankruptcy petition he is likely to be throwing good money after bad, because he will incur significant legal costs and face very low recovery in the bankruptcy.

[The best prospect of your client recovering the debt is to agree to me repaying him over 36 months at the rate of £300 per month. Although there is no guarantee, I expect to earn around £1,500 a month for the next few months; and after deducting my own personal expenditure and repayments to my other creditors, £300 per month is the most I can afford. It is in your client's best interests for me to be able to focus on my work because that makes it most likely that he will be repaid.]

OR

[The best prospect of your client recovering the debt is to agree to me repaying him in 6 months' time. Although there is no guarantee, I expect to earn around

£30,000 within the next few months; as I continue to trade profitably; and other debts are in turn paid to me. I will also explore the possibility of obtaining external financing from other sources. It is in your client's best interests for me to be able to focus on my work because that makes it most likely that he will be repaid.]

OR

[I am currently exploring the possibility of an Individual Voluntary Arrangement with Rose White, a qualified debt counsellor who volunteers at Citizens Advice in Shrewsbury. Although the details remain to be agreed, one possibility would be that my parents would agree to give £5,000 to my IVA Supervisor to repay my creditors. In return, the creditors would accept a 75% reduction of the debt. The Supervisor's fees would be £1,000, including VAT. The Supervisor would then distribute £4,000 to the creditors immediately, and I would be in a position to repay £500 every two months to my creditors beginning in six months' time for the next year. Overall my creditors would receive £8,000, i.e. approximately 13p in the pound. Your client would receive £2,400. This is a better outcome than if he continues to petition for my bankruptcy, where, as I have explained above, he is unlikely to receive anything at all after his legal costs. Since your client holds approximately 23% of the votes he does not have a blocking share in the IVA but his support would be useful. Would your client, in principle, be in favour of such a scheme? If so I will tell Rose White and I will make further enquiries about the IVA. If you would like to contact Ms White directly, her email address is Rose. White@ShrewsburyCAB.org.uk.

I am contacting the other creditors at the same time to seek their 'in principle' approval. I anticipate that it will take a further twelve weeks for me to obtain this and to instruct an IVA who will be in touch in due course with the full agreement.]

I attach a copy of my bank statement and details of my other creditors so that your client can verify the matters in this letter.

Please confirm that your client consents to this arrangement and that he intends to *[withdraw or adjourn]* the bankruptcy petition. If he does so before 4pm on *[the date in two weeks' time]* I will not need to instruct solicitors. This will only further reduce the money in my estate; and so reduce your client's prospect of recovery. I am aware of the possibility of spending my remaining assets on legal fees to contest the bankruptcy petition. It is not in either parties' interest to bring this petition. I would prefer to use the money to repay my creditors rather than contest a petition which I consider unjust.

Yours faithfully,
[Debtor]

Comment

This type of letter is suitable when the debtor has several creditors and not many assets with which to repay. If the numbers are appropriate, a creditor would be likely to withdraw the petition. The third option offers an IVA as described in Chapter 1.

Although there is some room for massaging the figures, in practice a creditor is likely to ask for evidence before believing the debtor. It follows that it is a mistake to underestimate the amount of money the debtor has in their estate; or to overestimate the total debts to make the particular creditor look smaller than they really are. By presenting the evidence upfront, the debtor will appear more trustworthy. Since the letter is being sent 'without prejudice', the attachments are also sent 'without prejudice' and the recipient cannot rely on them in court unless a) the sender discloses them in open correspondence; b) the court orders their disclosure; or c) some exception to the without prejudice rule applies. By exaggerating, the debtor will appear to be hiding something, and the creditor may not trust the evidence provided when it is true.

Notice how the costs of bankruptcy can make it unprofitable to make someone bankrupt even if they have assets of as much as £40,000 and the debt owed to the creditor is £14,000. The debtor would have been in an even stronger position if this argument was made when opposing a statutory demand, because the letter could add that, even if the application were to be dismissed, the creditor's costs would not take priority over the debtor's other costs, and so only a small proportion would be repaid.

This letter does not disclose why the bankruptcy petition will be opposed. This is to keep the debtor's options open for opposition. If there are strong reasons for dismissing the petition it would be sensible to include them. However where, as here, an individual might be able to instruct solicitors, it is best not to disclose the grounds of opposition until they are considered by a professional in case the reasons are changed.

Application to set aside a statutory demand on the grounds that the debt is disputed

There are two parts of an application: the completed application form and the supporting witness statement. This application is to set aside a statutory demand, but it applies for all insolvency proceedings.

Form IAA
Rule 1.35

Insolvency Act Application Notice

See Form IAA-N for guidance notes on how to complete this Form IAA

Insert case number if the court has assigned one

Case No:
[Leave blank]

Delete/complete as necessary:

IN THE COUNTY COURT AT [*nearest County Court* – see Chapter 5]

(a) High Court, London
(b) High Court B&PCs DR
(c) Non-B&PCs DR
(d) County Ct

Insert name of Debtor/bankrupt or company

IN THE MATTER OF ANDREW BRENTFORD AND IN THE MATTER OF THE INSOLVENCY ACT 1986

BETWEEN

Insert name(s) of applicant(s) **ANDREW BRENTFORD**

APPLICANT

-and-

Insert name(s) of respondent(s)

CHRISTIE DENMARK

RESPONDENT

Delete/complete as applicable

This application is made under rule 10.4 of the Insolvency (England and Wales) Rules 2016

Insert required details (name, address, etc) of applicant(s)	The Applicant is: Andrew Brentford 14 The Dale Manchester M23 4JD
Insert required details (name, address, etc) of respondent(s)	The Respondent is: Christie Denmark 13 Pickles Street Leeds L10 4AS
Insert required details of the debtor or company that is the subject of the proceedings	The application concerns Andrew Brentford
Identify level of judge and court or hearing centre (as per heading)	This application is made to the District Judge in [*Local County Court*]
Delete as applicable and if YES, insert the number assigned by the court	Is this application within existing insolvency proceedings? NO
	The Applicant seeks the following relief: (a) The statutory demand dated 1 December 2021 be set aside (b) Costs
Provide details of basis for application or identify the witness statement made in support	The matters on which the Applicant relies are set out in the witness statement of Mr Brentford dated 5 January 2022.
Insert names, addresses of those on whom the application is to be served (if any)	The names and addresses of the persons on whom it is intended to serve this application are: The Respondent (details above)
Insert names, addresses of those to whom notice of the application is to be given (if any)	It is not intended to serve any person with this application.
This is the address that the court will use for all communications to the Applicant until notified otherwise in writing	The address for service for the Applicant is: Andrew Brentford 14 The Dale Manchester M23 4JD Tel. 07891234567 email: [ ]
If the Application is authenticated by the sole member of a body, this fact and the body in question must be identified	Dated: 5 January 2022 Signed: Andrew Brentford The Applicant Name: Andrew Brentford

For court use

(Where the Application is issued by e-filing, the endorsement will normally be on the front of the Application, beneath the seal)

Insert address of court in which Application is to be issued

Endorsement by the court

This application will be heard:

Date ....

Time ....

Place ....

This application was issued at [*address of local court centre*]

Comment

The application form does not need to give the reasons if they are set out in a parallel witness statement. The information in the left hand column gives guidance on what needs to go where in the form. There is no court fee for an application to set aside a statutory demand.

CASE NO.

IN THE COUNTY COURT AT [*place*]

IN THE MATTER OF ANDREW BRENTFORD

AND IN THE MATTER OF THE INSOLVENCY ACT 1986

AND IN THE MATTER OF THE INSOLVENCY RULES 2016

BETWEEN

ANDREW BRENTFORD

Applicant

-and-

CHRISTIE DENMARK

Respondent

WITNESS STATEMENT OF ANDREW BRENTFORD

I, Andrew Brentford, of 14 The Dale, Manchester, M23 4JD do say as follows

1. I am the Applicant in these proceedings and I make my statement in sup-
    port of my application to set aside a statutory demand dated 30 December
    2020. Unless otherwise stated, the contents of this statement are based on
    my own knowledge and are true to the best of my knowledge and belief.

2. I shall refer to copy documents exhibited to this statement and marked
    'AB1'. The references to pages below are to pages of this exhibit.

3. The Respondent is a car mechanic.

4. On 1 February 2021 I was given a statutory demand outside of my house
    in 14 The Dale, Manchester, M23 4JD. A copy of this demand is exhibited
    at AB1/p1. This was the first time I became aware of the statutory demand.
    I dispute that the debt is owing, and so I ask the court to set aside the stat-
    utory demand.

5. The Respondent claims that I owe her £12,350. She says this is for an unpaid
    invoice from October 2020 which she issued when she sold me a Toyota car
    with registration LL03 5JD on 15 September 2020. A copy of this invoice is
    exhibited at AB1/p3.

6. I admit that I bought a car from the Respondent on 15 September 2020. However, I specifically asked the Respondent to sell me a car that was road-worthy, and which would not require any repairs within the first year. I explained to her that I intended to let my daughter use the car when she travels for work, and it was very important that the car did not break down.

7. However, on 20 September 2020 at around 12 noon, the car broke down in the middle of the M26 motorway. Three wheels came off the car and the engine started smoking. I only just managed to safely steer the car towards the hard shoulder. It subsequently emerged that the wheels were held on using superglue instead of using bolts; and the engine was in fact the wrong type for a Toyota to use. I was driving the car at the time to my daughter's house. I had to wait for six hours for the car to be recovered by the AA motorway maintenance team, who arrived at around 6pm.

8. I was informed by the AA engineers who attended the scene that the car was damaged beyond repair. They advised me to sell it to the AA for scrap rather than fix it. I was told that they would only tow the vehicle to my house if I paid them £500 to do so; and that it would not be safe (and potentially illegal) for me to drive it away myself. I called the Respondent from the side of the motorway, but I could not get through to her. I asked the AA to tow away the car. I attach the receipts I have been given from the AA at AB1/p5.

9. In a telephone conversation at around 9am on 21 September 2020 I told the Respondent that the car she sold me had broken down after only five days, and that I refused to pay her for the vehicle. The Respondent asked me to return the vehicle, and I explained that acting on the advice of the AA engineers, it had been towed away and scrapped. The Respondent started shouting and said that it was a perfectly good car, and that I still had to pay for it. I hung up the phone. I immediately left a bad review on the website SecondHandCarReviews.com which I exhibit at AB1/p10.

10. I have not spoken or communicated with the Respondent since then. I was very surprised to receive the statutory demand which came without any notice. I dispute that I owe the Respondent any money whatsoever.

Statement of Truth

I believe that the facts stated in this witness statement are true. I understand that proceedings for contempt of court may be brought against anyone who makes, or causes to be made, a false statement in a document verified by a statement of truth without an honest belief in its truth.

Full name: Andrew Brentford

Signed: Andrew Brentford

Dated: 5 January 2022.

Comment

The statutory demand is probably going to be set aside and the debtor will be awarded indemnity costs. This is because the debt is disputed, and that the creditor should have known it was disputed. The creditor may put in a witness statement to show that the debt was still owing, perhaps because the car was in perfectly good condition; or that Mr Brentford is lying; or that she sold the car on a 'buyer beware' basis. This is unlikely to affect the outcome: it is not the role of the bankruptcy court to determine the dispute. It is sufficient that there is a 'genuine trialable issue': see Paragraph 4.12. If Ms Denmark wants the money from the sale, she will have to bring a claim in the County Court. It is an abuse of process to issue a statutory demand.

The witness statement must provide the date on which the debtor first became aware of the statutory demand: see rule 10.4(6)(a) of the Rules.

Note that the witness statement does not aim to make a legal argument based on the facts. It states the facts from the witness's perspective, and allows the reader to infer why Mr Brentford does not owe the purchase price. This is the best drafting strategy when the author does not fully understand the legal argument.

Notice of opposition

Rule 10.15
Form Bank 6

Debtor's notice of opposition to petition

IN THE COUNTY COURT AT LUTON

IN THE MATTER OF JASON GRIPFORD

AND

IN THE MATTER OF THE INSOLVENCY ACT 1986

(a) Insert
name and
address which
will be used
for service
by the court

Take note that I, Jason Gripford, of 29 Elmstree Road, Luton, LU23 1OP intend to oppose the application to make a bankruptcy order on the following grounds:

1) The debt is disputed because it is based on a contract which the creditor had breached

2) The bankruptcy petition was not properly served

Dated 15 August 2021

To the County Court at Luton

and to LawFirm LLP, solicitors for the petitioner.

Comment

Unless the opposition to the debt is so strong that by setting it out the petitioning creditor will voluntarily withdraw the petition, it is better to say as little as possible in the notice of opposition. The court will set directions at the first hearing for the exchange of evidence which will set out the real grounds of opposition in full. There is also the possibility of receiving free legal advice, and a badly written notice of opposition may undermine the debtor's future case.

Note that since the petition is opposed, it will need to be heard at the appropriate hearing centre (see Chapter 5).

Application for a validation order

The application itself is made using the same form IAA as in the precedent above to set aside a statutory demand. It should be either to seek an order to validate all transactions into or out of certain specified bank accounts or to validate a particular transaction under s284 of the Insolvency Act (bankruptcy) or s127 of the Act (corporate insolvency). It is more common to seek an order in respect of companies because a winding up order is more publicised and so a bank is more likely to freeze an account in advance of the hearing of the petition. It is often sought on an urgent basis because without a validation order, the transaction would be void. An application for a validation order in corporate insolvency should contain a draft of the order sought: paragraph 9.11.8 of the PDIP. It is best practice to include a draft order with every application regardless of the rules, so it is clear what is being sought.

An example supporting witness statement is:

Case No: CR-2022-00001

IN THE HIGH COURT OF JUSTICE BUSINESS AND PROPERTY COURTS OF ENGLAND AND WALES

INSOLVENCY AND COMPANIES LIST

IN THE MATTER OF HIGHLIGIITER (GREEN) LIMITED

AND IN THE MATTER OF THE INSOLVENCY ACT 1986

BETWEEN

HIGHLIGHTER (GREEN) LIMITED

Applicant

-and-

HIGHLIGHTER (BLUE) LIMITED

Respondent

WITNESS STATEMENT OF WILLIAM HARRY SAMUELS

I, William Harry Samuels, director of Highlighter (Green) Limited ("**the Company**"), of 5 High Street, Bristol, BR1 0JX, do say as follows:

1.   I make this witness statement in support of the Company's application for

a validation order to permit it to trade using its HSBC account number, 12345678 ("**the Account**"). The company's registered address is 5 High Street, Bristol, BR1 0JX. It has 100 paid up shares of £1.

2. The Company is currently the respondent to a winding up petition presented by Highlighter (Blue) Limited ("**the Creditor**"), CR-2022-00001, on 1 January 2022. The Company was served the petition on 1 February 2022. The petition is to be heard on 1 April 2022.

3. The Company disputes that it owes any debt to the Creditor. However, I did not realise that it was possible to apply to prevent a winding up petition being presented. I discovered on 1 March 2022 that the Account was frozen and it is impossible to trade. This is why I have applied for a validation order.

4. The debt claimed in the petition is £12,000. Although the petition does not say where this has come from, and there has been no statutory demand made for the amount, I believe that this relates to a dispute between the Company and the Creditor over an unpaid invoice for the 15 boxes of stationary in 2021. I exhibit the correspondence between the Company and the Creditor at WHS/1 p1-p10. The Creditor is correct that the Company has not paid these sums: the stationary was of inferior quality and it was returned to the Creditor within a month. The Creditor has refused to accept the return. I had said to Mr Reyeman, director of the Creditor in a call in around August 2021 that we did not consider that we owed the Creditor any further sums. I told him that he should not present a winding up petition, but he apparently ignored me.

5. The Creditor has also refused to give consent to this application before it was made.

6. The Company is a wholesaler of stationery. It has just agreed an order of £15,000 for the purchase of additional supplies from its primary manufacturer, Le Highlighter s.a.r.l in France: see the invoice at WHS/1 p11-23. We consider this was a particularly good deal: the UK sales value for these products is in excess of £25,000. Already we have agreed the sale of £5,000 items to one particular customer, PlaceMat Ltd: WHS/1 p24.

7. The Company has had a tough trading year, but it is still able to pay its debts. Its most recent management accounts and its filed statutory accounts are at WHS/1 p25-p45. I also include a cash flow forecast at WHS/1 p46 – this was prepared on the basis that the Company was still able to trade. It shows that the Company is cash flow solvent.

8. The cash flow forecast shows the likely transactions for the next few

months. These all require disposition of Company assets: either stationery or cash. Nonetheless, if these transactions do take place the Company is expected to trade profitably. If the Account remains frozen, however, none of these transactions will be able to take place and the Company would be unable to pay its debts.

9. I ask that the court grant an order validating a) all transactions using the Account made in the ordinary course of business of the Company; and b) all dispositions of Company property made in the ordinary course of its business until such time judgment is given on the petition.

Statement of Truth

I believe that the facts stated in this witness statement are true. I understand that proceedings for contempt of court may be brought against anyone who makes, or causes to be made, a false statement in a document verified by a statement of truth without an honest belief in its truth.

Full name: William Harry Samuels

Signed: William Samuels

Dated: 5 January 2022.

Draft order:

Case No: CR-2022-00001

IN THE HIGH COURT OF JUSTICE BUSINESS AND PROPERTY COURTS OF ENGLAND AND WALES

INSOLVENCY AND COMPANIES LIST

BEFORE:

DATED:

IN THE MATTER OF HIGHLIGHTER (GREEN) LIMITED AND IN THE MATTER OF THE INSOLVENCY ACT 1986

BETWEEN

HIGHLIGHTER (GREEN) LIMITED

Applicant

-and-

HIGHLIGHTER (BLUE) LIMITED

Respondent

[draft] ORDER

ON the application of Highlighter (Green) Limited ("the Company") dated 2 March 2022

AND ON reading the evidence

AND ON hearing Mr Samuels, appearing in person on behalf of the Company and counsel on behalf of the Respondent

IT IS ORDERED THAT

1. Notwithstanding the presentation of a petition for the winding up of the Company presented on 1 January 2022 ("the Petition")

    a) Payments made into and out of the HSBC bank account 1234567 made in the ordinary course of business of the Company; and

    b) Dispositions of the property of the Company made in the ordinary course of its business for proper value.

Between the date of the presentation of the Petition and the date of judgment on the Petition or further order shall not be void by virtue of s127 of the Insolvency Act 1986 in the event that an order for the winding up of the Company being made on the Petition. HSBC shall be under no obligation to verify for itself whether any transaction made by the Company is in the ordinary course of business or represents full market value

2. The Respondent is to pay the costs of this application, summarily assessed as £X

Comment

This application seeks a validation order on the basis that (1) the petition debt is disputed (and so the petition is an abuse of process); (2) the transaction would be net positive for creditors. The underlying aim is to persuade the court that the company's creditors are unlikely to be prejudiced by the payments for which validation is sought (see Box 7 on page 24).

Since validation orders are often made urgently, there is not much time to prepare evidence in support. It is more important to focus on preparing the underlying exhibit so the judge has the relevant background and financial information, than giving a full description of these documents in the witness statement.

Statement of costs

Litigants in person are able to claim £19 an hour for their time preparing the case (see Chapter 16). This can add up to a substantial sum.

There is an official form for claiming costs, the N260. This can be found at https://www.gov.uk/government/publications/form-n260-statement-of-costs-summary-assessment. It is not easy to fill out and is not designed for litigants in person. An alternative is below:

CASE NO.

IN THE COUNTY COURT AT [*place*]

IN THE MATTER OF ANDREW BRENTFORD

AND IN THE MATTER OF THE INSOLVENCY ACT 1986

AND IN THE MATTER OF THE INSOLVENCY RULES 2016

BETWEEN

ANDREW BRENTFORD

Applicant

-and-

CHRISTIE DENMARK

Respondent

STATEMENT OF COSTS FOR THE APPLICANT

---

1. I have acted as a litigant in person in this case. I have also had assistance of Mrs Roth who volunteered her time on behalf of Advocate. I seek my own costs under CPR r46.5; and a pro bono costs order in respect of Mrs Roth.

2. The court has the power to make a pro bono costs order under CPR r46.7. I attach a schedule from Mrs Roth, who is of ten years' call. In total Mrs Roth spent 5 hours working on my behalf. At her usual hourly rate of £300 an hour, I seek a pro bono costs order of £1,500. I understand that this will be made out to the Access to Justice Foundation.

3. In addition, I have spent 20 hours of my own time on this case:

a) 4 hours researching the law

b) 2 hours applying for pro bono assistance

c) 5 hours writing my witness statement, skeleton argument, speaking notes and this costs schedule

d) 4 hours writing to the solicitors for Ms Denmark

e) 2 hours travelling to and from this hearing

f) 3 hours at this hearing and waiting

4. I seek my costs at the rate of £19 an hour as per PD46 paragraph 3.4. In total this is £380.

Statement of Truth

I believe that the facts stated in this witness statement are true. I understand that proceedings for contempt of court may be brought against anyone who makes, or causes to be made, a false statement in a document verified by a statement of truth without an honest belief in its truth.

Full name: Andrew Brentford

Signed: Andrew Brentford

Dated: 5 January 2022.

Comment

It is worth filling in a costs schedule like this if the outcome may lead to the litigant in person being successful. Although claiming £380 for 20 hours' work may seem too little, it is better than nothing and certainly worth asking for. It is also an extra incentive for the creditor not to make a speculative application or wrongly issue a statutory demand.

As stated in Chapter 16, always bring three copies of a costs schedule (or any documents relied upon): the additional two are for the judge and for the opponent.

Skeleton argument opposing the making of a bankruptcy order

CASE NO.

IN THE COUNTY COURT AT [*place*]

IN THE MATTER OF GEOFFREY HANKS AND IN THE MATTER OF THE INSOLVENCY ACT 1986AND IN THE MATTER OF THE INSOLVENCY RULES 2016

BETWEEN

ELEN FRANKS LTD

Petitioning Creditor

-and-

GEOFFREY HANKS

Debtor

SKELETON ARGUMENT FOR THE DEBTOR

---

1. This skeleton argument is filed on behalf of Geoffrey Hanks ("D"). D seeks dismissal of the bankruptcy petition dated 10 October 2020 which was presented by Elen Franks Ltd ("C"); or alternatively that it be adjourned for four weeks while D seeks a loan from a family member.

2. D is a litigant in person and has prepared this skeleton himself.

Dismissal of the petition

3. D seeks dismissal of the petition on three bases:

    a) First, the petition was not properly served.

    b) Second, D has a cross-claim against C which will extinguish the debt.

    c) Third, it is an abuse of process.

The petition was not properly served

4. C obtained an order permitting substituted service of the bankruptcy petition before District Judge Indigo on 30 September 2021. D was not given notice of this hearing and C has refused to share a transcript or counsel's note of what happened.

5. As set out in the Debtor's witness statement at paragraphs 8 to 13, C never even attempted to serve the petition personally. On 10 June 2021 Ms Franks, the sole director and shareholder of C, gave a copy of the petition to the Debtor's former colleague, who sent the Debtor a text message on 11 June 2021 suggesting they met up for coffee. They did so on 15 October 2021.

6. In the meantime, C had evidently applied for an order permitting substituted service. The first D knew about the petition is when it arrived by email on 2 October 2021.

7. There are serious concerns about the process C followed:

   a) Firstly, C was in breach of the r10.14 of IR 2016 and Insolvency Proceedings Practice Direction paragraph 12.7, by failing to carry out any steps to effect personal service.

   b) Secondly, C appears to have misled District Judge Indigo. Since C refuses to share any information about what took place at this hearing, D cannot give more particulars.

   c) Thirdly, C failed to inform D about the hearing before District Judge Indigo. No reason has been given for this failure.

8. From this behaviour, court can infer that C has deliberately tried to avoid its obligations to serve the bankruptcy petition personally. Further, it is likely that the order for substituted service was wrongly obtained and should be reviewed.

9. Service of a bankruptcy petition personally is a fundamental requirement of bankruptcy law. C has shown complete disregard for this rule, and for the proper rules of procedure in obtaining an order for substituted service. The petition should be dismissed by virtue of the court's inherent discretion to make a bankruptcy order. At the very least, C should be ordered to effect personal service of the petition, and this hearing should be adjourned with an indemnity costs order against C.

There is a cross-claim against C

10. D has a cross-claim against C for the reasons set out in C's witness statement at paragraphs 15 to 21. This cross-claim is valued at substantially more than the petitioned debt. In summary:

 a) The petition debt relates to an unpaid invoice for C's building services incurred in August 2019. C fitted double-glazed windows at D's house in Peterborough.

 b) On 13 September 2019 C was also instructed to redo the roof which was leaking. C charged £35,000 for the services. D paid C a deposit of £3,500 on 6 October 2019.

 c) C did not begin the services in a timely manner. Instead, the roof continued leaking and it lead to substantial damage to the premises.

 d) C claimed to have finished the work on 31 October 2019 and fixed the leak.

 e) There was heavy rain overnight on 2/3 December 2019. All of D's furniture in the upper floor was ruined, and so was the carpet. D estimates this will cost £10,000 to repair/replace.

 f) D was also forced to instruct a different roofer, Marsons Ltd, to carry out repairs. This cost D a further £50,000, which he borrowed from his brother's girlfriend. The higher fee was needed because the work had to be done urgently.

11. Even if D owes C £15,000 for the double-glazing, C owes D at least £25,000 for the roof and possibly more.

The petition is an abuse of process

12. As set out in D's witness statement at paragraphs 22 to 35, D is married to Elen Franks and they are in the process of separating. As the court can infer from the bankruptcy petition before it, there is a great deal of animosity between the two individuals. The divorce proceedings are heavily contested. One particularly contentious element is who gets custody over their two young children.

13. The real reason Ms Franks presented the bankruptcy petition is to get some improper advantage in the divorce proceedings. She seeks to show that D is financially irresponsible and so cannot be trusted to provide for their children. C's purpose behind presenting the petition is decisively not for

the interests of D's creditors.

14. Even if D owes the money to C, this was not a typical arms-length commercial debt. Instead, he took on the liability on the understanding that he was doing his wife a favour by helping her business.

15. The court has general discretion whether or not to make a bankruptcy order. D does have other creditors and accepts that he cannot repay them in full at present. However, D has written to them and they are prepared to give him a few additional months' grace provided he makes minimal repayment sums between now and then: see the correspondence in the exhibit to D's witness statement at pages 20 to 25.

Adjournment

16. D recognises that he has had notice of the petition since October 2021. However, in the event that the court is minded to reject the arguments set out above, he would request a further four weeks to pay off the debt. As set out in paragraphs 36 to 41 of his witness statement, D seeks to negotiate a loan from his parents. His parents themselves are trying to re-mortgage some property, which takes time.

17. There is minimal prejudice to the creditor of an adjournment. D accepts that this hearing would have resolved the substantive issues between the parties. He simply asks for more time to pay the debt. Through the generosity of his parents, he expects to be in this position in the next two or three weeks.

18. The mortgage application is exhibited at page 14 of D's witness statement. It is likely to succeed.

    a) The property in question has been valued at approximately £230,000 and has more than £100,000 of equity remaining. D's parents seek to secure a loan of just £30,000.

    b) The application for a mortgage was made on 10 November 2020 following a comment of DJ Littleton at an earlier hearing which was adjourned.

    c) The opinion of the mortgage broker was that this was likely to succeed: see paragraph 37.

19. The court can therefore be satisfied that D will be able to pay the debts by the next hearing.

Conclusion

20. The debtor respectfully asks that the petition be dismissed, or alternatively adjourned for 4 weeks for the reasons given above.

Comment

This is the sort of skeleton argument which would be filed in the second or third hearing of the bankruptcy petition, once all the debtor's evidence is included. It is unusual to have cross-examination in bankruptcy proceedings because the factual evidence of the debtor is commonly taken at face value even if the court does not draw the same conclusions. However, in the case that the petitioning creditor disputes the debtor's account of what happened when he was served, the court will need to make a factual finding about what actually happened. In this case, cross-examination is likely.

It is unlikely that any individual debtor will be able to run so many arguments at once. This precedent includes these arguments so the reader will be understand how each argument can be phrased. Three reasons are given for the petition to be dismissed and one reason why the petition should be adjourned.

Service of the petition: In this example, the bankruptcy petition was properly served, i.e. it was served according to the order permitting non-personal service of the petition. However, this order was improperly obtained. In my view, it is fairly balanced whether a judge will be prepared to dismiss the petition on that basis; or say that even if there was a procedural irregularity, it is of no consequence to the debtor. The tipping point will be whether the judge is persuaded that this was a deliberate breach of the rules. It is unclear why the creditor would deliberately break all of these rules, when it is not difficult or expensive to comply with them. On that basis, a judge may find it was incompetence by the petitioning creditor rather than a conspiracy to harm the debtor. On the other hand, it is suspicious, and potentially improper, for a party who attends a 'without notice' hearing not to tell the other party what happened. In the absence of a good explanation, it is logical to infer that there was a deliberate breach.

Debtor has a cross-claim against the creditor: Here a relatively strong argument is made that there is a cross-claim against the creditor. The judge is not going to resolve the factual dispute between the creditor and the petitioner. Instead, the judge will dismiss the petition on this point.

Abuse of process: These arguments rarely succeed, because a creditor with an uncontested debt is usually entitled to seek a bankruptcy order if their motive is to seek a distribution in the estate (see Chapter 5). However, in this case a judge will be having second thoughts about making a bankruptcy order because a) the petitioner's purpose seems tainted by the divorce proceedings, and b) other creditors do not support the petition.

Adjournment: Typically a debtor who disputes a debt and loses will be unable to seek a further adjournment because they already would have had several months from between the presentation of the petition and the substantive hearing to gather funds to pay. This part of the skeleton tries to explain why it would nonetheless be fair to have a further adjournment.

Grounds of appeal

The applicant wishes to appeal the bankruptcy order made by DDJ Zelda on 14 June 2021 on the following grounds:

1. The learned judge was wrong not to exercise her discretion to adjourn the hearing, given that the debtor was in the process of securing a mortgage on his property in order to pay the debt

2. The learned judge was wrong to hold that the petition had been properly served: the judge found that the creditor sent the demand by post.

3. The learned judge was wrong to hold, in the alternative, that she had the power to waive defects in service: she had no such power.

4. Alternatively the learned judge was wrong to exercise her discretion to waive the defects in this instance.

5. The applicant will be filing a skeleton argument in support of this appeal.

Comment

Grounds of appeal should be as short and concise as possible.

It is difficult to appeal on the grounds of incorrect exercise of discretion (grounds 1 and 4) and the debtor will need to show that the judge had acted unreasonably. The matter will turn on the facts. Grounds 2 and 3 are purely legal questions and so the bankrupt will succeed if the judge incorrectly stated or incorrectly applied the law. The skeleton argument can give more detail about precisely what happened, what the judge said in their judgment, and why that was wrong. The advantage of filing a separate skeleton argument is that an appellant only has 21 days to file a notice of appeal, which must include the grounds of appeal, but they have an extra 14 days to file a skeleton argument. This is particularly important if it has been difficult to get a transcript, and so to say precisely why the first judge was wrong.

Annex 2   Checklists

These checklists set out the technical rules which a statutory demand, bankruptcy petition and winding up petition need to follow. As set out in the main text, a minor defect is likely to be waived, a more serious one may require adjournment and correction, and one which causes prejudice to the debtor will likely lead to the dismissal of the petition.

The checklists were compiled by Guy Olliff-Cooper of 4 Stone Buildings and are used with his permission.

Statutory demand for bankruptcy

The Demand		
Rule	**Content**	**Check**
IR 10.1(1)(a)	The heading either "Statutory demand under section 268(1) (debt payable immediately) of the Insolvency Act 1986" or "Statutory demand under section 268(2) (debt not immediately payable)".	
(b)	Identification details for the debtor.	
(c)	The name and address of the creditor.	
(d)	A statement of the amount of the debt, and the consideration for it (or, if there is no consideration, the way in which it arises).	
(e)	If the demand is made under section 268(1) and founded on a judgment or order of a court, the date of the judgment or order and the court in which it was obtained.	
(f)	If the demand is made under section 268(2), a statement of the grounds on which it is alleged that the debtor appears to have no reasonable prospect of paying the debt.	
(g)	If the creditor is entitled to the debt by way of assignment, details of the original creditor and any intermediary assignees.	
(h)	A statement that if the debtor does not comply with the demand bankruptcy proceedings may be commenced.	
(i)	The date by which the debtor must comply with the demand, if bankruptcy proceedings are to be avoided.	
(j)	A statement of the methods of compliance which are open to the debtor.	
(k)	A statement that the debtor has the right to apply to the court to have the demand set aside.	

The Demand		
Rule	**Content**	**Check**
(l)	A statement that rule 10.4(4) of the Insolvency (England and Wales) Rules 2016 states to which court such an application must be made; and name the court or hearing centre of the County Court to which, according to the present information, the debtor must make the application (i.e. the High Court, the County Court at Central London or a named hearing centre of the County Court as the case may be).	
(m)	A statement that any application to set aside the demand must be made within 18 days of service on the debtor.	
(n)	A statement that if the debtor does not apply to set aside the demand within 18 days or otherwise deal with this demand within 21 days after its service the debtor could be made bankrupt and the debtor's property and goods taken away.	
IR 10.1(3)	A demand must name one or more individuals with whom the debtor may communicate with a view to: (a) securing or compounding the debt to the satisfaction of the creditor; or (b) establishing to the creditor's satisfaction that there is a reasonable prospect that the debt will be paid when it falls due.	
IR 10.1(4)	The postal address, electronic address and telephone number (if any) of the named individual must be given.	
IR 10.1(5)	A demand must be dated and authenticated either by the creditor or by a person who is authorised to make the demand on the creditor's behalf.	
IR 10.1(6)	A demand which is authenticated by a person other than the creditor must state that the person is authorised to make the demand on the creditor's behalf and state the person's relationship to the creditor.	

The Demand		
Rule	**Content**	**Check**
IR 10.1(7)	If the amount claimed in the demand includes: a) Any charge by way of interest of which notice had not previously been delivered to the debtor as a liability of the debtor's; or b) Any other charge accruing from time to time, the amount or rate of the charge must be separately identified, and the grounds on which payment of it is claimed must be stated.	
IR 10.1(8)	The amount claimed for such charges must be limited to that which has accrued at the date of the demand.	
IR 10.1(9)	If the creditor holds any security in respect of the debt, the full amount of the debt must be specified, but: a) The demand must specify the nature of the security, and the value which the creditor puts upon it at the date of the demand; and b) The demand must claim payment of the full amount of the debt, less the specified value of the security.	
IR 10.1(10)	When the statutory demand is to be served out of the jurisdiction, the time limits of 18 days and 21 days referred to in sub-paragraphs 10.1(1)(m) and (n) above must be amended as follows: (a) For any reference to 18 days there must be substituted the number of days which is the appropriate number of days set out in the table accompanying the Practice Direction supplementing Section IV of CPR Part 6 plus 4 days; and (b) For any reference to 21 days there must be substituted the number of days which is the appropriate number of days set out in the table accompanying the Practice Direction supplementing Section IV of CPR Part 6 plus 7 days.	

Service		
Rule	**Content**	**Check**
IR 10.2	A creditor must do all that is reasonable to bring the statutory demand to the debtor's attention and, if practicable in the particular circumstances, serve the demand personally.	
PDIP 11.2	A creditor must do all that is reasonable to bring the statutory demand to the debtor's attention and, if practicable in the particular circumstances, serve the demand personally.	
PDIP 12.7.1(1)	Where personal service of the bankruptcy petition is not practicable, service by other means may be permitted. In most cases, evidence that the steps set out in the following paragraphs have been taken will suffice to justify an order for service of a bankruptcy petition other than by personal service: One personal call at the residence and place of business of the debtor. Where it is known that the debtor has more than one residential or business addresses, personal calls should be made at all the addresses.	
PDIP 12.7.1(2)	Should the creditor fail to effect personal service, a letter should be written to the debtor referring to the call(s), the purpose of the same, and the failure to meet the debtor, adding that a further call will be made for the same purpose on the [day] of [month] 20[ ] at [ ] hours at [place]. Such letter may be sent by first class prepaid post or left at or delivered to the debtor's address in such a way as it is reasonably likely to come to the debtor's attention. At least two business days' notice should be given of the appointment and copies of the letter sent to or left at all known addresses of the debtor. The appointment letter should also state that: (a) In the event of the time and place not being convenient, the debtor should propose some other time and place reasonably convenient for the purpose;	

Service		
Rule	**Content**	**Check**
	(b) In the case of a statutory demand as suggested in paragraph 11.2 above, reference is being made to this paragraph for the purpose of service of a statutory demand, the appointment letter should state that if the debtor fails to keep the appointment the creditor proposes to serve the demand by advertisement/ post/ insertion through a letterbox as the case may be, and that, in the event of a bankruptcy petition being presented, the court will be asked to treat such service as service of the demand on the debtor; (c) (In the case of a petition) if the debtor fails to keep the appointment, an application will be made to the court for an order that service be effected either by advertisement or in such other manner as the court may think fit.	
PDIP 12.7.1(3)	When attending any appointment made by letter, inquiry should be made as to whether the debtor is still resident at the address or still frequents the address, and/or other enquiries should be made to ascertain receipt of all letters left for them. If the debtor is away, inquiry should also be made as to when they are returning and whether the letters are being forwarded to an address within the jurisdiction (England and Wales) or elsewhere.	
PDIP 12.7.1(4)	If the debtor is represented by a solicitor, an attempt should be made to arrange an appointment for personal service through such solicitor. The Insolvency Rules permit a solicitor to accept service of a statutory demand on behalf of their client but not the service of a bankruptcy petition.	
IR 10.3(1)	Where section 268 requires a statutory demand to be served before the petition, a certificate of service of the demand must be filed with the court with the petition.	
IR 10.3(2)	The certificate must be verified by a statement of truth and be accompanied by a copy of the demand served.	

Service		
Rule	**Content**	**Check**
IR 10.3(3)	If the demand has been served personally on the debtor, the statement of truth must be made by the person who served the demand unless service has been acknowledged in writing by the debtor or a person authorised to accept service.	
IR 10.3(4)	If service has been acknowledged in writing either by: (a) The debtor; or (b) A person who is authorised to accept service on the debtor's behalf and who has stated that this is the case in the acknowledgement of service; then the certificate of service must be authenticated either by the creditor or by a person acting on the creditor's behalf, and the acknowledgement of service must accompany the certificate.	
IR 10.3(5)	If the demand has been served other than personally and there is no acknowledgement of service, the certificate must be authenticated by a person or persons having direct personal knowledge of the means adopted for serving the statutory demand, and must contain the following information: (a) The steps taken to serve the demand; and (b) A date by which, to the best of the knowledge, information and belief of the person authenticating the certificate, the demand will have come to the debtor's attention.	
IR 10.3(6)	Where paragraph (5) applies the statutory demand is deemed to have been served on the debtor on the date referred to in paragraph (5) (b) unless the court determines otherwise.	

Service		
Rule	**Content**	**Check**
PDIP 11.3	A creditor wishing to serve a statutory demand out of the jurisdiction in a foreign country with an applicable civil procedure convention (including the Hague Convention) may and, if the assistance of a British Consul is desired, must adopt the procedure prescribed by CPR rule 6.42 and CPR rule 6.43. In the case of any doubt whether the country is a 'convention country', enquiries should be made of the Foreign Process Section of the Queen's Bench Division, Room E16, Royal Courts of Justice, Strand, London WC2A 2LL.	

Certificate of Service		
Rule	**Content**	**Check**
Para 6(1), Schedule 4	Certificate of Service	
IR 7.12(1)	Filed as soon as reasonably practicable, or with the certificate of compliance, at least five business days before the hearing of the petition.	
	Sufficient detail (clearly visible through letterbox etc.)	
Para 6(2), Schedule 4	Identify the application or petition;	
	Identify the company, where the application or petition relates to a company;	
	Identify the debtor, where the application relates to an individual;	
	Identify the applicant or petitioner;	
	The court or hearing centre in which the application was made or at which the petition was filed, and the court reference number;	
	The date of the application or petition;	
	Whether the copy served was a sealed copy;	
	The person(s) served;	

Certificate of Service		
Rule	**Content**	**Check**
	The manner of service and the date of service; and	
	Statement of truth.	
Para 6(3), Schedule 4	Sealed copy of the order for substituted service (where applicable).	

Bankruptcy Petition

The Petition		
Rule	**Content**	**Check**
IR 10.7(a)	Name and postal address of the petitioner.	
(b)	The name, postal address and telephone number of the solicitor.	
(c)	Statement that the petitioner requests that the court make a bankruptcy order against the debtor.	
(d)	Whether the debtor's centre of main interests is within the United Kingdom or within a member State, whethe the debtor has an establishment within the United Kingdom and whether he debtor carries on business as an Article 1.2 undertaking.	
(e)	Whether the debtor is resident in England and Wales.	
(f)	Where the petition is presented to.	
(g)	The reasons why the court or hearing centre to which the petition is presented is the correct court or hearing centre under rule 10.11.	
IR 10.7(2)	If more than four months have elapsed since the statutory demand, the reasons for the delay.	
IR 10.7(3)	A blank box for the court to complete with the details of the venue for hearing the petition.	
IR 10.8(1)(a)	The debtor's identification details.	
(b)	The occupation (if any) of the debtor.	
(c)	The name or names in which the debtor carries on business, if other than the name of the debtor, and whether, in the case of any business of a specified nature, the debtor carries it on alone or with others.	
(d)	The nature of the debtor's business, and the address or addresses at which it is carried on.	

The Petition		
Rule	**Content**	**Check**
(e)	Any name or names, other than the name of the debtor, in which the debtor has carried on business at or after the time when the debt was incurred, and whether the debtor has done so alone or with others.	
(f)	Any address or addresses at which the debtor has resided or carried on business at or after that time, and the nature of that business.	
(g)	Whether the centre of main interests or an establishment of the debtor (as defined in Article 2(10) of the EU Regulation) is in the UK or another member State.	
IR 10.8(3)	If to the petitioner's knowledge the debtor has used any name other than the one specified under paragraph (1)(a), that fact must be stated in the petition.	
IR 10.9(1)(a)	The amount of the debt, the consideration for it (or, if there is no consideration, the way in which it arises) and the fact that it is owed to the petitioner.	
(b)	When the debt was incurred or became due.	
(c)	If the amount of the debt includes any charge by way of interest not previously notified to the debtor as a liability of the debtor's, the amount or rate of the charge (separately identified).	
(d)	If the amount of the debt includes any other charge accruing from time to time, the amount or rate of the charge (separately identified).	
(e)	The grounds on which any such a charge is claimed to form part of the debt, provided that the amount or rate must, in the case of a petition based on a statutory demand, be limited to that claimed in the demand.	
(f)	That the debt is unsecured (subject to section 269).	

The Petition		
Rule	**Content**	**Check**
(g)	Either that the debt is for a liquidated sum payable immediately, and the debtor appears to be unable to pay it, or that the debt is for a liquidated sum payable at some certain, future time (that time to be specified), and the debtor appears to have no reasonable prospect of being able to pay it.	
IR 10.9(2)(a)	Where the debt is one for which, under section 268, a statutory demand must have been served on the debtor, the petition must specify the date and manner of service of the statutory demand; and	
(b)	State that, to the best of the creditor's knowledge and belief the demand has been neither complied with nor set aside in accordance with these Rules, and that no application to set it aside is outstanding.	
IR 10.9(3)	If the case is within section 268(1)(b) (unsatisfied execution or process in respect of judgment debt, etc.) the petition must state which court issued the execution or other process and give particulars of the return.	
PDIP 14.2.4	The date of service of the statutory demand should be recited as follows: (1) In the case of personal service, the date of service as set out in the certificate of service should be recited and whether service is effected before/after 16.00 hours on Monday to Friday or before/after 12.00 hours on a Saturday. (2) In the case of substituted service (other than by advertisement), the date alleged in the certificate of service should be recited. (3) In the strictly limited case of service by advertisement under rule 6.3, the date to be alleged is the date of the advertisement's appearance or, as the case may be, its first appearance (see rules 6.3(3) and 6.11(8)).	

The Petition		
Rule	**Content**	**Check**
PDIP 14.3.1	Pending petitions presented against the debtor and shall include the following certificate at the end of the petition: "I/we certify that within 7 days ending today I/we have conducted a search for pending petitions presented against the debtor and that to the best of my/our knowledge information and belief [no prior petitions have been presented which are still pending] [a prior petition (No [ ]) has been presented and is/may be pending in the [court] and I/we am/are issuing this petition at risk as to costs]. Signed..... Dated...."	
IR 10.10(3)	A Statement of Truth.	

Corporate Insolvency

Winding Up Petition		
Rule	**Content**	**Check**
IR 7.5(1)	Name of the court.	
	Name and address of the petitioner.	
	Identification details for the company subject to the petition.	
	The company's registered office.	
	The date the company was incorporated and the enactment under which it was incorporated.	
	The total number of issued shares of the company and the manner in which they are divided up.	
	The aggregate nominal value of those shares.	
	The amount of capital paid up or credited as paid up.	
	A statement of the nature of the company's business if known.	
PDIP 9.5	Where the petitioning creditor relies on failure to pay a debt, details of the debt relied on should be given in the petition (whether or not they have been given in any statutory demand served in respect of the debt), including the amount of the debt, its nature and the date or dates on or between which it was incurred.	
IR 7.5(2)	A blank box for the court to complete with details of the venue for hearing the petition.	

Witness Statement		
Rule	**Content**	**Check**
IR 7.5(1)(n)	A statement whether the proceedings will be COMI proceedings, establishment proceedings or proceedings to which the EU Regulation as it has effect in the law of the United Kingdom does not apply and that the reasons for so stating are given in a witness statement.	
IR 7.6(8)	The witness statement must give the reasons for the statement that the proceedings will be COMI proceedings, establishment proceedings or proceedings to which the EU Regulation as it has effect in the law of the United Kingdom does not apply.	
IR 7.6(6)	If the petition is based on a statutory demand and more than four months have elapsed since the demand was served, the reasons for the delay.	
IR 7.6(1)	Statement of truth "*[I believe][the (claimant or as may be) believes] that the facts stated in this petition] are true*".	
IR 7.6(4)	Authentication including (if not by the petitioner): a) The name and postal address of the person making the statement; b) The capacity in which, and the authority by which, the person authenticates the statement; and c) The means of that person's knowledge of the matters verified in the statement of truth.	
PDIP 9.6	The statement of truth must be signed no more than ten business days before the petition is issued at court.	

Filing Checklist		
Rule	**Content**	**Check**
	The original petition.	
IR 7.9(1)	An additional copy of the petition for the court and for each person on whom the petition will be served or delivered.	
	Statement of truth (if not included in petition).	
Para 3.3, Schedule, The Civil Proceedings Fees (Amendment) Order 2014 (SI/2014/874)	Court fee – £280.	
Article 2, Insolvency Proceedings (Fees) Order (SI 2016/692)	Official Receiver's deposit – £1,600.	
Paragraph 10.3, Schedule 1, Civil Proceedings Fees Order 2008 (SI 2008/1053)	Search fee – £11 (may not be applicable if the petition has carried out a winding up search immediately before presentation).	

Service Checklist		
Rule	**Content**	**Check**
Para 2, Schedule 4, IR 2016	Service at the company's registered office.	
Para 1(4), Schedule 4	Service in accordance with section 1139(2) of the Companies Act 2006 (overseas only).	
IR 7.9(3)-(5)	Service within three business days after the day on which the petition is served on the company on any voluntary liquidator, administrative receiver, administrator, supervisor of a voluntary arrangement or EU member state liquidator appointed to the company; the FCA or Prudential Regulation Authority (as appropriate).	

Certificate of Service		
Rule	**Content**	**Check**
Para 6(1), Schedule 4	Certificate of Service.	
7.12(1)	Filed as soon as reasonable practicable, or with the certificate of compliance, at least five business days before the hearing of the petition.	
	Sufficient detail (clearly visible through letterbox etc.).	
Para 6(2), Schedule 4	Identify the application or petition;	
	Identify the company, where the application or petition relates to a company;	
	Identify the debtor, where the application relates to an individual;	
	Identify the applicant or petitioner;	
	The court or hearing centre in which the application was made or at which the petition was filed, and the court reference number;	
	The date of the application or petition;	
	Whether the copy served was a sealed copy;	
	The person(s) served;	
	The manner of service and the date of service; and	
	Statement of truth.	
Para 6(3), Schedule 4	Sealed copy of the order for substituted service (where applicable).	

Gazette		
Rule	**Content**	**Check**
IR 7.10	Notice given in the Gazette.	
IR 7.10(2)	A petition has been presented for the winding up of the company;	
	In the case of an overseas company, the address at which service of the petition was effected;	
	The name and address of the petitioner;	
	The date on which the petition was presented;	
	The venue fixed for the hearing of the petition;	
	The name and address of the petitioner's solicitor (if any); and	
	That any person intending to appear at the hearing (whether to support or oppose the petition) must give notice of that intention in accordance with rule 7.14.	
	If the company address has changed since the presentation of the petition, the old and new addresses.	
IR 7.10(4)	Not less than 7 business days before the hearing, and not less than seven business days after the petition was served on the company (clear days).	
PDIP 9.8.2	A copy of the notice (or, if that is not reasonably practicable, a statement of the content of the notice) must be filed with the court as soon as possible and in any event not later than 5 business days before the hearing of the petition.	

Opposing the Petition		
Rule	**Content**	**Check**
IR 7.16(1)	Witness Statement.	
	Deliver a copy of the witness statement to the petitioner or his solicitor.	
	At least five days before the hearing.	
IR 7.16(2)	Identification details for the proceedings (IR 1.6(2)).	
	A statement that the company intends to oppose the making of the winding up order.	
	A statement of the grounds on which the company opposes the making of the order.	

Certificate of Compliance		
Rule	**Content**	**Check**
IR 7.12(1)	File a certificate of compliance.	
	At least five business days before the hearing.	
	Authenticated (see IR 1.5).	
IR 7.12(2)	Date of presentation of the petition.	
	Date fixed for the hearing.	
	Date or dates on which the petition was served and notice of its was given in compliance with rules 7.9 and 7.10.	
IR 7.12(3)	Copy of the gazette notice or, if that is not reasonably practicable, the contents of the notice.	

List of Appearances		
Rule	**Content**	**Check**
IR 7.15(1)	List of people who have given notice of intention to appear at the hearing.	
IR 7.15(2)	The date of the presentation of the petition.	
	The date of the hearing of the petition.	
	A statement that the creditors and contributories listed have delivered notice that they intend to appear at the hearing of the petition.	
	Their names and addresses.	
	The amount each creditor claims to be owed.	
	The number of shares claimed to be held by each contributory.	
	The name and postal address of any solicitor for a person listed.	
	Whether each person listed intends to support the petition, or to oppose it.	
IR 7.15(3)	Hand list of appearances to the judge or registrar before the hearing commences.	
IR 7.15(4)	Add to the list anyone who has been given permission to appear by the court.	

Sources of help

A range of organisations provide advice to debtors.

Legal advice organisations

There are many charities offering debt advice: National Debtline, StepChange, the Debt Advice Foundation, and the Money Adviser Network all have national coverage. These charities specialise in addressing problems before they escalate into insolvency proceedings. The equivalent for business debt is Business Debtline. Shelter and Christians Against Poverty are two other charities which have experience helping people in financial difficulty.

If a court hearing is listed, a reader's starting point is likely to be a local branch of Citizens Advice: https://www.citizensadvice.org.uk/. Citizens Advice can also be contacted through its national phone line service: 0800 144 8848 (England) and 0800 702 2020 (Wales). They also have a special debt helpline: 0800 240 4420. The Citizens Advice based in the Royal Courts of Justice (rcjadvice.org. uk) is particularly good, and can be accessed by emailing debt@rcjadvice.org.uk or by phoning 0203 869 3195 on Thursday or Friday.

Alternatively, there may be a specialist legal advice centre able to offer support. These can be found via the LawWorks website: https://www.lawworks.org.uk/legal-advice-individuals/find-legal-advice-clinic-near-you. In particular, Mary Ward Legal Centre in London specialises in bankruptcy matters.

The flagship organisation offering free legal advice by barristers is Advocate. Advocate has a partner scheme specifically for bankruptcy cases, known as PILARS. Advocate does not accept self-referrals, but an application for help can be made through the RCJ Advice Bureau, Citizens Advice, National Debtline or Business Debtline.

There are organisations like PayPlan which will offer advice and help organise an 'individual voluntary arrangement' for no upfront fee. If the arrangement is successful, they will take a cut of the funds from the creditors. These organisations can also provide useful advice.

The Samaritans will not offer legal or financial advice, but they do provide critical emotional support to anyone having a difficult time.

Further reading

Although this is the only in-date book on insolvency law guide for litigants in person, Muir Hunter's *Going Bust* (2007) offers an alternative perspective. Robin Meynell's *Book of Bankruptcy* (2009) also has further information about bankruptcy, focussing on what happens after the bankruptcy order is made.

The main textbook a professional lawyer would consult is *Sealy & Milman*. This is an annotated guide to the Insolvency Act and the Insolvency Rules with commentary under each section explaining how the provisions apply, and what the key cases are. It costs £350, which is cheaper than going to a lawyer. However, unlike a professional lawyer, it does not tell you what the answer is: it simply sets out what the law is, and it is up to the reader to apply the law to the situation they are facing. The book is also not designed to be read by someone without a working knowledge of insolvency law and so it may be impossible for a lay reader to use, unless they are comfortable with the technical language.

Resources online

There are many useful resources online which can be accessed by simply typing in the key legal terms on Google. For example, professional lawyers frequently publish short articles about the law in order to attract potential clients. Although it seems obvious, make sure that the article is about English law. The same keywords can attract articles on bankruptcy law in other countries. In general, it will not be useful to rely on any authority from any other country's law.

Table of cases

Ardawa v Uppal [2019] EWHC 456
(Ch)   80

Aslam v Finn [2013] EWHC 3405
(Ch)   126

Birdi v Price [2018] EWHC 2943
(Ch)   129

Black v Sale Service and
Maintenance Ltd [2018] EWHC
1344 (Ch)   201

Boulton v Queen Margaret's School
[2018] EWHC 3729 (Ch)   96

Bramston v Haut [2012] EWCA Civ
1637   125

Bucknall v Wilson [2020] EWHC
1200 (Ch)   22

Bush v Bank Mandiri (Europe) Ltd
[2011] BPIR 19   55

Coulter v Chief Constable of Dorset
Police [2004] EWCA Civ 1259   54

Crabbe v Day [2020] EWHC 222
(Ch)   78

Decker v Hopcraft [2015] EWHC
1170 (QB)   84

Ebbvale Ltd v Hosking [2013]
UKPC 1   98

Edgeworth Capital v Maud [2020]
EWHC 974 (Ch)   91

Financial Conduct Authority v
Avacade Ltd [2020] EWHC 26 (Ch)
                                        84

Freeburn v Hunt [2010] C.L.Y. 1903
                                       126

Gate Gourmet Luxembourg IV
SARL v Morby [2016] EWHC 74
(Ch)   80

Gravesham Borough Council v
Titilayo Orebanwo [2020] EWHC
107 (Ch)   87

Haworth v Cartmel [2011] EWHC
36 (Ch)   100, 198

Heath v Tang [1993] 1 WLR 1421
                                       126

Howell v Lerwick Commercial
Mortgage Corporation Ltd [2015]
EWHC 1177 (Ch)   51

Jones & Pyle Developments v
Rymell [2021] EWHC 385 (Ch)   38

Lilley v American Express Europe
Ltd [2000] BPIR 70   75

Lockston Group Inc v Wood [2015]
EWHC 2962 (Ch)   151

Lock v Aylesbury Vale District Council [2018] EWHC 2015 (Ch) 91

Martin v McLaren Construction Ltd [2019] EWHC 2059 (Ch) 157

McKenzie v McKenzie [1970] 3 WLR 472 227

O'Donnell v Bank of Ireland [2012] EWHC 3749 (Ch) 56

Official Receiver v Doganci [2007] B.P.I.R. 87 136

Papanicola v Humphreys [2005] EWHC 335 (Ch) 197

Re Bremner [1999] 1 FLR 912 115

Re Debtor (No. 340 of 1992) [1996] 2 All E.R. 211 63

Re: Kevin Stanford [2019] EWHC 595 (Ch) 88

Re Leigh Estates (UK) Ltd [1994] B.C.C. 292 98

Revenue and Customs Commissioners v Garwood [2012] BPIR 575 95

Shepherd v Official Receiver [2006] EWHC 2902 (Ch) 126

Supperstone v Hurst [2006] EWHC 2147 (Ch) 126

Whig v Whig [2007] EWHC 1856 (Fam) 143

Yang v Official Receiver [2013] EWHC 3577 (Ch) 198

Yu (also known as Lau) v Cowley [2020] EWHC 2429 (Ch) 80

Table of legislation

Practice Directions

Practice Direction - Insolvency
Proceedings
  Part 1
    para 3.2 — 121
    para 3 — 76
    para 3.8 — 78
  Part 2
    para 9.10 — 199
  Part 3
    para 12.7.1 — 80
    para 11.4.4 — 52
    para 12.5.1 — 79
    para 12.7 — 48
    para 12.7.1(4) — 80
  Part 4
    para 17.2 — 197
  Part 6
    para 21 — 140

Statutory Instruments

Administration of Estates of
Insolvent Deceased Persons Order
1986 (S.I 1986, No. 1999) — 149
  Sch 1
    Part II
      para 2 — 153
      para 5 — 150
      para 10 — 151
      para 24 — 151

Civil Procedure Rules 1998 (S.I.
1998, No. 3132)
  Part 81 — 121

r40.7 — 202
r44.7 — 216
r44.10 — 216
r46.2 — 216

Corporate Insolvency
and Governance Act 2020
(Coronavirus) (Suspension of
Liability for Wrongful Trading and
Extension of the Relevant Period)
Regulations 2020 (S.I. 2020, No.
1349) — 168

Insolvency (England and Wales)
Rules 2016 (S.I 2016, No. 1024)
  r10.1 — 47
  r10.1(1)(c) — 47
  r10.1(1)(l) — 47
  r10.1(7) — 47
  r10.1(8) — 47
  r10.1(9) — 53
  r10.1(10) — 47
  r10.2 — 48
  r10.4(4) — 50
  r10.4(5) — 50
  r10.4(6) — 50
  r10.5(1) — 57
  r10.5(2) — 58
  r10.5(3) — 58
  r10.5(5) — 50
  r10.5(5)(a) — 51
  r10.5(5)(b) — 52
  r10.5(5)(c) — 53
  r10.5(5)(d) — 54, 56, 57
  r10.5(8) — 60
  r10.9 — 75

r10.11	76
r10.11(6)	78
r10.11(7)	76
r10.14(2)	79
r10.24(1)	78
r10.40	44
r10.48	50
r10.125(1)	30
r10.125(4)	29
r10.149	33
r12.5	76
r12.31	78
r12.64	80
r14.1(3)	25
r7.10(4)	178
r7.24	178
r8.33	144
r8.34(k)	145
r10.7(2)	76, 90
r10.18(1)	82
r10.21	82
r10.26	100
r10.27(1)	102
r10.27(2)	102
r10.28	102
r10.29	103
r10.35	142
r10.101	36
r10.103	36
r10.103(5)	36
r10.103(6)	36
r10.122	106
r10.133(2)	140
r10.134	140
r10.135	143
r10.136	140
r10.142(2)	133
r10.143	133
r10.144	134
r10.144(4)	134
r12.59	197
r12.59(1)	199
r15.31(3)	173
r18.35	142
Sch 4	

para 6(3)	80
Sch 6	77

Insolvency Proceedings (Monetary Limits) (Amendment) Order 2004 (S.I. 2004, No. 547) — 113

Insolvency Regulation (Regulation (EU) No. 2015/848 — 73

Insolvent Companies (Disqualification of Unfit Directors) Proceedings Rules 1987 (S.I. 1987, No. 2023)
r3(3)	191

Statutes

Administration of Estates Act 1925
s25	148

Administration of Estates Act 1925 (Insolvent Estates Order)
s44	148

Bill of Sales Act 1878	25

British Nationality Act 1981
s41A	29

Civil Evidence Act 1968	121

Companies Act 2006
s172	174
s771(5)(b)	18

Company Directors Disqualification Act 1986 (CDDA) — 185
s6	185
s7(2)	186
s7A(5)	186
s11	26, 122, 146, 188
s11(4)	122
s13	122

s16	189	s270	49
		s271(2)	75
Corporate Insolvency and		s271(3)	93
Governance Act 2020		s276	7, 103
s12	168	s278	133
Sch 10		s279	37
para 9	175	s279(1)	133
		s279(4)	133
County Courts Act 1984		s281	134
s112	10	s281(3)	38
		s281(5)	38
Criminal Justice Act 1988		s282	133, 197
s101	103	s282(1)(a)	143, 146, 202
		s282(3)	139, 203
Family Law Act 1996		s282(4)	144
s30	111	s282(4)(b)	144
s33	111	s283	147
		s283(1)	30
Insolvency Act 1986		s283(2)	14
s122(1)(f)	177	s283(2)(a)	129
s132	183	s283(3A)	107
s147	204	s283A	109, 116
s213	168	s283A(4)	115
s214	167	s284	23, 61, 152
s216	183	s284(4)	23
s217	169	s285	34, 107
s235	183	s290	36
s235(3)(c)	183	s290(2)	36
s251O	9	s290(5)	36, 121
s251Q	9	s298	123
s251Q(3	9	s303	123
s260(2)	100	s304	123, 127
s261	144	s304(3)	129
s261(2)	100	s305	14
s262(2)(d)	144	s306	17, 150
s265	72	s307	34
s265(4)	73	s307(5)	30
s266(2)	79	s310	30
s266(3)	90	s310(3)(h)	31
s267	45, 76	s310(6)	31
s267(2)(c)	90	s310A	32
s268	46, 76, 90	s310A(2)	32
s268(1)	157	s310A(6)	33
s268(2)	57	s312	14, 121
s269	46	s313A	113

s315	18, 107	s435		21
s315(4)	18	Sch 4A		135
s320	107	para 10		146
s329	34	para 11		146
s333	34, 35, 121, 123	Sch 9		
s333(3)	38	para 18A		25
s333(4)	30, 123	Sch 10		120
s335A	113			
s336	113	Land Charges Act 1972		
s336(2)	111	s8		145
s336(5)	112			
s337	110	Legal Aid, Sentencing and		
s337(2)(a)	110	Punishment of Offenders Act 2012		
s337(4)	111	Sch 1		
s337(6)	111	para 33(2)		225
s338	114			
s339	20	Limitation Act 1980		93
s340	21			
s342	22	Limited Liability Partnership Act		
s342A	25	2000		
s343	25	s7		27
s344	25	s7(3)		27
s350	146			
s350(5)	117	Mental Capacity Act 2005		
s352	119	s1(2)		100
s354(3)	119			
s356	119	Perjury Act 1911		
s358	74	s3		112
s360	119			
s360(1)(a)	28	Statute of Frauds 1677		
s360(1)(b)	27, 29	s4		156, 160
s363	121			
s364	20, 75, 120	Theft Act 1968		119
s365	17			
s366	36	Trustee Act 1925		
s366(1)	36	s61		148
s367(3)	36			
s369	37	Trusts of Land and Appointment of		
s375	197, 198	Trustees Act 1996		
s382	114, 151	s14		113
s421A(2)	151			
s423	24, 169			

Index

A

Administration   166, 170
   floating charge   171
   moratorium on legal
   proceedings   171

Administrators   166
   power to review the
   transactions of the company
     174

Advocate (Charity)   232

After-acquired property   30

Alternatives to bankruptcy
   Breathing Space   11
   County Court Administration
   Orders   10
   Debt relief orders   7
   Debt Respite Scheme   11
   Individual Voluntary
   Arrangements   3
   voluntary bankruptcy   43

Annulment   139, 197, 202
   advertising   145
   and divorce proceedings   143
   application   203
   challenging expenses of the
   Trustee   140, 142
   court fee   139
   effect of   144
   failure to attend court   204

   grounds for   139
   debts and expenses have been
   paid   139
   IVA has been signed   144
   order should not have been
   made   139
   removing entries at the Land
   Registry   145

Appeals   197, 199
   annulment   197, 202
     application   203
   common areas of appeal   201
   grounds for   199
     serious procedural
     irregularity   200
     wrong: error in the exercise of
     discretion   200
     wrong: error of fact   200
     wrong: error of law   199
   rescission   199
   review   197
     purpose   198
   stay of judgment   202

Application for permission to be a
director   192

Assigning a claim   15

Assignment of book debts   25

B

'Balance sheet' solvency   40

Bankruptcy
  and employment 27
  annulment 133, 139
    advertising 145
    and divorce proceedings 143
    challenging expenses of the
    Trustee 142
    court fee 139
    effect of 133, 144
    expenses of the Trustee 140
    grounds for 139
      debts and expenses have
      been paid 139
      IVA has been signed 144
      order should not have been
      made 139
    removing entries at the Land
    Registry 145
  conclusion of
    discharge and annulment 133
  death 147
    after presentation of the
    bankruptcy petition 153
    after the bankruptcy order is
    made 153
    beneficiaries v creditors 149
    beneficiary 148
    CPR Part 64 application 150
    distribution from estate 149
    failure by PR to pay deceased's
    valid debts 148
    how insolvent estate can be
    administered 149
    Insolvency Administration
    Orders 150
    insolvent estate 148
    Personal Representative 147
    PR taking on role of Trustee
    149
    statutory order for the
    priority of payment of debts
    149
    'Survivorship' and jointly
    owned property 151
    third party debt orders 148

  default discharge date 133
  definition of xxix
  discharge 133
    bankruptcy restriction orders
    135
    certificate of discharge 134
    effect of 134
    long term impact 138
    suspension of 133
  effect on immigration status 29
  effect on the bankrupt's career
  and business 26
  extension of 133
  inability to obtain credit 28
  leaving E and W 75
  length of 37
  meaning of discharge from 37
  necessary conditions 45
  ongoing obligations of
  discharged bankrupt 38
  publicity of 34
    London Gazette 34
  running the bankrupt's business
  29
  stages of 13
  start date 133
  time limit for making
  bankruptcy order 44
  voluntary 43

Bankruptcy hearing 82
  adjournment 83
    appeal of the underlying
    petition debt/tax assessment
    87
    enable debtor to satisfy the
    court of their power to pay
    debts 85
    evidence required 84
    if an IVA can be made 87
    illness 84
    length of 84
    second hearing 84
    technical defect 83
    voluntary adjournment 89

Bankruptcy offences 117
   annulment and discharge 120
   application for an arrest warrant
      120
   contempt of court 121
   defence of innocent intention
      119
   defence of reasonable excuse
      119
   in the Insolvency Act 117
   outside of the Insolvency Act
      122
   prosecution 120
   punishment 120
   standard of proof 121
   statistics 117

Bankruptcy petition 69
   additional steps 78
   bankruptcy order 103
   centre of main interests 73
   certificate of continuing debt
      79
   change of carriage 103
   choice of court 76
   grounds to dispute 89
     bankruptcy would be
     disproportionate 92
     bankruptcy would have a
     serious psychological impact
     on the debtor 99
     court has no jurisdiction to
     make the bankruptcy order
      100
     creditors guilty of improper
     behaviour towards the debtor
      99
     debt is disputed 93
     debt is not for a liquidated
     sum 92
     debtor has made an offer to
     settle 93
      debtor able to pay all their
      debts 94

      offers unreasonably rejected
      94
     debtor has no assets 91
     debtor is very elderly or
     unwell 99
     debtor lacks capacity 100
     IVA has been approved 100
     petitioner does not attend the
     hearing of the petition 100
     petition is an abuse of process
      96
     serious procedural
     irregularities 90
   jurisdiction 69
     carrying on business 73
     disputing COMI 74
     domicile 74
     residence 73
     rules for determining 72
   notice of opposition 82
   other forms of bankruptcy 103
     criminal bankruptcy orders
      103
     petitions following a failed
     IVA 103
   removing estate property
   outside E and W 74
   search for ongoing bankruptcy
   proceedings 79
   service 79
     personal service 79
   statement of truth 78
   substitution of creditor 102
   timing of the hearing 82
   when brought 75
   withdrawal 79
     permission for 79

Bankruptcy restriction orders 135
   length of 136
   statistics 137
   undertakings 136

Bankruptcy restriction
undertakings 136

Barristers 226
  direct access 226
  fees 211

Beneficiary 148

Breathing Space 11

C

Carrying on a business
  definition 74

Cashflow insolvency 40

Cause list 58

Centre of main interests (COMI)
  73

Challenging expenses of the
Trustee 140, 142

Change of carriage 103

Choice of lawyer 226
  barristers 226
    direct access portal 228
    finding appropriate direct
    access barrister 228
  County Court advocates 227
  legal executives 227
  McKenzie friends 227
  solicitors 226
    finding appropriate solicitor
    227
  solicitors' agents 227
  word of mouth 229

Christians Against Poverty 295

Circuits of England and Wales 77

Citizenship applications 43

Civil restraint order 123

Class of creditors xxxi

Company Insolvency Pro Bono
Scheme 181, 182

Company Voluntary Arrangement
(CVA) 166, 173

Compounding a debt 94

Compulsory liquidation 177
  statutory demand 177

Compulsory winding up 167

Conduct of the bankrupt
  review of 20

Contesting a bankruptcy petition
  40
  factors to consider 41

Contingent creditor
  definition of 4

Coronavirus
  transaction avoidance 175
  winding up petitions 178

Corporate insolvency 165
  administration 170
    floating charge 170
    definition 171
    moratorium on legal
    proceedings 171
    selling company as going
    concern 171
  before a company goes into
  liquidation 170
  contesting a winding up
  petition 170
    correct court 178
    definition 166

difference between bankruptcy
and winding up petitions   177
general process   166
  administration   166
  Company Voluntary
  Arrangement (CVA) 166, 173
  compulsory winding up   167
  Creditors' Voluntary
  Liquidation (CVL)   167, 173
injunction restraining
advertisement of the petition
                             178
  correct court   178
limited liability   167
  exceptions
    company being used as a
    vehicle for a fraud   169
    directors in breach of their
    duties   169
    fraudulent trading   168
    'phoenix' company set up
                             169
    someone has signed a guar-
    antee   169
    someone takes property
    belonging to the company
                             169
    transaction which defrauds
    a creditor   169
    wrongful trading   167
  liability for debts of company
                             169
    personal liability   170
liquidation
  compulsory   174
  voluntary   174
liquidation process   173
moratorium outside of
administration   172
pre-pack arrangements   172
restraining presentation of
winding up petition   177
standards of a 'reasonable
director'   170
statistics   166

statutory demand
  service   177
winding up petitions
  advertisement   178
  wrongful trading   170

Costs   207
  assessment basis   217
    indemnity   217
    standard   217
  bankruptcy or winding up
  petition   217
  barristers' fees   211
  claims by litigants in person
                             215
  costs schedules   219
  court fees   213
    help with   214
  fees of the Trustee in
  Bankruptcy or liquidator   220
  improper conduct   218
  in the case/petition   215
  no order as to   216
  principles of costs awards 215
  process server's fees   214
  reserved   216
  solicitors' fees   208
  summary assessment   217
  third party costs orders   216

Costs schedules   219

County Court Administration
Order (CCAO)   10

County Court advocates   227

Court bundle   241

Court fees   213
  help with   214

Court's review of decision   197

Creditors
    class of   xxxi
    contingent   4
    future   3
    secured   xxxi
    unsecured   xxxi

Creditor's meeting   4

Creditors' Voluntary Liquidation
(CVL)   167, 173

D

Debt Relief Orders (DRO)   7
    application for   8
    challenge to   10
    conditions for   7
    fee   8
    nearly qualifying for   9
    revokation of   9
    schedule of debts   8

debt relief restriction order   10

Debt Respite Scheme   11

Debts of the bankrupt
    calculation of   25
    secured on property   26

Defective statutory demand   47

Department for Business, Energy
and Industrial Strategy (BEIS)   13

Direct access   226

Directors
    definition   165
    disqualification hearings   185
    duty to act in the best interest of
    the company's creditors   174
    duty to act in the best interests
    of the shareholders   174

Directors' disqualification hearings
    185, 191
    director's defence   191
    statement by the Secretary of
    State   191

Directors' disqualification orders
    xxxi, 185
    application for permission to be
    a director   192
      imposition of safeguards   193
    avoiding   188
    breach of   187
    compensation   187
    definition   185
    definition of unfit   186
    disqualification hearings   191
    disqualification undertakings
    187, 189
    advantages of offering
      undertakings   190
    length of disqualification   187
    liquidator's report   185
    number of   185
    proceedings commenced   189
    statistics   189

Directors' disqualification
undertakings   187, 189
    advantages of offering
    undertakings   190
    statistics   190

Directors' guarantees   155

Disclaimer of property   18

Dispositions
    definition of   23

Disputed debt   236

Domicile
    definition   74

E

Estate of the bankrupt 14
    sale of 17
        bankrupt's business 29

Excessive pension contributions 25

Execution of judgment 62

Expedited demand 49

Extortionate credit transactions 25

F

Fees of the Trustee in Bankruptcy
or liquidator 220

Fixed charge 171

Floating charge 170

Future creditor
    definition of 3

G

Going concern 171

Guarantees xxxii
    challenge to 158, 159, 160
        evidence required 160
    debts that are covered 156
    definition 156
    Guaranteed Obligations 157
    independent legal advice for
    guarantor 158
    proper demand 157
    unenforceable 156
    validity 158
        duress 158
        misrepresentation 159
        undue influence 158

written by non-lawyer/lawyer
155

I

Inability to pay
    definition of 46

Income Payments Agreements
(IPA) 32
    duration of 32
    variation of 32

Income payments order/agreement
138

Income Payments Orders (IPO)
16, 30
    duration of 32
    pension included in income 16
    variation of 32

Indemnity
    definition 156

Indemnity basis of assessing costs
217

Individual Voluntary Arrangements
(IVA) xxx, 3
    challenge to 5
        material irregularity 5
        unfair prejudice 5
    definition of 4
    failure of 7
        second IVA 7
    interim order 5, 6
        fee 6
    length of 7
    negative features 6
    process 4
        creditor's meeting 4
    providers of 4
        Creditfix 4
        Hanover Insolvency 4

StepChange 4
statistics 6

Insolvency Act 1986 xxi

Insolvency Administration Orders
(IAO) 150

Insolvency, definition of xxix

Insolvency law, corporate xxxii

Insolvency law, principles of xxxi
Trustee in bankruptcy xxxi

Insolvency Practitioner 13

Insolvency register 138

Insolvency Register 34

Insolvency Service xxx, 13, 31, 43

Interest on debt 25
statutory rate of 25

J

Judgment debt 15

Judgment returned unsatisfied 62

L

Lawyers 226
fees 208
how to best use them 229
pro bono legal advice 232

Legal executives 227

Legal professional privilege 36

Limited liability 167

Liquidated debt
definition of 45

Liquidation
compulsory 174
definition 165
process 173
voluntary 174

Liquidator
definition 165
first interview after winding up
order 183
power to review the
transactions of the company
174

Litigation tips 225

London Gazette 34

M

Material irregularity 5

McKenzie friends 226, 227

Moratorium outside of
administration 172

N

Notice of opposition 83

O

Offers unreasonably rejected
test for 95

Official Receiver (OR) 13

Online Debt Solutions 43

P

PayPlan 295

Personal Representative 147

Personal service 48

Petitioning creditor xxxii

Possession hearings 105
  bankrupt's rights 108
  contesting 108
  cost order 114
  dismissal of Trustee's
  application for possession 115
  failure to oppose an application
    115
  if bankrupt was renting 106
    vesting order 107
  low value homes 113
  mortgage payments 113
  objecting to sale 114
  orders for possession 110
  possible steps by Trustee
    agreement 110
    charging order 110
    selling the interest 109
  rights of occupation 110
  selling bankrupt's house 105
  time limit for Trustee to take
  steps 109

Pre-action protocol 237

Preferences 21
  definition of 21

Preliminary Information
Questionnaire 182

Pre-pack arrangements 172

Pre-trial review 60

Private examination 36

Privileged advice 37

Pro bono legal advice 232

Process server 48
  fees 214

Property
  after-acquired property 30
  assignment of book debts 25
  bankrupt's business 29
  definition of 14
  disclaimer of 18
  dispositions of 23
  exceptions to transfer to Trustee
    14
  excessive pension contributions
    25
  extortionate credit transactions
    25
  jointly owned 16
  pension rights 16
  preferences 21
  sale of 17
    distribution to creditors 33
    treatment of family mem-
    bers 33
  sale of bankrupt's house 18
  suing for debts owed to the
  bankrupt 20
  transactions at an undervalue
    20
  transactions defrauding
  creditors 24
  transfer to Trustee 14

Proprietary claim
  definition of 46

Public examination 36

R

Remote hearings 243

Removing entries at the Land Registry 145

Representing yourself 233
  appearing in court 242
   order of speaking 245
   remote hearings 243
   speaking to the judge 244
   what clothes to wear 245
  correspondence with petitioning creditor 233
   disputed debt 236
   'pre-action' correspondence 237
   sending documents 236
   settlement 234
    open offer 235
    without prejudice privilege 235
    without prejudice save as to costs 235
   using the creditor's resources wisely 238
   who to contact 237
  written documents for the court 238
   court bundle 241

Rescission of bankruptcy petition 199

Residence
  definition 74

Reviews 197
  purpose 198

S

Samaritans 296

Schedule of debts 8

Secured creditors xxxi

Securing a debt 94

Service
  bankruptcy petition
   personal service 79
  statutory demand
   certificate of service 76
   failure to serve 49
   if personal service is not practical 48
   incorrect service 55
   personal service 48
   process server 48
   substituted service 48
  waiver of defects or irregularities 80

Settlement 234

Shareholder, definition 165

Shelter 295

Skeleton arguments 238, 240
  exchange 241

Solicitors 226
  agents 227
  fees 208

Sources of help
  Advocate 295
  Business Debtline 295
  Christians Against Poverty 295
  Citizens Advice 295
  Debt Advice Foundation 295
  LawWorks 295
  Money Adviser Network 295
  National Debtline 295
  PayPlan 295
  PILARS 295

Samaritans 296
Shelter 295
Step Change 295

Stages of bankruptcy 13

Standard basis of assessing costs
217

Standard of proof 121

Standards of a 'reasonable director'
170

Statement of truth
definition 76

Statutory demands
challenging 60
consequences of 49
defective 47, 54
overstated debt 54
understated debt 54
definition of 47
disputing demand or
bankruptcy petition? 60
expedited demand 49
in respect of a contingent debt
57
in respect of future debts 57
reusing argument at bankruptcy
hearing 60
service 48
certificate of service 76
failure to serve 49
if personal service is not
practical 48
incorrect service 55
personal service 48
process server 48
substituted service 48
setting aside 50
contents of application 50
directions hearing 58
first hearing 58

evidence 59
genuine triable issue 51
grounds for 50
jurisdictional argument 56
making the application 50
possible orders 59
Pre-Trial Review 60
review of application 57
substantive hearing 59
undisputed net debt 51
time to pay if in E and W 49

Staying the petition 88

Stay of judgment 202

StepChange 4

'Substantial purpose' test 24

Summary assessment of costs 217

'Survivorship' and jointly owned
property 151

Suspension of discharge 133

T

Third party costs orders 216

Third party debt orders 148

Transaction avoidance 175

Transactions at an undervalue 20

Transactions defrauding creditors
24

Trustee in Bankruptcy xxix, xxxi
acting in bad faith 126
challenges to 123
civil restraint order 123
common complaints 124

compensation for breach of
duty 127
complaints to the regulator
129
  statistics 130
general control of Trustee by
the court 124
failure to cooperate with 35
investigation powers 35
  private examination 36
  public examination 36
obligations of 125
removal of 128

Trusts 16

U

Undertakings 10

Unfair prejudice 5

Unsecured creditors xxxi

Usual compulsory order 179

V

Validation order 23, 238

Voluntary bankruptcy xxx, 43
  adjudicator 44
  application fee 43
  false representation 44

Voluntary liquidation 174

W

Winding up
  definition 165
  petition
    adjournment 180
    after usual compulsory order
    is made 182
      duty to cooperate with the
      liquidator 183
      first interview with liquida-
      tor 183
      Preliminary Information
      Questionnaire 182
      prohibition on phoenixing
      183
    defect 180
    during coronavirus 178
    hearing format 179
    hearing second time round
    181
    location 178
    rescission of winding up
    order 199
    useful tips 182
    usual compulsory order 179

Without prejudice privilege 235

Wrongful trading 167, 170